The Story of Ellacoya

To Jewell ~
my closest and most
inspiring friend through
many years of Joy.

Jenne Clark

HERIMA
tells

THE STORY OF ELLACOYA

by
Jeanne Clark

Beech River Books
Center Ossipee, New Hampshire

BℝB

Beech River Books
P. O. Box 62, Center Ossipee, NH 03814
603-539-3537
www.beechriverbooks.com

LIBRARY OF CONGRESS CATALOGING-IN-PUBLICATION DATA

Clark, Jeanne, 1931–
  The story of Ellacoya / by Jeanne Clark.
    p. cm. -- (The Herima series)
Summary: "A prose poem saga that celebrates female
strength and wisdom, as personified in the fictional story
of an Abenaki heroine"--Provided by publisher.
ISBN 978-0-9793778-9-1 (pbk. : alk. paper)
1. Women--Poetry 2. Prose poems, American. I. Title.
PS3603.L3643S76 2009
811'.6--dc22
                    2009040694

Cover and interior artwork by Gene Matras,
Pittsfield, New Hampshire

Photo of author on back cover by
Ken Quiet Hawk

Printed in the United States of America

For Lisa Elaine Simon
and all daughters everywhere
who share Snow Owl's fate.

The HERIMA series
by Jeanne Clark:

The Story of Ellacoya

Goldenrod

Thomas Clark's Journal

Herima, the storytelling old woman's name, is an invention linking the feminine *her* with the masculine *[h]im*, and ending with *a*.

While her *Story of Ellacoya* arose from the shadowy legend of Ellacoya, Kona, Ahanton, and the description of Lake Winnipesaukee as a "Smile of the Great Spirit," it is not an anthropological or historically accurate treatise. Few customs and no characters are real. What *is* real and what permeates the story is her respect for the land, for the enduring spirit of the Northeastern Woodlands Abenaki and their descendants.

Preface

Joseph Campbell, the twentieth century's noted mythologist, once said in a conversational documentary with journalist Bill Moyer (*Joseph Campbell and the Power of Myth*, first broadcast on PBS 6/20-6/28/1988):

> It is hard for a boy to become a man, but it is easy for a girl to become a woman...[A] boy about to become a man is told by his mother, "Go and find your father." He is pushed out. And he must gather all the mother's energies into himself and go out and search and struggle and fight.

He gave this as his reason why it is only men who write epic poetry, what he calls "mythopoetic readings of the place and destiny of man in the universe."

He also said:

> The sleeping beauty myth is just a girl resisting becoming a woman until a prince (a boy just completing the transition into manhood) awakens her and shows her it is pleasant to be a woman. A girl has no trouble becoming a woman. With the onset of menses, she is transformed. *Boom!* That's it!

Ah, Joseph, there is a bit more to it than that.

All the mother's energies the boy gathers into himself
never came from any Sleeping Beauty.

— Jeanne Clark, Wolfeboro, New Hampshire

Herima sat on the rooted stump rejoicing,
Hearing the hiss and the slap of the wind-stirred lake,
Heeding the whistling whine of the wind-tossed pines,
Watching the white-crested foam caps shivering shoreward,
Seeing the shuddering aspen shimmering silver,
Feeling the fleeting strokes of floating filaments,
Catching the wafting caterpillar threads,
Smelling the streaming smoke of the morning campfire,
Sniffing the subtle scent of sun warmed sap,
Tasting the minted tang of loose wet tea leaves,
Licking the sweet bleeding wound of a bee-stung finger,
Stretching the drum-taut skin of her sunburned back,
Thinking the name of the Indian maid, Ellacoya,
Liking the Indian lake name Winnipesaukee,
Singing the names of the numerous isles and islands,
Sounding Sandy and Jolly, Steamboat, Dollar, and Mud,
Calling Guernsey, Rattlesnake, Barndoor, Mark and Three Mile,
Crying out Pine, and Five Mile, Stonedam, Black Cat and Hen,
Shouting out Blueberry, Whortleberry, Mink, and Little Bear...
Laughing aloud on the shore of the smiling Great Spirit,
Herima roared on the rooted stump, rejoicing,

    And the children,
        hearing, ran
            to her, begging a story.

"Tell us a story of Indians cruel and savage.
Tell us of settlers' children stolen and sold.
Tell us of tomahawks, tumplines, tom-toms, toboggans.
Charm us with sagas of sachems, shamans, and Sagamores.
Chill us with ancient lore and legend eerie.
Tell of the teeming tribes of the Algonquin.
Describe the Contoocok, Pennacook, Abenaki.
Sing to us Indian place names, songs of mystery.
Tell us a tale of this lake, these mountains and woodlands.
Smuggle us sidewise out of the tent of time.
Float us back over tracks of the raccoon, black bear and vixen.
Collapse the years between us and the basket weavers.
Carry us quickly to quiet and shaded shallows.
Catch us a slippery salmon flashing past birch bark canoes.
Cry us the cries of the wild goose, the loon, and the hoot owl.
Weave us a web that ensnares us in wonders.
Splice a wily design of words to amaze and stun us.
Trap past delights and perils in present word-song.
Seduce our senses with sounds of lost voices lilting.
Tell us a story of people who lived here before us,
Tell us a story of woman, wild and courageous."

Then the listeners,
        settling,
                watched Herima grow swarthy and young.

"I am Ellacoya," said Herima. "Ellacoya's my name.
Courage, intelligence, strength are mine in abundance.
My feet are tough to the trail, my palms to the paddle.
My back is strong to the pack, my legs to the climb.
I am skillful in guiding, in building good campfire and shelter.
I gather the wild berry, honeycomb, safe green and mushroom.
My nose never misses the scenting of warm-blooded quarry.
My eye ever glimpses the glint of the fish and the bird.
My keen ears can detect the slightest suggestion of danger.
My skin can predict each imperiling change in the weather.
My tongue tastes and savors delicate leaf and root spices.
My voices are many. I call with the loon and blue heron.
I can summon the hoot owl, hush the inquisitive deer.
I can trill the red squirrel's rancor, chatter jay's squall.
I can whisper a sound even softer than green grasses growing,
Or hiss like the sizzling wavelets assaulting the shoreline.
I listen on guard through black night for the noises of nothing.
I know where I am, though in spaces where no one has been.
The whole breast of Great Earth is my home, and her woodland's
         my shelter.
All the tribes of the upright walkers belong in my family.
All their little ones crawling and creeping are my adored children."

   Come now,
         everyone breathing,
            enjoy Ellacoya's adventure.

I first espied Kona, the Eagle, when I was a maiden.
He was barely a youth of an enemy tribe to the south.
My father, Ahanton, sole son of late chief of our village
Would murmur at night for the ear of my mother
His confounding awe of the prowess and craft of his rival,
The father of Kona, a warrior he must defeat,
So that he, my father Ahanton, might justify fate,
By slaying the enemy prove his own fitness for chieftain.
When he slew him, he sobbed through the night on the breast of
        my mother.
The sounds tore my belly. Next morn I first bled as a woman,
Was sent with my basket and deerskins and packets of corn
By my mother, her eyes filled with pride, commencing my walkabout.
"Go out a maiden, come back a woman, my daughter.
This blood is the constant of women, sweet sign of our power.
So, cherish your ripening body and relish its structure.
Heed well your heart's message and learn to be true to your nature.
Examine original visions. Seek out your soul.
For you now are the new chieftain's offspring, both stalwart and kind,
Fit to fly with the eagle, to spiral and glide with the hawk.
Go. In five days return, if at all, Ellacoya,
Wholly clean of the remnants of childhood's frail caul."

    People, I went,
        seeking
                the slain chieftain's orphan.

For two days I hiked, hugging the eastern shore.
Holding my back to the crimson hill of home harbor,
I traced this solemn and soundless lake's lip southward.
I stopped only to bathe my scarlet-stained thigh flesh clear
And to study reflections fertile in waters untroubled,
To glory in autumn rednesses as rich as my own.
Hidden in mist, I skirted a circle of mountains,
Unseen by the vigilant eye of the fine Ossipee.
I trod the stout dams of the beaver by stagnant backwaters.
Then, descending a slope, stood at last on the ledge of Long Bay
While the pain in my sweating belly lay heavy and hard.
I wept with the hurt and the gripe of becoming a woman.
I felt lonely and hungry and mortal, and somewhat afraid.
I had failed to outrun the red river of ripeness within me,
Had carried it onward, an onerous tiding from Moon.
Growing colder and shivering badly, I surveyed the valley
Seeking a suitable shelter where sunlight might wake me
With warmth and bold brilliance at dawning, but night's frost not chill.
On an escarpment below me, a glister of sinewy shoulder
Warned of a climber, unaware of my presence, approaching.
'Twas a lone youth, lean face, tear-streaked, with eyes of an eagle.

　　So climbed Kona,
　　　　good people,
　　　　　　chief's orphan of enemy tribe.

I whistled the warning for "Woman space—do not come nigh me."
He kept right on scaling the ledge face, as though he'd not heard me.
Then, over the ledge lip he struggled, scratched and weary.
His breathing was rapid and harsh and half strangled with sobbing.
His knuckles and knees were red, raw from the rub of the rocks.
His slim body was hairless and bare except for a breechclout.
In his uneven teeth he clenched bone knife and moccasin laces.
'Round the crown of his head a thin band bound back his thick hair.
Down his backbone, his ribcage, his thin calves, clear sweat droplets
       trickled.
On his smooth flesh the past summer's sunlight had painted rich hue.
Supple as woodland sapling, lithe as flame,
This heartbroken boy/man, slender, rose straight up before me,
Eyes opening wide as he spied me, so close to him, standing.
His heat was so high and so near that my cold skin absorbed it.
His odors were pleasing. He smelled like a glade of sweet moss,
And his breath when it mingled with mine was more pungent than cider,
And strong in his hair hung the campfire's comforting fume.
I watched as he let fall his slippers and resheathed his bone knife.
"I'm taboo," I warned him. He reached out his right hand to touch me.
"I'm Kona," he responded. "You are new friend. Taboo changes nothing."
Face to face, we stood tasting our tears while deep recognized deep.

    Gold sun, setting then,
        fading,
                left us on the ledge in cool shadow.

Down the mountain slope, steep at our backs, rolled the chill evening air.
In the valley a gathering mist obscured harbor and shoreline.
Lifeless calm, like a birdless feather, came to settle upon us,
While above us the unclouded sky supplied nightfall's first star.
"I am Ellacoya. Taboo is my task," I told Kona.
He drew himself taut. "Your father killed mine!" he exclaimed.
When he spoke, the gray grip of bereavement remodeled his features.
His pleasure at meeting me vanished, as anguish revived.
"Your loss has been grievously sudden and cruel," I acknowledged.
"Like a vulture devouring prey, death is ripping your heart,
And your spirit is blazing with anger at the hostile Ahanton.
Now your body is restless with fierceness unused and untried.
Fear winds like a fast-climbing vine 'round the roots of your courage.
Your soul's talons grapple with sadness and disbelief.
Your mind yearns for return to this earth of the dead one's presence.
The whole world seems savagely sterile." "Nothing's the same,"
Kona moaned in the eddying silence my words left behind them,
His somber expression confirming the truths I had framed.
"I am orphaned now, angry and lonely," he haltingly whispered.
"I hurt, and I need, and I feel as I did when a child,
Without power to alter disaster, or make myself stronger."

    Kona shivered then,
       shuddered,
            moved nearer a boulder for warmth.

It appeared he intended to linger all night at my campsite.
We'd spoken together of feelings that scratch at the soul.
But I had to proceed with the challenge of learning my selfness.
I needed my woman space, free of distraction, serene,
So I talked to him gently concerning the business before me.
"You may not remain here, sad Kona. I must be alone.
Already the lights in the north sky have started their dancing.
Already my medicine animal stirs in her lair.
Tonight I become Ellacoya the dream-weaving woman.
Tonight I grow strong, celebrating my joyful taboo.
You may hinder no longer my realization of Spirit.
Friend Kona, I greet you as kindred and bid you depart."
"But I need to remain with you. Here, I feel comforted, calmer.
Ellacoya, you nourish my hungry and hurting young heart.
Please delay until sunrise whatever your task that wants doing.
Tonight let me share in your campfire, absorb your sweet warmth."
"You entreat me unwisely, dear brother, to defer my becoming.
The source of your life force is elsewhere. My power lies here.
In your village the elders wait eager to treat you with wisdom."
"You speak as a sister, with firmness and care. I descend
To the valley, remembering friendship first found on this mountain.

   Farewell, Ellacoya,"
      Said Kona. I waved.
         He went homeward.

I then scurried to fashion a shelter, consume a scant meal,
To supply myself much needed comfort, reduce pain's annoyance
In order to concentrate fully upon the details
Of my ritual mystery, make from a blending of forces,
Within and without, an apt pattern designed for my growth work.
At last, standing warm and contented, well wrapped in soft deerskins,
I opened my senses completely to what whirled around me.
I widened my eyes to the sights of the north sky,
Devoted my ears to the musical hum of the woods.
To appreciate musky aromas, I wrinkled my nostrils,
Extended my tongue to collect the mild flavors of air.
In my palms felt the delicate heft of great nature's sensations.
I stood until I was at one with external conditions.
No boundaries squeezed my perceptions. I no longer stopped
At my skin but stretched endlessly, endlessly outward,
Infiltrating everything liquid and solid and void.
My bare toes stirred the core of our Earth in her rolling.
My braids agitated dark planets. My brow disturbed stars.
I grew huge with awareness of BE-*ing*. I *felt* my existence.
I *knew* that I *was*, that I *lived* that I *breathed,* that I *moved*
Manifesting aliveness, I shouted, "My BE-*ing* is *real!*

> I exist on my *own* all alone,
> > in the *now* of
> > > *my* lifetime.

My shouts set up echoes that sang through the mountains and rang
Out my BE-*ing* to all of creation in loud celebration.
Head back, face uplifted, I saw the aurora a-ripple with awe,
For there flickered above me bright fingers of light that would linger,
Like hands smoothing strands of invisible hair, soothing care.
It was Creator's hands weaving heaven. Then, leaving Her basket
Inverted on high and heaving Her sky-splinters north,
Set them blazing: a green glow with green coals and green flame amazing.
The smoke from Her green fire soon spread a great blanket of red
Overhead, turning everything red on the earth and in heaven.
The trees and the mist and the ledges, the stars and the sky,
Grew all-scarlet in hue, and the lake surface burned like a meadow
Ignited by lightning on summertime's driest of nights.
Then a terror, with cold fingers probing, grabbed hold of my marrow.
I watched my own death stalking toward me, to mock my small life.
It was hideous, glaring, relentless, devoid of compassion.
My knees could not bear me erect, so I fell on the ground,
While a whirlwind of glittering eyeballs encased me in visions,
Which leered from all sides as I groveled and tearfully cried.
I was shaking and dizzy and woefully sick in the stomach.
In this vortex of horror, I cowered bewildered by doom,

　　For a panic had
　　　　blown away reason,
　　　　　　paralyzed will.

Isolation oppressed me. I felt out-of-touch, set apart,
Unconnected to anything real or familiar. Not even
My body's sensations could ground my awareness in fact.
How I wished there were someone beside me, stronger than I was,
Whose hand on my shoulder might serve to connect me to earth
And my life more securely than ever, whose voice, calling sweetly
The name Ellacoya, could summon my senses again.
But the funnel of bodiless eyes caged me captive, and no one
Was out there to break through the spell. So I huddled in fear
Half the night on the ledge, while I waited for something to happen,
Some sign to appear for my guidance, some external force
To dispel my bad dream. Nothing happened. I waited until,
From the seed of my fears, a fresh energy sprang. In my center
It burned like the flames of a campfire. It pulsed through my blood
And it set my heart pounding this message: "There's nobody stronger
Than you, Ellacoya. There's no one who's stronger than you.
There are many *as* strong, and with them all your years will you travel,
But always remember that no one is stronger than you."
With this energy's message my confidence joined. I imagined
Myself as a shaman, shutting each eye in the whirlwind,
Closing, with thumbs most tender, the eyes of my death.

    And at peace then, I knew
        I would live to become
            ancient woman.

Not sooner could anything kill me. I'd seen my own death.
For the rest of my very long journey, a dangerous woman
I'd be, unafraid for my life ever after. Secure
In this knowledge, I opened my own eyes and stared all around me.
The night held no colors but charcoal and chalk. while full Moon,
With Her light, was a hole through the Sky. On black water below Her
A white dancing pathway led straight through dark thighs to The Womb
From which woman was born, in the First Birth, Original Mother.
I ran up the pathway. I sat by Her side. Moon embraced
Me and spoke to me: "Well done, my daughter. You've withstood a panic,
Confronted fear's fantasies, trusted your soul. You've sustained
Your aloneness, enhanced your taboo with interior growth work,
Prevailed over troubling temptations to keep yourself child.
It is time you specifically name me now, make Me your Sister.
You share in My Rhythms now, shed My Great Seed with your own.
The names you will choose for Me come from events of your birth month.
Rekindle, each time you address Me, in secret, the feel
Of the earth at the hour of your birth, for you chose your arrival
With careful attention to nature's receptive design.
You were winter-born, brave Ellacoya, by blizzard delivered.
On elegant elements, wild, your nativity thrived.

    Now envision your birth season's
        might.
                Create Moon-name reminders."

"Oh, Moon of booming ice, of longest dark,
Of dancing gale, of gleaming ground, of whitened
Weasel, dreaming tree, of frozen bark,
Of rattling leaf, of snoring bear, of frightened
Doe, of smoky breath, of squeaky snow,
Of bawling wolf, of yowling fox, of crackling
Vine, of stifled stream, of stinging toe,
Of splitting lip, of teary eye, of cackling
Owl, of squalling hare, of tinkling hail,
Of icy thong and rigid hide, of aching
Eardrum, ringing air, of newborn's wail,
Of startling quiet, ghostly light, of quaking
Cold. Oh, Moon of all these things and more—
Eye of my Earth nights, Drum of my life's fierce rhythm,
Shield of my birth rights, Sign of my source within—
Anoint, with your oily light, each joint and limb
Of my body. Bathe me with lustrous balm of renewal,
As here in these woods, on this ledge, by this lake, I undress,
And expose, for your loving reflection, perfection of flesh
And of frame that from all of my probable selves has become I,
Ellacoya, of tribe Abenaki and cluster Algonquin,

    By Winnipesaukee's
        far northern shore,
            in wintertime born."

That was how I addressed Mother Moon on my night of renewal.
I danced in Her light and Her shadows, moon-bathing myself
In the clearing as morning approached. Then, exhausted, I rolled up
In deerskins and lay down to dream-weave my medicine animal,
Learn my true spirit name: told by the images, colors
And feelings contained in whatever events my deep sleep
Would design. I grew warm and relaxed as my breathing rate lessened.
My mind, as it sifted the present, soon broke free of time,
And collected my pasts and my futures together, as if gathering
Grasses, and spread them, like matting, on the floor of my brain.
Then, in comfort and wonder, I waited, expecting the dream.
First, a song like crickets and wind enlivened the grasses.
The melody swelled in my skull to an unnerving buzz,
'Til I thought I could stand it no longer—when all of a sudden,
It ceased, and I found myself floating along through the trees
To the banks of a faraway river I never before had
Been near. On a rock in the river's green middle, there stood
A black bear, who with one paw was swatting up trout for three cubs
On the shore. How the droplets of rainbow-hued water did sparkle
In arcs, as each fish sailed through air in a quivering flight.
When I saw how that she-bear's teeth gleamed with each toss of her head,

 Then I knew that my true
   spirit-name
     was to be Laughing Bear.

For the bear, in her natural actions, appeared to be laughing
Directly at me, as I hung in my dream state above her,
Admiring the powerful swipe of her forepaw, the grace
Of her balancing, ponderous bulk. I felt bonding and kinship
With her and her cubs, as though I were once part of their circle,
And died in the birthing but wouldn't move on, so kept watch
As they frolicked and prospered in nature's rich gift of survival.
I wondered if I was as real to the bear's eye as she
Was to mine. Could she spy a bright hover of consciousness dancing
In light nearly over her nose? Could she sense how I longed
To be born to her den and her flesh? I so wanted to tell her
I loved her thick fur and wild odor. How often I'd heard
Her gruff chant in the woodlands of home and been drawn to her song!
How I prayed she would leave me a hint of her nearness as omen,
Some symbol to signify bear as my medicine animal:
Hers, as the spirit inherited, Hers, as the force
And the presence to call on. Intuitive knowledge of healing.
At-one-ness with all of Creation. Acceptance of life,
Of its fear and its love, of its jealousy, grief and its anger.
Enjoyment of effort, and beauty and danger. Belief
In the purpose and meaning of every least creature and tree.

    Oh, magnificent bear
        of the forest,
                please send me a sign!

My dream shifted then, setting me down in a steep, sloping meadow.
I held in my arms a sick, pitiful infant, unloved
And abandoned, in need of my care. I don't know where it came from
But I had to help it. I carried it gently, in search of the herbs
That would smooth its chafed skin.

                                    Something moved in the meadow
          below us.
A trio of black bears stood feeding. I watched as the nearest one
Scented us, saw us, came charging right at us, uphill.
Her blunt muzzle lunged forward, her paws were a blur, and her light-
          struck
Black fur seemed to surge in a rippling, galloping rhythm,
As animal instinct gave chase. In great dread, I then whirled
And fled, clutching the infant, afraid bear would catch and destroy us.
I stumbled and struggled to flee through the brambles ahead
Of her charge, but could feel her draw closer, could hear her harsh panting.
I knew I might never escape her alone.
Then I called on my dream friends to help me and turned to confront her.
She skidded in midstride, her claws raking grass and her rump
Plowing mud, as she slid with ridiculous grumblings, jaws clicking.
She awkwardly stopped, when I gestured with upraised hand.
By surprise, I had stolen her power to scare me, confronted
And conquered that danger, asserted my natural will
In defeat of her threat.

                                    As my dream friends arrived, they
          applauded.

     I strode to the
          muttering bear
               and demanded a gift.

Though my fear was still with me, I made myself stand without trembling
In reach of her claws, and continued demanding she give
Me a gift of significant value. She rose on her hind legs
And roared, but the infant I held in my arms made a sound
Like the clamor of hungering eaglets, which shocked the bear silent,
As if by a blow. Then shaking her great head, bear dropped to
Her forelegs, and spat out a gleaming white tooth at my feet.
As I knelt to examine the gift-tooth, the infant transformed itself
Into an eagle, and flew from my arms to the sun
With one sigh of its wide wings. I took up the tooth, and awakened
So swiftly, I hardly had time to cry thank you to bear,
For I knew that my vision was given at last, and that I would
Return to my people a woman of spirit: the powers
Of bear for my medicine animal; knowledge of self
To depend on for courage; the body of woman to nourish,
For strength; the sure promise of long life; a daughter of Moon;
The brief meeting with Kona, a secret, sweet friendship to relish;
The chant of my birth month, a bold celebration of flesh.
I had done all taboo had required of me, save find the token,
The amulet placed by my spirits somewhere on my path
For discovery, trying my keenness for subtle connections.

        Preparing my breakfast,
                I sang,
                        for I soon would be home

I felt strangely unsettled in body and spirit, 'though happy.
My visions and dreams and the meeting with Kona all swam
In my brain like trout trapped in a weir. I could not release them.
They circled and darted, eliciting colorful moods
That were strong and, distressingly, lasting. A new way of being
Alive had begun to make use of me: vital, intense.
I was not sure I liked it. It felt too consuming, too restless,
Too raw. And I sensed, from then on, I would live the world differently.
Breakfast and rain brought my thoughts back to plans for the homeward
Bound journey. Around the big lake, to return from the west,
Was the pathway I wanted to follow. I needed to hurry.
Arriving at home in five days, as my mother had said,
Would mean running long sections of trail in the daylight and walking
At night many miles through deep woods. I would rest in dead trees
Or in slots between rocks. Never stop to make camp or to cook a
Full meal. Yet I welcomed the challenge, expecting to quell
The brain's moil with the body's exertion, creating a homecoming
Attitude: peaceful, triumphant. I wanted to stride
Through my village a woman of obvious stamina, purpose
And will, fit to rule when maturity granted, to serve,
In the meantime, with power and promise apparent to all.

   I felt eager
       and proud,
             setting out on my homeward bound course

Though I first had to skirt Kona's village without being seen.
Allowing myself to be taken for ransom would anger
Ahanton, cause mother dismay. I felt certain of Kona's
Assistance, if captured, but losing my freedom and choices
Would be a great trial. So I stood on the ledge and I studied
Both shores of the long narrow bay. To the south lay the enemy
Village, obscured by the rain, and below me a rocky
Peninsula pointed across the deep bay toward the opposite
Shore. Could I swim in this weather without being spotted?
The rain was quite heavy. The water, however, was calm.
Only with luck could I swim it, unsighted, and only
If no one was fishing, or trapping, or gathering wood.
Down the face of the boulder-strewn ledge to the edge of the water
I skidded and crawled, using bushes and uprooted tree
Trunks for cover. I came to a small, sheltered pocket of beach,
Where I hastily stripped off my garments and crouched in the pelting,
Cold rain as I carefully folded the wet items tightly in
Deerskins and bundled them all in my sturdy grass basket.
I entered the water. How wonderfully warm it felt! Not
Like the rain… Without making a ripple, and floating face upward,
I settled my basket to ride on my chest, near my chin.

    Then I cautiously sculled,
        without splashing,
            but sensed something near.

Quite close, something curious, cunning and cautious, came swimming
Around me. It bumped my bare shoulder. It breathed at my ear
And went under. I felt no alarm, for its antics were joyous
And gentle: an otter—perhaps a bold, young one—aware
Of her marvelous movements in water, and playfully eager
To tease with exuberant freedom a slow, hampered human.
The animal suddenly surfaced, surprisingly close
By my thigh, and exhaled with a snort as she stared at me staring
At her through the rain. As we, side by side, lazily lay
In the bay, stroking shoreward, amused and amazed at each other's
Strange features, friend otter's large eyes sent the sting of intelligence,
Making connection with mine. The feeling was eerie,
As though she had purposely sought me to show me some sign,
But before I could summon an image, she dove and swam under
Me, stirring the water and swirling in circles. Then, surfacing,
Diving and swirling again, she drew farther and farther
Away with each turn, and I laughed at her creature dance, so
Full of glee. With her sleek form cavorting along, she had helped me
Sustain the long swim, without tiring, almost to shore,
And then left me alone, with my memory teeming with questions
About her appearance, her startling intelligent gaze.

    I crawled from the water
         and knelt
                 in a crevice, well hidden.

I wrung out my wet braids and opened my bundle of clothes
To get dressed. Then I heard, in the water behind me, a ripple.
Believing bold otter had swum back to find me, I turned
To see Kona afloat in the shallows, his hands on the bottom,
Slithering toward me in silence, but smiling and calm
In the cold, morning rain. He was naked as I, when he waded
Ashore. From his mouth to his hand, he transferred a small stone.
I could see the stone, oval and pink in his palm, as he offered
It to me. I took it and marveled: a stream-tumbled pebble
Of pink-tinted crystal he'd cleverly carved, to make plainer
Its natural look of a wee, crouching rabbit. The tail,
Ears and eyes and frail whiskers, the haunches and forepaws and nostrils,
All showed. It was warm and its surface surprisingly smooth.
"What a fine little rabbit you've made, clever Kona," I whispered.
"For you, Ellacoya," he said, looking pleased. "Oh, I like it,
Friend Kona, and thank you, I'll carry it always."
He watched as I turned it and turned it, admiring his skill
And his accurate eye. I expected the rabbit to squeak.
It looked so like a newborn, alive and expectant. How could
He have wrapped so completely the spirit of rabbit in crystal?
This Kona, my new friend, seemed talented, tender and open,

   Courageous,
       and loving adventure.
           I liked him a lot.

"How did you know I'd be swimming the channel?" I asked him.
"I guessed," he replied, "you would not be content to retrace
The way you had come, but would circle the lake to return
To your village the long way. You seemed so adventuresome, healthy
And proud when I met you last evening. I tried to decide
What would I do, if I had to slip by my village unnoticed.
'I'd swim 'cross the bay,' I decided, so early this morning I hid
On the shore there and waited. But you, Ellacoya, are stealthy.
You must have passed close, but I missed you. I wanted to swim
The bay with you but otter, instead, kept you company. Otter,
Whose ripples attracted my eye to your waterborne course,
Caused more stirrings than you did. I've had to swim swiftly to catch you."
"I'm glad you caught up with me, Kona," I answered, "and glad
For your gift of the beautiful rabbit. I, too, have a token for sharing."
I opened my amulet pouch and unwrapped a clear stone
Of no color. "This stone has rare properties, Kona," I told him.
"It's harder than any hard rock you can find, disappears
Underwater, and captures the rainbow from sun without rain.
I have carried it years since I found it atop a high mountain,
And wondered about its strange magic quite often. I give
It to you now for treasure and keeping, replacing sweet rabbit."

He took up the stone
        to examine it,
                smiling and pleased.

"I have heard of such magical stones, but not seen one," said Kona.
"My thanks to you for it, new friend Ellacoya: with this
I remember you always. Now come, I will show you a path
To your village. This morning my people are sitting in council
To name a new chieftain. No one may suspect you are near.
You must hurry, for soon will the women emerge from the shelter
To gather ripe corn ears, and squashes and acorns to roast
For the feast. The best acorns lie close by, so you must be running."
I took up my basket and followed swift Kona from shore
To the edge of a well-beaten pathway. He pointed direction,
Then left me in silence. I hastily dressed, tied my braids back
And ran. All was stillness, so deep in these woods. The rain
Hardly reached me. As Kona had promised, the pathway lay empty.
I went without fear of detection, enjoying my breath,
And my energy sensing the strength of my young, running body,
And feeling the glorious rhythms of muscle and bone,
As they sped me along. I was loose and relaxed from the swimming,
Quite fit to keep running for hours in this way, if I chose.
All around me the arrow-straight conifers, close-standing, towered.
The tent top of interlaced branches admitted low light,
And no undergrowth rose through the blanket of thick, fallen needles.

    The forest kept from me
            no secrets,
                    as northward I ran.

I felt strong, unrestricted, acutely alert, for although
My ripe body still honored Moon Mother, the pain in my belly
Had gone overnight. I was lithe in my tissues again,
And restored to my former condition before I first bled
As a woman and was banished by mother to do my taboo.
How astonishing life was becoming for me! How surprising
The changes! How calming the samenesses. Now I could sense
My own power as separate and personal, quite independent
Of others' permissions. Was this the great purpose taboo
Was designed to accomplish, I wondered. Were feelings so joy-filled
And fraught with the promise of full-fledged maturity, meant
To arise on this trek in their natural flourishing? Body
And spirit, in unison, thriving when challenged and freed
At the time of first blood? Yes, this must be the purpose taboo was
Designed for: to meet one's own selfness; to learn both one's fears
And one's powers, directly with no interference; no hiding
From growth work in daily distractions of chatter and busy
Group duties, familiar routines. Oh, how simple it all
Was, and yet how complex! What if I hadn't discovered
My selfness, as I was supposed to? What if I had hid
In the cave close to home, as some others had done in their terror?

I thanked, as I ran,
           my sweet spirits
                  for keeping me bold.

The journey grew long. I walked often. Toward evening, I rested.
When birds hid in treetops and deer with their fawns bedded down,
I withdrew a short distance away from the trail and assembled
A bedding of needles and fern in a hollow between
The two halves of a boulder that split long ago. I intended
To nap little more than a gnat's life, but Moon shone in clear
Sky before I awoke. The wet weather was ended, the temperature
Falling. My breath was a cloud in the crisp, midnight air.
I walked swiftly. The pathway lay sandy and wide, within sight
Of the shore now, and level as untroubled water itself.
No round roots, nor rough pebbles tormented my feet as I traveled,
And moonlight that filtered through forest and flickered on water,
Lit up the broad path with a dim, silver glimmer amid
The great hemlocks. Toward dawning, I reached a sand beach of great
            beauty.
With moonset behind me and sunrise before me, I stood
For a moment between night and day as they balanced each other
Exactly: a magical moment of death and rebirth,
Like the story my grandmothers tell of Old Glooskap, the Crafty,
Who formed, from his mother's dead body, the Sun and the Moon.
As I stood at the edge of the water, rejoicing at morning,
I saw the great paw prints of black bear pressed deep in wet sand

    They were recent,
            made after the rain,
                    so I followed them warily.

Better surprise bear, than be surprised by her, I reasoned,
Excitement increasing with every curve of the shore.
Was she fishing or berrying, napping or traveling homeward,
Even as I was, I wondered. Perhaps she had already
Heard me behind her, and started to gallop away.
I was frightened enough by her nearness to pray she was running,
Yet curious feeling enough to half-hope to approach
Her unseen and unsensed, and to watch her just being herself
In her natural freedom: untroubled by hunters, unthreatened,
Unthreatening. Dream and reality mingled in mind
Now, so weirdly I had the uncanny impression that all this
Had happened before. I was certain that 'round the next bend
I would see she-bear berrying calmly. Be able to watch her
As long as I liked, undisturbed. Bear was my medicine
Animal, source of my power. I yearned to observe her.
The gentlest of breezes arose as the sun lifted higher.
It blew in my face very softly and told by its rich,
Pungent scent that the bear was upwind of me, close and not moving.
I halted then made myself still as an oak trunk and listened.
At first, all was silence, except for the breeze. Then I heard
A low rumbling of animal pleasure and saw bear erect

On her hind legs,
        not far from me,
                scratching her back on a tree.

Such a young one she was, standing upright no taller than I,
But much heavier: ready for winter, well larded with fat,
Her black fur long and glossy, her muzzle and eyes bright with moisture.
In excellent health and full strength, she stood rubbing her back
On the tree with great energy, causing the branches and leaves
High above her to jiggle and quiver and rustle, like dancers
Performing a prayer for Creator, grateful for life
And for vigor, for sunrise, for beat of warm blood in their bodies.
Bear, too, was a dancer—in balance, deliberate, graceful—
And tree was her partner, responding in rhythm. I laughed,
Much too loudly for wisdom, but bear kept on happily scratching,
Not hearing my laugh, or not letting it lessen her bliss.
Did she recognize humans, I wondered, or never been hunted,
Not asked to give up her great soul, so that humans could eat
And keep warm by her bounty? She did not seem wary nor watchful
At all, and that puzzled me. Then I saw why! Her huge dam
Loomed nearby. I took cover and froze. There was nothing to do, then,
But wait 'til they left or discovered my presence. I shook
Like the outermost leaf on the slenderest branch of bear's scratching
Tree, fearful and wholly unwilling to give my own soul
To bear's claws. I was certain the elegant dam had been hunted.

    An old one and wily,
        she was,
                or I'd sooner have seen her.

She lifted her muzzle and sniffed at the air, now alert
To some change or some danger approaching. Was I the unwelcome
Intruder she sensed, or were hunters out early to try
For her beauty? Perhaps there was nothing the matter. A wary
Old bear dam, like this one, would constantly check on the space
That surrounded her, guarding her cub and herself from intrusion.
The cub stopped its scratching and dropped to a standstill, aware
Of its mother's attentiveness: quiet, obedient, ready
To follow her signal. Then I sensed things, too, some subtle
Disturbance. The mood of the woodland was altering, peace
Seeping out of it, tensions arriving by stealth and in numbers.
Old bear began swaying uneasily, shifting her weight
From one side to the other, and swinging her head as though summoning
Thought. Then she charged at her cub and the two of them raced
For the water. They scampered right past me, unheeding my trembling,
Thin body, hugged close to a tree. As they brushed me, I saw
The old she-bear's right haunch bore a scar that her coat couldn't cover.
It looked like a burn or a scrape wound from falling, not large
But distinct and significant, marking her hide with her history,
Making my sighting of her unforgettable. Stark
In my memory hovered that scar, as the bears hit the water;

　　　Then, yelling and whooping,
　　　　　　from out of the woods
　　　　　　　　burst the hunters...

The bears in the water swam easily, swiftly, their heads
Very low to the surface, presenting unfavorable targets,
Not worthy the wasting of arrows and soon out of range.
I was glad they were safe, but felt bad for the hunters, who needed
Their flesh and their hides to survive the long winter ahead.
At the shoreline, the hunters stood watching the widening ripples,
Intent upon tracing the wake of the bears as they made
For the far wooded shore. By my tree, I watched, too, keeping hidden,
Although there were men of my tribe with the hunters, and I
Would be safe. I was pleased with my loneness, enjoying my journey,
Unwilling to come into company, liking taboo
And its freedom too much to be found here before it was ended.
Old bear and her young one emerged on the opposite shore.
They stood, shaking their coats free of water and pawing their faces.
The hunters spoke quietly, pointing out possible ways
That the two bears might travel. I knew that the hunt wasn't over.
The bears would be tracked to their deaths in the mountains. I mourned
Them and thanked them for sharing taboo with me, hoping that somehow
The wily, old matriarch still might escape with her cub
And sleep well through the winter. The hunters were soon joined by others
Who carried canoes on their shoulders. All quickly embarked,

And with strong strokes they paddled
        across
                to the far wooded shore...

I watched 'til they landed, then slowly I walked to the waterline,
Where in the wet sand the story lay printed of bear
Paws and moccasins, keels of the hunters' canoes. In the water,
Small bubbles escaping from under dislodged bottom stones,
Pocked the surface with delicate popping sounds, almost inaudible.
Crouching, I heard their soft musical whispers expire,
Then I splattered my face with cold water and drank. Time to travel
Again, 'round another long bay lying northward and west
Of my home. The large party of hunters was closer to Red Hill
Of home now than I was. Perhaps I would come upon traces
They'd left of their chase on my way. As I turned toward the path,
I caught sight of the tree where the young bear stood happily scratching
A short time ago. Clumps of black fur still clung to the bark.
And the twigs of surrounding small bushes bore fuzzy black flowers.
I smiled at the sight of them. Funny young bear, giving bushes
Fall blooms of such shaggy, soft texture! I picked some and sniffed
Their wild odor: a scent not unpleasant, yet signaling danger
Down deep in the bone. I untied my small amulet bag
And took out the carved rabbit stone Kona had given me yesterday,
Wrapped little rabbit in bits of black fur, and repacked
The small bag with both cherished taboo tokens safely inside.

On the path toward the river,
     I ran.
          I was ready for home.

I could feel myself stronger and leaner, 'though tired and hungry
And cold. All the rest of the way I'd be pushing myself
To my limit. I wanted my mother's anxiety eased
By my timely arrival. I longed to receive father's welcome
Embrace. I soon came to the riverbank. Breathless, I rested
A moment before I disrobed and walked into the fast
Flowing water, my clothes in my basket held high on one shoulder,
My other arm outstretched for balance. I waded almost
To the middle before the swift current entangled my footing
And toppled me headlong. Down river I tumbled, afloat,
And then under, on belly, on backside, head first, and then toes,
I went whirling and plunging—forever, it seemed, to my fanciful
Senses. Blurred sky, spinning trees and white bubbles were all
I could see. In my ears, water gurgled. My nostrils were stinging.
My basket was ripped from my grip, as it caught on a branch
And broke open. My shoulder was wrenched by the pull of the handle.
I gasped, without thinking, and swallowed some water. I choked
And went under, afraid for the first time I might not recover
Control of my breathing enough to survive. If I surfaced
And choked and went under another time, how would I see
What I needed: a branch, or a log, or a sandbar to save me?

    Lungs burning, I surfaced
        and retched
            and again I went under...

My shoulder scraped rock, then I felt myself falling through air
A brief instant before hitting water once more. It was calmer.
I surfaced with ease and was able to draw in deep breaths
Without coughing. The current was gentler. The river had widened,
Was emptying into a bay. With relief I reached shore
And sat waist deep in water, reclaiming my wits and my shaken
Belief in dream's promise of long life. Then laughed! Promise kept!
I was naked and cold, but alive. I looked down for my amulet
Bag. It was still on its thong 'round my neck. I was glad.
On one hand and both knees, I crawled out of the water and sat on
A rock in the sun to unfasten my braids spread my hair
Out to dry. My right shoulder, abraded and bleeding, was stinging
A little, but otherwise normal. My left shoulder hurt
Deep inside, like a sprain, and my arm, badly swollen, was aching:
To move it was torture. I needed to bind it up tight
To my side, but with what? Both my clothing and basket
Of deerskins were gone, not to mention the last of my food,
Torn away by the river. I shivered and carefully rose to
My feet. Walking close to the edge of the bank, I ascended
The slope by the falls and surveyed the wild river where rocks
And felled tree trunks diverted her flooding, clear waters, where eddies
Twirled circles of froth in the shallows, and bright sunlight danced.

    My respect for such beauty
        and power
            was painfully learned.

I belonged to the river now. Heart of swift river had captured
My body and breathing, then given them back as her gifts
To tomorrow's unfoldings: whatever they might be; wherever
My living could carry me; however long I might dream
This existence; my futures were already ended, yet barely
Begun. In a few seconds' tumbling and terror and throe,
I was taught by swift water that whatever would happen already
Had. She had smuggled me sideways out of the tent
Of time for that instant, to string me a hammock of ever
And never. Had tangled and tethered and teased me, and tossed
My imaginings downstream and skyward, from yesterday's ecstasy,
Present day's pain to my hopes for a hundred years more
On my earth before leaving. I yearned to experience all Earth
Held out to me. Willing to suffer and struggle and sing,
Make her mountains long echo my life song, my laughter, my agonies,
After my last sigh had faded, my body but leaves…
So my reverie ended. I rallied when spotting a deerskin
Afloat on an eddy, another one caught on a log.
Though my basket was shredded, dried berries and corn kernels vanished,
The woods still held mushrooms and seeds, also nuts and sweet roots,
So I bound up my shoulder, wrapped up in wet deerskins, then barefoot

I limped toward Red Hill
        and slept restlessly,
                one day from home.

In the morning, the low clouds made promise of snowfall and winter's
Arrival. The path was a river of acorns and leaves
Leading straight to my village, a path I knew well. I expected
To meet someone soon. Children racing. Men scouting for moose
Spoor or deer tracks. A party of foragers. Some face familiar
With welcoming nod to accept my return, but the first
Face I saw was my sister's: the youngest of all, barely seven,
Concealing herself off of the trail by a tree stump and rock.
When she peered out and saw me, she ran from me homeward, feet flying.
No greeting, no cry; her expression of terror, of shock.
Had she thought me a spirit, I wondered, a ghost come to frighten
Her? No, she was braver than that, her young heart was a fox.
I was baffled and sad she would leave me to stumble the rest of
The way all alone when I wanted a greeting, a smile,
A small shoulder supporting me, chatter and gossip and stories
She always was full of, distracting my last painful mile.
But I entered the village alone and without celebration.
My mother stood waiting for me in the center of camp
Where the fire in the circle was cinders The elders sat silent.
The children all gawked. No one moved, as I straightened and walked
On cut feet and in tatters, but proudly, right into the circle,

    To nod at the elders,
        And bow to my mother,
            And grin.

For my sister had shouted my homecoming, winning her wager.
I learned soon enough, she had bragged I would take the long way
'Round the lake, return home from the west, while her playmates were
                waiting
To see me appear from the east, from the way I had gone
Only five days before. When I asked why she ran from me, Mother
Spoke up: "Ellacoya, you had to complete your taboo
Trek unaided, no one be allowed to assist you, not even
Those last halting paces relieved, so the journey holds true.
It is good you are thinner and limping and injured and weary,
The proofs of your struggle quite evident, plain to be seen,
To be witnessed by all. Now, your courage and bravery, proven,
Can never be questioned: your womanhood earned and your place
In the village assured." "Welcome home, Ellacoya," the elders
All chanted. The drums, softly beating, announced my return.
And the children danced, whooping and leaping, surrounding me, eager
To hear my adventures, but Little Fox, sister, demanded they pay
Up her winnings and Mother said: "Come now, the sweat lodge is ready.
The time for your rest and reflection is here, time to heal
Your young body, be comforted, cared for and soothed by the women
Who love you as I do. You're one of us now—not a girl
Any longer—our womanhood secrets sustaining you also.

    Then, children, I crawled in
            the sweat lodge
                    with pride and relief.

In the darkness and heat, I relaxed, as the steam eased my muscles,
And helpers brought water to pour on hot rocks in the pit.
While the women undid my torn deerskins, massaged the strong essence
Of rosemary into my shoulder, rubbed oil of the witch
Hazel onto my cuts, brushed my hair and perfumed it with balsam.
Then, rocking me gently, they sang me to sleep on their laps.
I was home, truly home, and the feelings of bliss and acceptance
Built the core of my soul a stout framework to trust and depend
On: my value undoubted, my heart unafraid, my grown body
Suffused with well-being, I slept without dreaming or care.
My aunties' sweet voices around me, now humming, now chanting,
Immersed my subconscious in murmurs familiar and old
As the rhythms once heard in the womb-waters' musical grotto,
An echo so ancient Creation itself lay enthralled.
For these brief, peace-filled moments, I rested in safety and love
Overwhelming, with nothing to do but to heal and remember
Events my taboo walk had granted me: dream's promise kept,
And the passionate grasp of wild river's rough wrench and releasing;
The swim with friend otter; two meetings with Kona; his gift
Of carved rabbit; the blackness of bear's fur abloom on the sapling;
My spirit name, Laughing Bear: totem to honor and serve;

    I recalled the bear hunters;
        dear people,
            and woke myself weeping.

The sweat lodge had cooled. All the women had left to prepare
A rich feast for my homecoming. Mother and I were alone, but
For Little Fox kneading the swelling and bruising my feet
Still endured, as our mother assured her my weeping was normal,
A healing response to my taxing ordeal and relief
At completing it nobly. "No, Mother, I weep for the hunted
Black bear and her cub I saw swimming for safety, while chased
By a party of our men and others." The mention of bear cub
Appeared to distress both my mother and Little Fox. Each
Frowned, demanding to know just how old did I think that the cub was.
"A year, maybe two, but no older," I answered. They sighed.
With a smile, Mother murmured, "She'll make it," and Little Fox whistled
Her happy trill softly, but I remained puzzled and dumb
To their secrets. The hour of the feast was commencing, so Mother
Led Sister and me from the sweat lodge to bathe in the lake,
And then dress for the meal and the songs and the speeches and dances.
As Mother bound up my hurt shoulder and Sister set quills
In my blouse, I could smell the food cooking: a meaty stew boiling,
Aroma delicious that made my tongue tickle with spit.
Then they led me to sit at the campfire upon Mother's bearskin
And gave me the first bowl of bear stew to taste and pray thanks

"To the Spirit of Black Bear,
        Your gift
                grants us winter survival…"

"Ingesting your energy, courage and powerful strength,
We now celebrate sacrifice, graceful surrender to arrow
And knife of the hunter, in full understanding of what
Your death serves. I salute you." "My totem is Bear," I announced to
My father, "my spirit-name, Laughing Bear, shown in a dream
On the mountain side next to Long Bay." As I spoke, I was seeing
The hide of a new bearskin stretched curing. My focus soon found
In the hide the rough scar so distinctive. I knew this was wily
Bear, keen on the beach where the hunters had tracked her with young
One and paddled to catch her on opposite shore of an island
Or neck of the mainland, (I wasn't sure which, but canoes
Were much swifter than swimming or walking), and so the hunt party
Was well into camp many hours with its quarry before my return.
Now, no wonder my mother and Little Fox worried, when mention
Of cub made them frown and ask questions, exchange secret looks.
To deprive a young cub of its guardian, leaving it helpless
To fatten and den itself snugly for winter was not
Our tribe's practice. The men must have judged the cub older
Than playfulness seen near the beach made it seem to my eyes.
When my brother, Loon Diver, the swimmer, stepped forward describing
Magnificent she-bear erect, standing huge to her kill

A deep rumble shook Red Hill
        like laughter
                inside the earth's belly...

The children stared startled, the men nodded wisely, the quake
Made the women sigh, knowing an omen of prosperous futures
Had sounded, while I in my heart knew my she-bear had laughed.
As the speeches proceeded the hunters assured us the age of
The young cub was two summers old, and her mother, grand dam
That she was, a great-grandmother many times over, an ancient
Of woodland and mountain and stream, her fertility spent,
No wee seeds in her tubes for the winter's long sleep and rebirthing.
The news made me glad only one life was taken to warm
And to feed us this night my emergent adulthood was honored.
My turn came to tell my adventures of vision and dread,
Of bold otter and waterfall, Kona and Moon. At the mention
Of Kona, concerned whispers hissed and my father grew stern.
"What of Kona?" he thundered. "What hurt or what harm did he threaten?
How did you escape him?" Before I could answer White Crow
Woman queried me, softly: "Sweet girl, did he touch you, caress you?
What aid did he render you?" Suddenly fearful taboo
Was undone, I felt tempted to lie, but I had to speak truly:
"Good people, brave Kona respected my woman space, left
When requested, a grieving young man, our chance meeting surprising
To him and to me, never touching, nor threatening harm,

    Only showing a pathway
        I traveled,
            the day of last raining."

"We did exchange tokens…" I ached to keep secret his gift
But knew better, so opened my amulet bag to hand rabbit
To White Crow who held it between thumb and forefinger, close
To her good eye and sucked in her cheeks, squeezing lips, tongue click-
        clicking,
Head wagging, a tear from her blinded eye seeping down cheek
To her chin, where it hung like a jewel, moon-red in the firelight.
I loved White Crow fiercely, had faith in her magical skills,
But I feared she might find something not to her liking: some essence
Of Kona confirmed in the carving I had not divined,
Some slight quirk in his nature, imbalance, some deviance lurking.
If that were the case, she would smash Kona's token.
I'd seen Her destroy countless bribes and false treasures belied in the giver.
I'd known one young boy to turn bully and coward as man.
One youth dressed in a woman's adornments refusing to husband,
To hunt or to carry. One married to live off his wife;
He contributed nothing but heartache: the blame for his actions
He laid upon her back, not caring for feelings, no love
In his heart, no remorse, no regret, without loyalty, lying
Full lips sweet as nectar, no truth in his mouth, that vitality
Missing of goodness and character staunch to life's trials.
Our village held one like that: mean, petty, grudging, a cheat.

    Cunning White Crow,
        I silently pleaded,
            find friend Kona flawless…

"Ha!" exclaimed White Crow, her fist clutching rabbit raised high
In a gesture of triumph. "Taboo well completed. The meeting
Intended. Exchanging of tokens a promise, a pledge
In all innocence made. This young man you shall marry, young woman.
His spirit name, Eagle Wing, yet to be granted, you know
From your dream on the mountain above his bereaved winter village.
Though enemies now, your betrothal unites both our tribes
When it happens." A scoff from the opposite side of the circle.
"Old woman, you babble. Taboo is invalid; her sport
With the enemy—treason. I order a quarantine, ten moons."
Confinement! My breath stopped. The venom was Yellow Snake's
        sneering.
The hatred he bore, more than that for himself, he bore White
Crow, who searched for his soul when he came to our village, found
        nothing
And warned his intended young bride, far too eager to wed,
To pay heed. So false Yellow Snake joined us, demanding we show him
Respect undeserved. Often fostering discord, ill will
By his treatment of Lame Fawn, his wife, he made family turmoil
Erupt in her brothers' protective endeavors. Again
He was fomenting trouble, negating chief's daughter's achievement,
Provoking Ahanton unwisely. The women all jeered
At his ignorance. "One moon suffices, erases suspicion,"

    Small Lame Fawn
            reminded him,
                    bravely rebuking his bluster.

When Yellow Snake reached out to strike her, my father arose.
"Your abuse and snide ranting offend us, exhausting our patience.
The Council will meet to decide how your insult to White
Crow and wild accusations, unfounded, against Ellacoya
Be dealt with, your arrogance tamed. In the meantime, this feast
Shall continue as though you'd not spoken, the rites of this passage
Proceed in accordance with custom." Then Loon Diver stood
And approached me as I stood to face him, my body still shaking.
Success and distress both at war in my heart, and my joy
Giving way to fatigue. "Ellacoya," he said, "I now give you
This eyetooth of bear for an amulet sign you have prayed
To receive. When you wear it, absorb to yourself that bear's vision,
Enhancing your own." "I am grateful, My Brother. Your gift
Is most precious. I thank you." I turned to the hunters surrounding
The campfire and bowed to their prowess, their talents, their skill,
Our dependence upon them deserving of honor. Then White Crow
Returned Kona's carving, announcing my true spirit name,
Laughing Bear, could be used. She declared me betrothed to young Eagle
Wing, Kona, no other allowed to come courting. I smiled
To imagine friend Kona's amazement to find himself promised
Without his consent or his knowledge, our futures ordained.

Just then, Yellow Snake,
        brooding and sullen,
                was summoned to Council.

His penance was swiftly pronounced by agreement of all.
He was banished to follow my trail, the same one I had taken
Around the great lake, but commanded to do it in four
Days, not five. "I will run it in three days," he scornfully boasted
And set out at once, unprepared as he was, hoping, we guessed,
To gain half-a-day's bonus by starting at night, though day counting
Commenced at each dawn, not before. His disdain for the rules,
Once again so apparent, amused Lame Fawn's brothers. His flip-flopping
Heels and his wib-wobbling behind retreating betrayed
His unfitness for physical effort and set them to howling
Derision. "I'll run it in three days." They mimicked his lisp
And his lumbering gait in a dance just so perfectly wicked,
We all had to cover our mouths and pretend to be shocked,
To spare Lame Fawn hurt feelings, or so we believed 'til we saw her
Cavorting, despite her game ankle, and laughing with glee
Seldom seen on her features since Yellow Snake entered her childless
Domain and upbraided her barrenness openly each
Time a live birth occurred in the village. Each time she assisted
New mothers to nurse, and her loving benevolence fell
On us all like sweet generous blessings, resentment was Yellow's
Response to our gratitude. He claimed neglect by mild Fawn.

    His departure relieved
        her oppression,
                but I felt uneasy...

He might, if he got that far, blunder right into the camp
Of young Kona, be taken for hostage, embarrass our elders,
Cause Lame Fawn disgrace in a new form, compel her to pay
Out a ransom she could not afford. But then, knowing the follies
Of Yellow Snake well, an alternative ploy he might try
Would be circling around to our north to re-enter from westward
As though he had done the trek ordered, appearance alone
Masquerading as fact. Soon the three days he boasted of, passing,
Brought nothing, nor four days, nor five… On the sixth afternoon,
Two tall hunters and Kona set Yellow Snake's stiffening body
Across the east entering boundary pathway and stood
Boldly, waiting our notice. "It's Kona," I whispered to White Crow,
"It's Kona." I ran to tell Mother but Lame Fawn's shrill scream
Of alarm brought her brothers with weapons confronting the strangers,
Unarmed and impassively watching, though Lame Fawn fell down
Right in front of them clutching her ankle and yelling at Yellow Snake.
"What have you done?" unafraid of the three who stood, arms
At their sides, as her brothers bent to her. My father, arriving,
Commanded her silence, demanded to know of the men
Who they were. "This is Kona," I told him. "Remember the union
That white Crow predicted," I urged him, in hope and in fear.

    "Are there any behind you?"
        asked Father.
                "Of course!" said the tallest…

"We come to return this man, Yellow Snake's, body because
Of the tale he has told us while dying of injuries suffered
From falling to rocks on the shore below cliffs at Long Bay."
"Come in peace," said my father, "and tell us this tale he has told you.
Lame Fawn and her brothers will tend to the body at once.
We shall eat and send food to your men in the woods by the women.
We'll listen for truth or for fable from Yellow Snake's lips
As you tell what he said." But when Lame Fawn was lifted, her ankle
Gave way and she fell with a cry, her small foot all awry.
She was carried to White Crow, her foot all a-dangle, fish-flopping,
Her face pale with pain as I hurried to help with her care.
I forgot about Kona, the strangers and Yellow Snake's dying.
My concern for our midwife, my friend of the life-coaxing hands
Was consuming. I paid little heed to the tallest of strangers,
The one who had answered "Of course," who now knelt facing White
Crow across Lame Fawn's leg. "I am healer, as you are," he told her.
"I've worked with such injuries, often successfully, gait
Restored well, in most cases to normal."   "But this one is lamed for
Some years now," said White Crow. "But not," I protested, "when young.
"For we ran and we jumped all together as children," I added
With passion. "Her ankle was broken alone on taboo.

> Fawn returned to us crawling,
>   too many weeks late
>   for true healing."

"The breaks have recurred," said the tall one. "And that may be good,"
He suggested. "I saw, as you ran to the dead one, the angle
Your foot had, the limping it caused you. I marveled the speed
You could move with." "Too much speed for safety," groaned Lame
      Fawn, unhappy
At being the patient instead of the helper. "I wish
I had been much more careful," she scolded herself." "Hush now,
      woman!"
Crooned White Crow. "The tall one speaks wisely. Together we'll bind
Up your leg and foot properly. Laughing Bear, fetch us some water
And hides, and send Little Fox after long thongs and stout sticks."
We were glad to have something to do to assist and ran quickly,
Returned to find Lame Fawn gone quiet and held in the strong
Gripping fingers the tall one had placed on her foot and her ankle.
First, slowly, he bent to hear bones tell their story beneath
Lame Fawn's skin, then he pulled and held firmly while White Crow
      worked surely
To wrap and bind tightly. Dear Lame Fawn lay squeezing our hands.
Not a sound did she utter, just widened her eyes and kept looking
In mine. I could see her relief as the bindings took hold.
She relaxed. We determined to serve her until she was walking
Again and so carried a bed to the circle and fed
Her there, waiting to hear what the visiting strangers intended
By bringing back Yellow Snake's body in peace and good will.

    They were enemies,
        fighting us often,
            not long ago warring.

Their numbers diminishing weakened their power. They lost
To us more than they triumphed, their bravery never in question.
My father, Ahanton, our chieftain had slain their last chief,
Kona's father, mere short weeks before: understanding their peaceful
Appearance with Yellow Snake's body a mystery not
Yet explainable. Legend of old told of two brothers fighting
For power once, splitting our village, with half going south
To Long Bay, where they'd prospered and lived for a hundred snow seasons.
No person alive now who knew that lost brother, no kin
Keeping contact, the story alone kept such history vivid:
A tale of betrayal, we thought it. I wondered how they
Told the legend, what feelings still harbored, what enmity lurking
Might fashion a ruse such as this to infiltrate our camp.
Lame Fawn's brothers, Gray Hawk and Red Elk, soon reported her
                husband's
Dead body bore multiple bruises, his stomach and rib
Cage distorted by internal bleeding consistent with impact.
No sign of a battle attack wound, or torture, or mark
To refute the account of the strangers, who claimed he had fallen.
"We need to believe them," they cautioned her. "Nothing can prove
Them untruthful. His body, still rigid, suggests that his dying
Occurred on the trail as they carried him homeward alive."

    So we fed them
        and ate with them,
            waiting to hear their strange story.

I noticed the tall one, who'd treated her, studying Lame
Fawn's expression for signs of discomfort or shock manifesting,
And saw White Crow watching him closely, convinced of his skill.
By the deference shown him by Kona's companion and Kona,
We sensed he had taken the place of their chief, but appeared
Not to want the distinction: his manner commanding, but gentle,
No arrogance evident, leadership talents inbred
In his nature, his stature, but healing his calling, his passion.
Reluctantly standing, beginning the story, he told
How their women had heard the faint, pitiful cries emanating
From Yellow Snake lying on rocks at the foot of the cliff,
The still waters of Long Bay enhancing his moans with far-carrying
Echoes to reach them and prompt them to follow the sounds
To his broken, soft body, surprised he was enemy nearly
Arrived at their village and babbling of Kona: a tale
Of delirium; wildly improbable ranting; betrothal,
Uniting of villages long kept apart, and a girl,
Ellacoya, whose fault it all was. Even weakened, his anger
Was sour, his desire to arouse their hostilities strong.
They mistrusted his motives, but trusted good omen when Kona
Recounted the meeting he had on the cliff with the girl

    Ellacoya,
        her swim with the otter,
            across their bay waters...

"I'm Medicine Otter," he told us, "the interim chief
Of our village and uncle of Kona, here standing before you.
We chose to return your man's body to show our good faith
And desire for a meeting between our two separate peoples
Who once lived as one, if the legend our elders insist
Is the truth be the same as the memories your elders carry."
"It is," agreed Red Feather, voice a mere scratch in the air
From a throat slack with age and lungs emptied by labors of gasping.
We listened amazed (he'd not spoken for days, next to death
As he seemed). He confirmed that the legend of Medicine Otter
Was our legend also. The Old One remembering best,
In retelling the tales we once begged of him, often preserving
Our history, passing it down, this instruction his last
Occupation as energy left him, still loved and respected.
Much drama he gave us in telling, enjoyably bright
Scenes describing events resurrected from dim years uncounted.
His guardianship of our heritage soon would be passed
To another. He'd lived long enough to endorse the tall Otter's
Disclosure. A blessing, it proved to be crucial for what
Happened next: a proposal so startling we hardly believed it.
Though Father and Red Feather saw it made excellent sense,

    Kona's uncle's suggestion,
        at first, made our Councilmen
        doubtful.

He wanted to merge our two villages back into one,
Recombining a peoples too long kept apart by the folly
Of brothers long dead, the betrothal of daughter and son
Of each chieftain a logical step in advancing the process.
"I gladly would marry friend Kona, one day," I agreed,
"If he wishes, but not right away and not merely symbolic
Of armistice." Medicine Otter just smiled at my bold
Protestation. "Young Kona has warned that your courage and character
Make you formidable, young as you are. But I swam
With you, looked in your eyes there in Long Bay, inhabiting otter,
My medicine animal, saw for myself Ellacoya: the girl
Turning woman, enchantress of Kona, my nephew. His grieving
Could well have made fantasy real to him forming a dream
For his panic and sorrow to feed on (distraught and distracted
And lost as he was at the time). The encounter proved real,
Brought him peace and a promise of futures both hopeful and fruitful.
A method to honor the loss of his father instead
Of avenging his death with more fighting and killing and hatred
Began to take form as he praised Ellacoya's wise words
To him. Gently concerned yet adhering to purpose, she altered
His view of her village, her manner disproving old tales
Of barbarity, cruelty, rampant disdain for our villagers.
Seeing in her a young person, the same as himself,

    Simply doing her growth work,
        They met on the mountain
          and parted.

"As friends, exchanged tokens of value next morning. I watched
Through the eyes of the otter from shallows and saw their affections
Develop in innocence: neither suspecting the change
Coming over them; neither aware of a possible future
Together (nor I, until Yellow Snake's tale told of White
Crow's prediction). Snake's scorn notwithstanding, his venomous
             energy,
Fierce, though his body was failing, lent truth to his rant.
This fed Kona's desire for a suitable end to the killings:
To honor his father with peaceful solutions; to bind
Up the hurt and the waste of good lives before perilous winter
Would weaken us further, and threatening flatlanders south
Travel north with their guns and diseases and pale skin to plunder
Our rivers, our woodlands, the deer and the beaver and moose.
As reported by dispossessed Sagamores fleeing to northward,
Grave troubles are coming. We need to make plans and be strong
To preserve our blest heritage, honor our ancestors, cherish
Our woodland, its creatures, its bounty. Protect Mother Lake
Where the fish people dwell. She reveals her approval, displeasure,
Abundance or drowning, her lessons (well taught), the uncouth
Do ignore at their peril. Strangers do war against land and pure waters:
No harmony shared with our Earth; no respect for Her Heart."

   And so, finished with speech,
       he sat down
           to await our responses…

I saw, as he glanced at me, eyes I had looked in before,
In Long Bay as I swam. I understood how he was gifted
To be a shape-changer who borrowed an animal, bird,
Or live tree to inhabit when needing to glean information
Not otherwise knowable. Few there were granted this art,
Even fewer enabled to suffer it, absent full madness.
A terrible talent to bear, but a sacred one too.
He could not see the future like White Crow, the past like Red Feather.
This Medicine Otter, tall uncle of Kona, still young
And unmarried, yet carried his duties, unsought and unwanted,
With dignity, character, purpose. Survival for all his
Main aim. He, by choice, could be everywhere, anywhere, nowhere,
Commanded respect. He held the attention of all of us, wrapped
In the quiet of night, as we pondered his words without speaking.
The crackling of fire logs collapsing, the sparks shooting up,
Dying out in the darkness, the kiss of the smoke…no distraction
From thoughts deep and heavy with dread of a future reports
Of the Sagamores painted. The benefits union of villages
Weighed against problems of enmity seared in some souls.
The expressions on faces reflecting the glow of the campfire
Bore clues to such thoughts, entertained and rejected by turns,

    Until Red Feather, gasping,
        suggested we meet
            with their peoples.

My father assented, saw merit inherent in talks
With the others concerning the future, the dangers our villages
Faced. "But the marriage," he said, as he looked down at me,
Then at Kona, "we do not consider at present advisable.
Both are too youthful, unformed as to character, wise
As their conduct has proven thus far. There remain many trials,
Much tasking that each must accomplish before they may wed,
If they choose. A betrothal agreement must wait until meetings
Between our two peoples conclude in good will and accord.
For if not, then no marriage can heal the longstanding division
Between us. My daughter speaks well to refuse such a scheme.
Though White Crow may be right, her prediction must ripen and prosper
As destiny wills." I was sad but relieved at his words.
As yet, Kona had not done his vision quest, found his true spirit
Name, taken his medicine animal's essence to heart.
Neither one of us knew who the other would be in adulthood,
If friendship now solid in youth would endure and would form
A stout basis for lifelong commitment, a bond in maturity.
Looking at Kona, I nodded so no one could see,
And he nodded to me, imperceptibly smiling in secret.
But Lame Fawn and Medicine Otter both watched us, sharp-eyed.

> Then they looked at each other
>   and blinked
>   their amusement.

All four of us giggled, upsetting the elders' grim sense
Of propriety. White Crow then clapped her hands smartly, and laughing,
Said, "Good for the young ones! They've not inhaled hatred or fear
From the milk of their mothers, have not been taught prejudice, bias.
There's hope we shall join with our sisters and brothers below,
Reuniting in harmony peoples once lost to each other.
And I, for one, welcome the unity soon to be gained."
"You seem certain the talks will succeed," said my father to White Crow.
"Full certain," she answered. "I've seen us together, and more
I'll not mention. But these two," she gestured at Lame Fawn and
            Medicine
Otter, "shall also be married to bind our two tribes.
Both are healers of body and spirit, are fit for the purpose
Of mending the rift of one hundred snow seasons gone by."
"It is time we retire for the night," said my father, "and ask in
Our dreams to be guided aright. Then tomorrow we'll choose
Who shall journey to Long Bay with Medicine Otter and Kona.
Thus kinsmen and women, advancing ideas, cause plans
To take form." "With permission," said Kona, "I go to my tribesmen
Who wait in the woods and inform them of what has been said
Here tonight." "And I with him," the quiet one added, his speaking
Voice musical, resonant, bidding us each a good night.

    And they left,
        while the rest of us
            thoughtfully sought out our dreaming.

I lay next to Lame Fawn, determined to rouse at first sounds
Of distress, but she made none. Her breathing, soft, even and restful,
Was lullaby. Dreamless I slept until dawn when she nudged
Me awake, said my name, and sat upright, forgetting her ankle
Was broken again 'til my hand on her arm stopped her move,
Her attempt to stand up. She remembered her fall and vain Yellow
Snake's dying, and all that had happened the long day before.
So we whispered together of wonderful changes. Expectant
And hopeful, we chirped like two nestlings. Mists melted away.
The pale sunlight emerging transformed morning's dimness and shadows
To flickering patterns of light all around, as a breeze
Came meandering over the treetops to rustle and rattle
Dry leaves of the oak, quake the aspen, awaken the camp.
"I must bathe and prepare my dear dead husband's body," she murmured,
Fresh tears in her eyes. Why she wept for his passing escaped
Me. But Lame Fawn was tender to all, never minding their meanness,
Or failings of temperament. Seeing in each, the hurt soul
Shrunk beneath the façade. I was far more judgmental, impatient
With foibles, than she. Just then Medicine Otter emerged
From the forest with branches he'd fashioned for aiding her walking.
He lifted her, taught her the use of them, tested her foot.

> He seemed satisfied
> White Crow had done a good job.
> He was smiling.

"Perhaps we shall have to create a new name for you. Lame
Won't describe you when healing's complete, although Fawn is still
            perfect."
I looked at the two of them standing together, his hand
At her elbow for steadiness, head and back bending to study her face for
Expressions of pain or unease. There were none.
She was calm, appeared eager to test out her walking, accomplished
Supported by branches he'd fashioned and brought for her use.
His enormous height dwarfed her small stature. They made quite a pair.
His concern for his patient a trait I much liked in him, trusting
His interest soon might grow deep. I could tell by her blush
Her attraction to him was surprising, perhaps a new feeling
She'd never experienced brushing her heart, downcast eyes
Not concealing confusion and pleasure from my lucky vantage
Ground, seated and watching their drama develop. How strange
This new day was! How whimsical! Change brought wild improbabilities
Pouncing like fox kits at play. It pummeled our lives,
Making sport of our certainties, wrestling and tumbling together
Our age-old beliefs in a future untroubled, benign.
Only yesterday feeling secure, now this morning new prospects,
Exciting and frightening, loomed: the unthinkable stooping
To clutch us and carry us off as the hawk plucks the kit

    In all innocence frolicking.
        I felt a chill
            And a shiver.

My mother, approaching, regarded my face with concern.
How I wanted to run to her, bury my threatening weeping
Between her soft breasts and give way to the child still within.
I'd expected my recent taboo journey ended all weaknesses,
Hardened me resolute, fit to survive without aid.
Yet my feelings from childhood persisted to mix independence
With neediness, courage with cowardice, envy with love.
Still uncertain, confused by conflicting emotions assailing
My reason, precarious balance achieved by sheer will,
I stood facing her as she came nearer, my lower lip quivering,
Giving my bravely-held posture the lie. But she held
Out her arms, drew me close, understanding, she said, how so baffling
It was to be my age: half child, half adult. "The profound
Alterations in body and mind brought about by the onset
Of menses destroys equilibrium," Mother assured
Me, and added, "In time you will find your own balance, your inner
Resolve. Learn to live with strong passions, to care and to serve,
To receive and to give, or to grieve or congratulate, welcome
Or speed on their ways all the people your life shall embrace.
Please stay open to everything. Shielding your heart is quite useless
And foolishly cramped, merely crippling creative pursuits."

So I wept and felt strong,
        reassured of my progress,
                much calmer.

Whatever the future would conjure could wait. My right now
Was exciting enough, what with meetings to settle our joining
Of villages, burying Yellow Snake's body (respect
For Lame Fawn our intent). Then, preparing for winter as usual:
Gathering wood, twigs and sticks and the curls of birch bark
For our cook fires and sweat lodge, repairing our clothing and shelters,
And storing up corn ears and acorns, and smoking our fish,
And the hunting and drying of deer meat and moose meat and berries.
We had much to do while the weather and water held soft.
When the ice again formed, we would chop holes for water. The fishing
For salmon and trout could resume. And the crossing to Long
Bay a much shorter walk on the new ice and snow, although dangerous.
Currents caused weaknesses under the drifts, so a man
Might fall through without warning, be lucky to surface, not drowning:
Trapped under the ice and unable to find the slim slit
He fell into. We lost one that way every winter by drowning,
Or freezing when wet, as the wind froze his clothes to the ice
Where he lay in exhaustion, intending to rest but succumbing
To cold unaware. All these thoughts filled my mind as I walked
Beside Lame Fawn to help preparations for Yellow Snake's burial.
Young as I was I had seen enough death not to fear.

    Although Yellow Snake's spirit
        still hovered,
                our songs would release him.

Much singing and many strong chants would be needed. A soul
Such as his had no wings of its own to fly skyward and homeward
Unless we assisted with loving goodbye songs to lift
And sustain its slow, faltering flight. And until our forgiveness
For every least insult, abuse and mistreatment he wrought,
For each lie that he told, for the hurts to Lame Fawn he delivered,
Erased from our hearts all resentments and memories sour.
It was more as a kindness to us than to him that we did this.
His power to rile our mild natures would dissipate, die
With him, tether us to him no longer. His malice forgiven,
His failings forgotten, his name never uttered again.
With our singing we freed ourselves from him and freed him from
          earthbound
Attachments. For all his intent to provoke us to war
With our brothers in Long Bay, his last act achieved quite the opposite,
Making us grateful and willing to aid his limp soul
In its passage. We all had been taught from our births that in order
To heal we must find in that person some small part to love,
Just a teensy bit, White Crow instructed us, pinching her fingers
To such a small gap we would laugh, understanding her point.
It was hard to find something to love in dead Yellow Snake's nature,
But Lame Fawn had done so, and we could oblige her in this.

     So we sang his dressed body
               to graveside
                         and chanted him cloudward.

Then talks were begun as to who would be chosen to go
To Long Bay for discussions on merger and who from that village
Remain with us here in good faith. When the young one who spoke
With the musical voice was selected to stay with us, Little
Fox barely suppressed her delight. He was double her age
But she thought him a suitable playmate, she said in a whisper.
"Perhaps," I agreed, "you can whistle and he can play drum
To your tunes." "Or we'll make up new songs for the evening campfire."
She added. I hoped for her sake he would not disappoint
Her fond scheme, would indulge her a little while, now and again if
Approached. Little Fox was not shy and her brashness appealed
To some people but turned many others away from her energy.
Kona's companion seemed quiet, reserved, although poised
In his manner, polite and quite sure of himself and his duties.
The chance he would pay much attention to her was in doubt
In my mind. But before the day's end, earnest Kona and Medicine
Otter and Father departed for Long Bay. While Lame
Fawn and Red Feather, Mother and I lingered watching and waving
Goodbye and good luck, I heard Little Fox asking his name.
"I am Song Maker," came the low answer. "I whistle my melodies,"
Little Fox told him and let loose her lively new air.

    His expression was comical,
        hearing her tune
            so inventive…

"How can one so young create melody out of slight breath?"
"I was born at the waterfall after spring rain," said my sister
In answer, "my very first Earth sound was water on rocks."
"Mine was hoot owl," said Song Maker, "singing me secrets from treetops
In darkness, now near and now far, to the coyote's call."
"Morning heat beetle's whirring," trilled Little Fox. "Red squirrel's
        rancor,"
Chirred Song Maker. "Frog in the rushes," croaked Little Fox. "Hawk
In the meadow," cried Song Maker. "Mice in the grasses." "The fisher's
        wild
Scream." "The gull's squawk from the seashore." "The seized rabbit's
        wail."
"The wave's thunder." "The whistle of wind." "And the crashing of
        branches."
The two of them vied to come up with original themes
For their music, in tempo and increasing volume that had us
All listening, clapping in rhythm, diverted, amused
By their good-natured contest, so pleasing, so joyful, so novel.
My sister an able contestant. She easily kept
Up the pace of invention. I doubted no longer Song Maker
Would pay her attention. The pair were one singer in two
Distinct bodies, enriching the harmonies Earth lends her children:
Both gifted with sensitive hearing; creative, quick minds;
Their abilities equal despite the age difference between them;
Capacities matching for mimicry; passionate grasp of Earth's pulse.

    What a wealth of sweet music
        and rousing fresh heartsongs
           they promised!

So Yellow Snake's curse once again became blessing, instead,
By acquainting two talented singers who otherwise never
Might meet in their lifetimes. Though during the days as we worked
At our duties, their separate tasks were dividing the two,
In the dusk before sitting to eat, we could hear them composing
Brief phrases of melody off at the edge of the woods.
They were frequently last to the meal, too engrossed in their sharing
Of snatches of song that had hummed in their heads all day long
To be bothered by hunger. My jealousy hurt in my marrow
To see how my sister, at seven, had found her true path,
While I floundered, unknowing and ignorant what my true calling
Would be. I could do any task set before me with ease,
But had never got lost in the doing as she did; had never
Dissolved into effort: oblivious, carried beyond
Myself, focused and pure to endeavor creative, enchanting.
So grounded and sober and practical I had become,
That my calling eluded me. Something essential was hiding
From conscious awareness; thought frivolous: stifled, suppressed.
On taboo trek, I reveled in freedom of thoughts and of actions.
Once home, I reverted, obedient, passively seeking
To please, which felt wrong for me now. A new quest must begin:

        To discover my bliss
                and to follow
                        wherever it led me.

I'll plunge myself into my tasks, I resolved in my mind.
I'll stay open, as Mother has urged, to my colorful passions,
Experiment bravely with scary new traits of the heart,
And indulge all expressions of joy as my sister is doing.
The core of my nature shall surface, as hers has. I feel
It is straining to free itself, spring into purposeful action.
Some clue must persist in emotions taboo journey drew
From me: moon dreams and visions; the dancing of lights in the North
        sky;
The dance of the leaves on bear's scratching tree; brilliance of Sun
Lending sparkles to flowing dark waters that tumble, a blinding
Display of swift motion; the stretch of the hemlocks; the pause
Of the rocks; the lithe sway of the birches and branches in hurricane's
Gale; or the wafting of spiders airborne on their webs;
The winged whirl of green seed pods all spinning to earth; or the dancing
Of fireflies, butterflies, grasshoppers, toads; and the thrush
In its swooping low arcs as it flies to its nestlings, heads bobbing.
How everything dances, I marveled. How movement prevails.
Even infants are constantly testing, extending their bodies,
Calm only while sleeping or nursing. And yet, even then
Their small fingers, uncurling and curling in rhythm with sucking,
Beat baby step dance of the fists on their mothers' full breasts.

> The enchantment of movement
>   seethes everywhere.
>   My dance emerges.

I felt in my sinews the rhythm of laughter. The pulse
In my blood made old sorrows recalled shake my ribcage.
The mix of sweet joys contradicting wet tears sought release.
I became the taut predator ready to spring, my lithe body
Explosive with energy, pinned, hesitating, unsure.
I sat motionless there by the campfire, my feelings in turmoil;
So distanced from everything normal, I thought I'd gone mad.
I was expert at seeming untroubled, but this was consuming
My skill at control. I was fearful of acting the fool
Until Little Fox, standing by Song Maker, whistled and warbled
A bird call while Song Maker's hum interwove it for depth.
And then, wordless, they sang a duet of pure melody, soaring
And dipping, first softly, then louder; first slowly, then fast
As the galloping deer in full flight race their fears through the forest;
Then, resting, return to their browsing untroubled, serene.
I had never heard Little Fox sing with such passion, such purity,
Voice as mature as a woman's and richer then most.
This was no childish tune but a glorious harmony blending
With Song Maker's vibrant low rumble of tones in true pitch.
As we listened, Song Maker encouraged the men to sing with him
And Little Fox beckoned the women to follow her lead.

So we sang this new music,
        this wordless new anthem,
                together.

I could not sit still as the voices around me took hold
Of their parts with more confidence, singing more surely, more sweetly.
The music, relaxing the old rigid rhythms of drum
Beat and hand slap, flowed water-like, liquid and tunelessly curling:
A vapor of echoes about the stout tree trunks and rocks
From the women; a thunder to level whole mountains, erupting
At times from the men. This was music to rattle the soul,
Seize the feet of the lame, yank the arms of the dead from their sockets.
And so, without thinking, I rose from my place by the fire
To begin a wild dancing that sprang from my innermost being,
A spirit unleashed in my body: an arrow, a hawk,
A bold eagle, a deer leaping boulders, a wolf lowly skulking,
A moose proudly pacing. First leaping, then whirling around the wide
        circle
Of singers, engulfed in my passion for movement, I spun
To the dark of the woods—disappearing as mist into shadow—
Then springing—a gust from a squall—reappearing, I soared
Into view again, landing as lightly as leaf upon water.
I drifted, at one with the melody, sank to the ground
As song tapered and came to its end. In the ensuing silence
I breathed my rank perfume of purpose, uncovered my bliss.

        In the sweat of my life dance,
                at last I had found
                        my true calling

My sister and Song Maker stared at me. Loon Diver smiled.
Mother's tears were high praise. Even Red Feather, White Crow, and
      Lame Fawn
Knew something both changeful and wonderful wakened in me.
When I danced, I was fierce and sublime, a strong storm and a zephyr,
A bat and a butterfly, avalanche, rain and bright dew
On the meadow, the flash of a fish in the shallows. All elegant
Elements, wild, coalesced and exploded and flowed
From my heart to my limbs, to the earth, to the sky, for my people's
Delight and amusement and wonder, transformed from a girl
Into agile, bright flame, fragile snowflake, bolt lightning and firefly.
Black bear that laughs as it romps with her cubs in the Fall
Between foraging, gorging on ants, grubs, and acorns for Winter's
Long sleep, was my totem's bold spirit. She burst herself free
In me, savage and raw, overwhelming, exhausting and glorious.
Power to be, just to BE, in exuberant glee,
This wee creature of Earth, born to dance on Her breast for a moment
In time and then vanish, perhaps, or persist in Her core
As an energy quenchless and pulsing, eternally vibrant,
Alive in new form, never dying. I felt myself one
With all creatures. The moil of white maggots asquirm on dead flesh did
A dance of stark beauty in reverent service to life.

   So might I, in my dance,
      elevate the mundane
         to Earth's glory.

High thoughts for a young girl to have. Grandiose. To be mocked
By the sober and stifled among us perhaps. But ignoring
Temptations to doubt myself, I would continue my dance
Through the life that was promised me, long-lived and fearless,
The laugh of black bear in my throat, my death rale at the end.
True to totem I'd live out my years by this lake and these mountains
As Earth has intended my people to do: in calm love
And abundance, in beauty and kindness, creative, expansive,
Reflective—the qualities humanly finest we owe
One another, well taught from our births to express and embody.
Not every tribe in the region believed, as we did,
That the purpose of life was to live it in harmony, peaceful
And sharing. The frequent attacks from the tribe in Long Bay
Proved their differing view, an inherited attitude. Conflict
Their aim until Kona's great grief at his father's brave death,
And Ahanton's black sobbing in sorrow the breast of my mother
Received on the night that he slew him, joined forces. Desire
For an end to hot slaughter grew strong in the hearts of both victims,
The slayer as trapped in his role as the slaughtered. All this
Came as clear to my mind in the instant I sank from my dancing
As if revelation had boomed with a thunderclap roar.

In my bosom, old teachings,
        but half-understood,
                I grasped fully.

The changes in me, coming rapidly, forcefully, hot
In my soul, set to shaping the passionate, purposeful woman
Emerging from innocent, stubborn grown girl I had been.
Now ecstatic, I wanted a tether to bless me with limits,
To keep me from shattering, bind this new me to adult
Form and wisdom. Again I was waiting for something outside me
To touch me, a power both wiser and stronger than I.
But remembering cowering fearful all night on that cliffside
Awaiting some aid on my walkabout, only to hear
From my innermost core a sweet message of comfort, assurance,
I crouched at the cooling low campfire, surrounded and loved
By the women who'd traveled this shifting terrain in their earlier
Days. Comprehending my turmoil, observant yet not
Interfering, they trusted the process unfolding to carry
Me safely. I sensed their restraint was their gift from the heart.
This was growth task to do on my own. I felt sure it amused them,
As well as concerned them, to watch my moods play with me, blow
Me about like white froth upon beach sand. My growth was essential,
A duty of service my people demanded of each
Of their children, not always discharged by the brash and the thoughtless.
Determined to hone my best self, to mature, to stand tall,

    I would claw through my tangles
        of changefulness,
            brambles of mystery…

Willingly struggle to grow without mishap, express
Myself helpfully, earn a position of trust with my people,
Recapture and hold the conviction of fitness to lead
I had felt on taboo. Much was owed because much had been given
Me: Mother and Father, each caring, intelligent, kind;
My small sister, big brother of outstanding personal talents;
A village determined on peaceful pursuits to enhance
Our survival. A bountiful lake and dense woodlands of plenty
Surrounding us. Grateful for all, but amazed at how long
It was taking, how buffeted, foolish and wild I was feeling,
I well understood how the young can get lost as they thrash
Through transition; how boys with mean fathers attack to destroy them,
Protecting and loving their mothers, or take out their rage
On the weakest around them in secret; how some girls, unfortunate,
Never know nurturing, cannot give love to a child
Unless someone more blest intervenes. I had watched her as Lame Fawn,
More crippled by uncaring mother than injury, strove
To become a whole woman, mistakenly marrying Yellow
Snake, fearful no other would want her, unsure of her gifts
Until White Crow and Grey Goose, my mother, enfolded her, taught her
The beauty and magic and worth of each child at its birth.

> Now her small loving hands
>   Were the first to soothe newborns,
>   heal mothers.

Ignoring vile Yellow Snake's cruelties, Lame Fawn, while wrapped
In the wings of White Crow and Grey Goose, hatched her last smothered
            fragment
Of self, understanding, belatedly, worth a birthright
Of existence. I watched dignity flower within, saw her brighten
In spirit, intent on her calling, effective, serene,
Fully four Spring's my senior. I failed at the time to appreciate
Just what had happened, but understood now what delayed
Her maturing, saw why she had clung to our friendship when differing
Ages and marriage would normally split us apart.
The hurt child in her relished the care I was given, the nurture
So vital, so taken for granted, I had that she lacked,
Yet absorbed from our friendship. But when after marriage to Yellow
Snake threatened grave harm, the two women who loved her adopted
The role her own mother neglected, a mother whose love
Was reserved for her sons, unaware how her daughter was pining.
This inner affliction her brothers detected but could
Not root out with their boisterous, loving attention and teasing
Assurances, telling her legends all saying the same
Thing: that women are equal, hold up half the sky on their shoulders.
A truth her experience failed to supply for her childhood,
Accepted now fully, and joyfully shown in her work.

    Her example had proven
            how love
                    subdues evil so subtly.

No flesh-piercing arrows, no battles, no warriors fierce
Were required to mislead and subdue generations of people
When prejudice, bias, and ignorance stunted their souls,
When brute force substituted for reason, rash feelings supplanted
Reflection, undisciplined actions, encouraged, admired
And mistaken for manhood, restraint branded cowardice, girlish,
And women ignored, were the rule. Many sagas of old
Warring tribal disputes were retold in our legends as lessons
In folly. A miracle we had survived with our peace-
Loving ways. We were able to fight, but we hated blood conflict,
Preferred confrontations in sportsmanlike games of great skill
And agility. Artful designs for our clothing and baskets
Competed with beauty, creative, original, bright.
Our dyed hues, clever quill work displayed at Fall powwows,
Were traded with others for productive sharing. We met
Again this Fall to demonstrate craftsmanship, heard frightful stories
Of armies of pale ones encroaching along the sea's coast
And the banks of wide rivers, invading our hunting grounds. Wasteful
And noisy, too careless of nature's precarious poise.
White Crow's vision of future catastrophe found confirmation.
She told it once more to us, soberly warning of change.

    Walking home from the gathering,
        downcast,
            I feared for our people.

I prayed that my father would safely return from Long Bay.
He had missed the Fall gathering, stayed to the south many sunsets,
Too long for my comfort. I wondered had progress occurred,
Or had enmity won and our party been slain, no provision
For Song Maker's safety considered. This waiting for news
Prompted action. Pretending to forage for herbs, I sped southward
To spy out whatever I could, keenly wishing to be
A shape-changer like Medicine Otter instead of a dancer.
What good was a dancer when peril came stalking, when fear
Ruled our days. With my mind on dark futures, attention distracted,
I heedlessly raced down the path and collided head down
With lone Kona on vision quest quietly standing and waiting
To see, he said, who could be crashing so carelessly toward
His position. Once stopped in his presence, I told him of White Crow's
Dire warnings, then asked if he needed alone time, as I
Had, to finish his walkabout. "No," he assured me while smiling,
"I'm Eagle Wing now, and have come in advance to your home
To announce our success with the talks and the pending arrival,
Quite soon, of the party from Long Bay to settle on terms.
While alone on the path, I reviewed how my vision was changing
Me deeply, a grieving and angry lost boy now is grown."

It was true he seemed sturdier,
        sure in his stance,
                much more confident.

"As Eagle, my vision is keen, all encompassing, clear.
I can see that our peoples must act for our future survival,
Combine our slight forces, employ our fine minds in the time
That approaches, avoid confrontations. We're destined to suffer
Grave illnesses never encountered before if we stand
In place stubbornly. Better to melt into woodland and mountains,
Retreat, be invisible, unified, stalwart, unseen
By the eyes of invaders. The Sagamores tell us of treaties
Ignored, hard-won promises broken, this alien grip
On the land claiming ownership, forcing them out of their fishing
And hunting grounds. Foolish to think men can own Mother Earth,
Keep another from sharing her bounty, traversing her meadows,
Or drinking her waters." He shook his head sadly, eyes down
For a moment, then rallying, asked me to walk with him back to
My village. But, eager to greet my dear father again,
I refused, yet assured him I soon would return with the party
Behind him. "Your love for your father is strong, as was mine
For my own," he said softly. I felt then a grief sharply piercing,
To think this young person so gently could treat me, the child
Of the man who had killed his own father in battle. No hatred
To blight our affections, no urge for revenge in his bones.

    Although some might regard him as weak,
        I saw well
            how he'd strengthened.

Rejecting old customs of conflict, embracing the past
That predated division of villages, seeking old unity,
Kona was steadfast. No meanness corrupted his soul
Or his spirit. A truly unusual youth, and I wondered
Whose influence guided his growing, whose heart held him safe
In her own when a boy? Who watched over and loved him? Who tenderly
Taught him to think and to feel and behave as he did?
He walked on down the path to my village. I ran to greet Father,
Together with Medicine Otter and others, who came
Slowly walking, assisting a woman appearing more ancient
Than Red Feather, older than anyone I'd ever seen.
Her great girth was magnificent, stunning, a marvel to contemplate.
How her small feet bore her weight was miraculous. How
She had walked all the way from Long Bay at her age and condition,
I could not imagine. She ought to have swum like a whale
With deep water supportive. No ten of our strongest could carry
Her. No one could lift her in case she should stumble or fall.
Yet she paced along slowly, allowing a steadying hand
At her elbow when roots or stones hampered her progress along
The rough pathway. I halted and stared in amazement, quite rudely.
She saw me and laughed at my gawking, while Father looked shocked.

    But her laughter prevailed
        over scolding,
            and everyone chuckled.

She had that effect on the company, Father as well.
I escaped his initial desire to have taught me my manners
Yet felt disapproval's mild sting as I stood with eyes closed,
My head bowed, to one side and awaited reproof or correction.
But Father dealt neither. His hand on my head broke the spell
Of contrition. His words whispered softly when all had proceeded
On past were some comfort. "I barely contained my own awe
When first seeing her," Father confessed. "You did well enough, all things
Considered. She's proud of her size. Your expression confirmed
Her conviction her figure contains massive import, a monument
Hewn in stout flesh to the glory of life and great joy
In the living. One cannot be sad or dismayed in her presence
For long, for she radiates energy, vigor, huge grace
And deliberate rapture. She's Kona's great-grandmother's mother,
Most ancient of ancients. The last to be born of our camp
On the day our tribe split, so she claims, none alive to gainsay her
Assertions. Whatever her age, we fall under her charms
When she laughs or speaks serious words of encouragement, planning
Our merger. The woman is Red Feather's counterpart, White
Crow's wise complement, mentor of Medicine Otter and Kona."
"She's big as a whale," I protested, "she'll eat all our food."

    "Yes, she will," he agreed,
        "and we'll offer her
            all we have gladly."

Regretting my selfish concerns, I so yearned to grow smart,
To be generous, sharing, and kind. We caught up with the party
And entered our village together to hear White Crow shouting
A greeting announcing that here was the great Spotted Whale
Come to council. I cringed to think White Crow could be so insulting
To someone she never had met. "Spotted Whale is her name,"
Murmured Father. "An apt one," I answered. We strove to seem serious.
There was no need. Spotted Whale screamed her pleasure with laughs
That spread gleeful hilarity echoing all through the campsite,
Caused babies to burble and children to skip to her side.
Old men struggled to rise in her honor, and young men went scurrying,
Finding and bringing four stumps to arrange for her seat
At our circle. She needed all four when she carefully lowered
Her backside, positioned precisely with fluid slow grace
Evidencing a musculature underlying astonishing
Fat which was sturdy, supporting her ably, control
Of her frame well maintained in old age. I assumed she could wrestle
A moose if need be. What an image that prompted. My mind
Ran away with the picture as, laughing, I brought her some water.
"I sit on moose. Too old for wrestling," she said to me, belched
With a rumble outdoing a man, and winked, wickedly sly.

> "I see into your thoughts,
> > Ellacoya, the dancer.
> > > Perform for me."

Signaling Little Fox, bowing to Song Maker, poised
I stood waiting for music but Spotted Whale shushed them, "Too easy,"
She said. "Anyone can be floated by melody, soar
On a song. You must conjure your dancing from deep in your marrow,
In silence make everyone feel what you feel as you move.
Let them witness your agony, ecstasy, efforts to sunder
Your earth-sodden bonds." Oh, now here was a test of my art
I had never conceived of. Now here was a taskmaster trying
My mettle. No mercy. No coddling. Excuses refused.
Hesitation forbidden. False start all too obvious. Patent
Uncertainty cause for harsh censure. Resolved not to quail
I extended my arms, palms uplifted to Spotted Whale's majesty,
Kneeling. Then sprung from the dirt as if stung by ground wasps
I flung lungfuls of breath to the treetops, which made dry leaves quiver.
And when watchers looked to the rustling, eluded their sight,
Disappeared as does frost in full sunlight, became but a memory
Vividly etched in their history, lost to their touch.
And, when mystery fluttered the beat of their hearts in irregular
Rhythms, I vaulted from shadow right over the stumps
Where imperious Spotted Whale sat in fat splendor, then spun in
A whirlwind of merriment. Saw I'd surprised her and pleased

Her enormously.
        Quaking with jollity
            Spotted Whale hugged herself.

"Well done indeed," she pronounced her approval. Some cheered.
I saw Kona's amusement greet Mother's relief, reassuring her
Spotted Whale's accolade genuine, meant as earned praise.
I was new to the dance, but if tempted to copy old patterns
In lazy reliance on styles of the past I was cured
Of that notion before it took hold, as were Song Maker, Little
Fox fashioning music unsung in this forest before.
They combined to create for us mystical wisps of pure natural
Cadence and pitch, unconstrained by dull drumbeat or droned
Monotone. I recalled Kona's words on the path when I met him,
Believing, he said, we must vanish, invisibly live
On in secret, conceal our great heritage safe in the mountains,
Survive as the thriving wise tribe that we have been and are.
My elusive new dances, new songs indistinct from the weather's
Sweet whistle and moan, from bird call, from the bugling moose
In the springtime, the clunk of black bear to her cubs in tree branches,
We'd sing and we'd dance undetected forever in peace
And good health. Was it possible? How could I know it would happen
That way? I was eager to speak of my wistful half dreams
With slim Eagle Wing Kona, to hear how he reasoned our futures
Might fare. We were young, inexperienced, no doubt naive.

   Who would listen to him
         or to me
              if we bleated such drivel?

To run and to hide violated our nature, except
As child's play in the games that prepared us for chasing and stalking,
Assisting the hunt by reporting locations of game
For the hunters to kill for our eating, I failed very often
To tell of the turkey or rabbit I saw. I played
In the woods as a child, letting sympathy lie with the creature
Instead of our stomachs until times grew harsh and game scarce.
Then I skulked off the trail with the keenest of eye, sparing nothing,
Necessity rooting out softness, my squeamishness gone.
I was thinking these thoughts as I worked beside Lame Fawn and Mother
Preparing to gut out and skin out and chop twenty hares
For the stew pot that already simmered on coals in the circle.
Wild onion grass boiling and spicy corms roasting were scents
Both familiar and promising, making me hungry and hopeful
Our guest Spotted Whale would leave some for the rest of us once
She was served. But I needn't have worried. She ate very little,
Surprising us all with her appetite small and her bowl
Barely drained of its juices before she was offered ripe blackberries
Which she declined with a shake of her head. Something ailed
Her. I watched her skin color turn ashen, a sheen of clear droplets
Break out on her brow. Then she beckoned me near as she said,

> "I want you to walk with me
> 　　well into the woods
> 　　　　and wait by me."

Supposing she needed to void, I set out on the path
To the soil trench, but Spotted Whale stopped me and called out to Kona
And Medicine Otter to help her along, warding off
The assistance of others concerned for her welfare and eager
To spring to her aid. I saw Red Feather whisper to White
Crow who shook her head sadly, laid hand on her heart, grasped his elbow
And, looking at me, ordered, "Do as she asks you. Go tend
To her," sternly conveying the serious nature of Spotted
Whale's ailment. "Oh, Moon," I lamented, "why me? What have I
Done to merit distinction, be chosen to witness her dying
So soon after meeting this merry and mountainous whale
Of a woman?" I wanted to know her, to listen to stories
Of Kona the boy as he grew, and the tales she could tell
From her earliest memories, happy, transporting us backward
To simpler pursuits of her joyous and sweet youthful days.
As she labored along on the arms of strong Kona and Medicine
Otter I sensed she was seeking particular ground,
Some place meaningful, special, important to her. We were nearing
A secret secluded small glade where a circle of trees
Made a worshipful site, contemplation in privacy possible,
Sacred to me from my wanderings. "Here I shall rest,"

  She said, reaching the glade.
    "In this place I was born.
     I am home now."

"This knoll is Wiscasset, the Place of Tall Trees. I recall
Plunging down through thick green watching Mother awaiting my
          birthing
Alone and no older than you, Ellacoya. My dead
Father, drowned under ice sheet before I was felt to be kicking,
Beside me and coaching my entry to Earth with his love
For my mother undying, and I, his last gift to her, living
Within then beside her, reminding by manner and mood
That his presence still hovered, caressing and palpably pleasing
Whenever I kissed her, adored her, drank up her salt tears.
On that day of my birth, half the tribe split off, first to the ocean,
Where squawking white gulls called huge whales to their breaching and me
To my appetite, making me ravenous, greedy, a laughing
Stock, ridiculed, mimicked, and teased for my size as I grew.
No one knowing but Mother that daughter and father united
As one in my spirit, my girth a necessity. Whale
Was my medicine animal. Right from the start my adventure
Was charted, no vision quest needed to flesh out my soul.
I am dying now. Relatives perch on the branches above us
To welcome me shortly. I die unafraid, so obey
My last wishes and let gray wolves gather to feed on my body.
Come back for my skeleton whitening, fleshless, and clean.

        I am too huge to bury.
              My bones must be flung
                    In the ocean."

When Medicine Otter had built a small fire and the dark
Slunk around us, I wept as one wolf circled closer while Spotted
Whale's breath pushed up bubbles of froth on blue lips. Slowing rales
Killed her laughter. She labored, collapsing against a stout tree root,
Half with us, half elsewhere in spirit. True Kona kept hold
Of her hands as he promised her gently we'd honor her wishes.
We sat through the night. The bright eyes of more wolves flashed and
            winked
Behind trees in the light of our fire as they paced panting nervously,
Wary of flame and the living, aware pending death
Filled the air. So her childhood was painful, her playmates abusive
And taunting. Her laugher a shield, a persuasion. Their scorn
Was subverted, made ignorant how she was charming their meannesses
Out of them. Grief overwhelmed me again and I sobbed,
Felt unfairly abandoned before I could know her. My sobbing
Aroused her. With effort she summoned me closer and sighed,
"Let me go now, my daughter. You'll know me and love me through Kona,
Whose heart is my own in its strength and endurance and care."
So I wiped the wet froth from her lips and I kissed her cool forehead
Goodbye. The sun rising illumined her features, relaxed
And at peace, exhalation a prayer. We waited and watching
Saw no inhalation to follow. Her chest did not rise.

    All was quiet. The wolves disappeared
            in the daylight,
                    retreating,

Awaiting the cover of darkness to work their grim task
And grow fat for the winter, well larded by Spotted Whale's carcass.
We could not begrudge them their natural duties which served
Such high purpose, fulfilling her wishes exactly as spoken.
Tall Medicine Otter knelt down to remove Spotted Whale's
Ample amulet bag from her neck, rose to hand it to Kona.
Her braid, white as ice, he cut off and then wound in a coil
To preserve as his own fond remembrance. For me, he took nothing.
My face must have shown disappointment, for Kona stepped close,
Said, "She gave your art blessing and value. Your dancing delighted
Her very last day. And she gave her approval to us
For our union. I should not have married without her agreement
No matter how much I have wished it." "Nor I without White
Crow's endorsement," I added. We stood in the glade, three together,
And gazed down at Spotted Whale's body, aware she was there
With us, waiting. "One duty remains," uttered Medicine Otter,
"And only the women may do it. That task falls to you, Ellacoya,
Her handmaiden chosen. Wait here 'til we bring you
Your helper. Do nothing until we return with Lame Fawn."
They soon left me alone. So I danced all my wishes and visions
To Whale's drifting spirit and thanked her for blessing me well.

    Then I sensed a departure,
        an energy
            languidly vanishing.

Knew she was gone from me, body an empty if generous husk.
She was right when she said she was too huge to bury. A lifetime
Of massive proportions conditioned her every thought.
Every action planned out to accommodate bulk. What a burden
She bore all her seasons on earth. She was free now to float
Where she willed, free to dance on the wind like gulls over the ocean.
No wonder she treasured my dancing, my freedom, my flight.
My agility pleased her, no envy, no critical comment
Escaped. Simply praise, with demand I create my own style.
How I loved her. I stopped in my dancing and studied tranquility
Clear in her face. Though it may have been only death's trick
Of the muscles relaxing, she seemed to have greeted her dying
As Friend-Who-Kindly-Stopped-For-Her-Who-Could-
Not-Stop-For-Death. Energetic and purposeful, pushing
Herself to effect the combining of tribes once again,
And to settle the lives of two grandsons before she relinquished
Her power, her ponderous influence, guidance, and will.
Left alone with her corpse a long time, I had plenty to ponder.
I understood nothing about how we all came to be.
Could not fathom design or mere chance to explain our existence.
So there I stood staring right down into mystery's mask

    With no answers at all.
        "Life is what it is,"
           I decided.

Content not to know, just to live as though dropped from a branch
Like an acorn becoming an oak but not knowing the reason,
Becoming, for now, Ellacoya the woman, and wife
Of brave Kona, perhaps bearing children. If so, I would birth them
Right here in this very same glade, a good place to be born.
Just then Medicine Otter with Lame Fawn astride his wide shoulders
Strode into the glade. Her hands, clasping his forehead, seemed more
For caress than security. Thighs by his cheeks was familiar
And welcome embrace, from the look of him. Each was well pleased
With the other, affections apparent. Behind them came Kona,
The Eagle Wing, carrying water and knives and sweet herbs
For our chore. Kneeling, Medicine Otter set down Fawn, reluctant
To quit him but able to bear her own weight now without
His assistance, although her slim ankle remained bound up firmly
In deerskin supports. "We shall leave you alone while you work.
When you finish, walk seven white rocks down the pathway to homeward
And whistle to signal that we may approach your return
Yet avoid violating Whale's privacy. Men must not witness
Such privileged honor as bathing Grandmother in death.
Tend our Spotted Whale lovingly. Bare her and bathe her with reverence.
Treat her with dignity, cherish her character fine."

>   Both men bowed and retreated
>   while Lame Fawn and I
>   grabbed hands tearfully.

"How they did love her!" she said to me, sighing. "And she
Cherished them with whole heart, reared them lovingly, sternly,
      demanding
Of them their best efforts, expecting much of them. I thank
Her for that," I agreed as we bent to her body and cut off
Her clothes at the stitching to save the soft skins for good use.
"I shall wrap my first child in this blouse front," I said as I folded
It carefully, certain that I would bear many. But Fawn
Only dropped her gaze sadly and murmured regretfully, "Children
Will never be mine." And she rested her head in her grief
Upon Spotted Whale's stomach. The pressure pushed gas from Whale's
      backside,
Magnificent grumble, surprising, derisive, a taunt.
"That's what Spotted Whale thinks of your fears," I said, both of us
      giggling.
"She's had the last word, made us laugh at her deathbed despite
Our sad duty." We dried up our teardrops, undressing and bathing
Her body. Her skin was unblemished except for nine spots
On her belly encircling her navel, which gave her her birthing
And spirit names right from the start of her life, as described
To me here in this Place of Tall Trees Spotted Whale called Wiscasset.
"Nine babies," said Fawn, counting spots with her finger. "They said
She had nine. Every one gone before her. Old age tragic blessing."
"And still she stayed merry," we marveled, resolving aloud

    To each other
        no matter what happened
            we'd live her example…

A vow humbly taken and earnestly meant to fulfill.
So together we bathed her and left her bare body as ordered
For wolves to consume. Sprinkling water and herbs all around
Her we sang our goodbyes. As I carried our bundles, and Fawn,
With one arm on my shoulders limped slowly beside me, we counted
The seven white rocks placed along the trail homeward and stopped
At the seventh to whistle for Kona and Medicine Otter
Who waited nearby. They appeared in an instant to join
Us, to carry Lame Fawn, and to scatter the rocks so no signals
Remained to lead others to Spotted Whale's altar of peace.
Though tonight be her busiest hour, we saw no contradiction
Between the night's frenzy to come and the image of calm
We had left in the glade. We had done as she wished and had willingly
Followed instructions. She wanted no grave, just return
To the sea and her medicine animal's wide-ranging freedom.
We talked as we walked of her wish for our marriages soon
And decided we wanted to have them together, then travel
To Long Bay to tell of old Spotted Whale's illness and death.
When we entered the village and spoke our desires, all agreed
With our plans and prepared for our weddings to take place tomorrow.
Canoes had been secretly made for us, hidden from sight,

    Now presented to us
        with great merriment,
            flourish and teasing.

It seemed they all knew before we did just what we would do.
We were happy, embarrassed, and nervous by turns, with attention
So focused upon us. The shift in emotions from grief
To elation was almost too sudden, defied comprehension,
Like laughter at graveside or joy in a dangerous storm.
I felt giddy, ungrounded and, glancing at Lame Fawn's expression
Saw she felt disquiet amidst all the joking and fun.
Although Kona and Medicine Otter seemed stoic, composed,
They were doing what I called "the man thing," impassive, no outward
Emotion, while inside the passions were bubbling and strong.
Their past gone in an instant, their futures upon them, immediate,
New, and untested, with everything changing their lives.
So tomorrow would join us all four to our fateful adventures.
Uncertainties founded on promises spoken and thrown
On the wind, only trust and intention of hearts to rely on.
As solid as smoke if one's character crumbled, or failed.
Or was never developed. Or twisted, like Yellow Snake's deviant
Nature. But Lame Fawn and I had the blessings of White Crow.
And Medicine Otter and Kona had Spotted Whale's word.
Thus the wisdom of elders confirming our choices felt strengthening,
Giving us courage. We bid one another good night

    And went thoughtfully off
          to our dreaming,
                awaiting tomorrow.

The morning dawned overcast, squalls in the offing. The lake
Might turn rough for our paddle to Long Bay, a hazardous journey.
Perhaps we should walk, though we wanted to use the canoes,
Spare Fawn's injury, demonstrate thanks, and explore a few islands
Along our way southward. We seldom went out very far
On the water, aware how the lake could turn instantly treacherous,
Squalls screaming over the hills without warning, and rain,
Dense, obscuring the shoreline and swamping canoes within moments
Of onslaught, a pleasant, brief outing turned fight-to-survive.
In discussing our wedding and plans for our journey, decided
Canoes should be chosen if only symbolically used,
A short paddle to prove our delight, then put up in the village
Before setting out on the path to Long Bay. We announced
We were ready to marry, so White Crow and Red Feather gathered
Our people around us to listen to promises made
With intention to live them—our sacred avowals of loyalty
Spoken aloud for the air to remember and Earth
To absorb, for the trees to uphold, and the sky to remind us
Endurance provides many faces for constancy's sake.
Then amongst all the others we launched our canoes in soft raindrops,
Were paddling the harbor when suddenly sunshine broke through.

"The Great Spirit
        now smiles for these four,"
                cried Ahanton, my father.

The harbor lay calm. Only paddles of many canoes
Churned the water around us as villagers, whooping and calling,
Good wishes. Long life. Many children. Much pleasure. Good luck,
Circled closer and closer to splash and torment us and threaten
Capsize in high spirits. With Little Fox rowdy and loud
In the melee and Song Maker urging her on, overturning
Their craft they collided with others until half the young
Ones were swimming and laughing and righting canoes in great turmoil.
The four of us, during the height of confusion, escaped
From the harbor and paddled with energy, changing our planning
As weather's benign opportunity lent us the chance.
Heading southward we found a large island before early nightfall
And landed to shelter beneath our two upturned canoes
Set a distance apart with our fire in between for the cooking.
Both Lame Fawn and I had packed food and the men had brought coals
In slim anticipation of just such good change in the weather
As happened. We ate and then settled down early to love's
Sweet fulfillment, familiar to Lame Fawn, I thought, unfamiliar
To Kona and me, though exciting. Sharp pain interrupted
My pleasure. My blood blessed the leaves. Kona's juices were wasted.
We lay in distressing perplexity, ignorant, tense,

    Hearing Lame Fawn and Otter
        cry out and then
            lapse into silence.

Left out of the secret, we lay skin to skin in the glow
Of the coals dying down, still excited but frustrated, baffled,
Expecting much more than we got from our first time of love.
In the morning the men went for wood for the cookfire, and Lame Fawn
Embraced me with joyous expression. She told me her first
Night with Medicine Otter brought pleasure she'd never experienced
Married to Yellow Snake. Happiness colored her cheeks,
Made her eyes pool with tears. "But love hurts me," I cried. "It was
        painful."
"But only the first time," she comforted. "Pain won't return.
Women heal very quickly. Perhaps by tonight you'll be better."
The men, reappearing with armloads of branches and pine
Cones and twigs, coaxed the smoldering embers with breath and deft
        fingers
And delicate care into faltering tendrils of flame
That soon crackled the pine pitch, consuming the cones and dry needles.
The fire lent some warmth to the morning's chill breeze and damp air.
They had seen from the top of the island a great storm approaching,
The water too rough for canoes. "We shall stay here a day
Or two more," we agreed, quite content for our sojourn's extension.
How little we knew then destruction would visit our world,
Topple trees, flood the rivers, and keep us unable to travel,
No sight of the moon or the sun to track nights by, or days,

    Only grayness and blackness,
        hard punishing rains,
            great limbs crashing.

We stayed countless days on the island. The raging storm made
Us climb higher, find shelter among overhanging huge boulders,
Away from the wind and the rain blowing sideways. We built
A stout wall out of rocks from the hillside and kept our fire going
Improbably bright by the efforts of all as we scoured
The wet forest for fueling deadfalls, dry wood fragments hidden,
And curls of birch bark that would sizzle and burn even damp
On account of the oil in their layers, kept feeding with constant
Attention those life saving flames. No one slept through the night,
Taking turns at the fire. By day searching for rabbit and squirrel
And berries and nuts in the downpour unending, the wind
A high screech, or by turns a deep thrum. Our sojourn was no idyll
Of blissful escape, what with love's promised paradise wracked
By harsh weather. And yet in our struggles I sensed a deep happiness.
We were together, surviving and strong and content
To be mated. Lame Fawn's reassurances came to fruition
As Kona and I learned to tend to each other the way
We would coax a full flame from red embers. Light hearted, exuberant,
Noisy, no shyness, no privacy either, for them
Or for us. But, no matter. Such caring, so joy-filled, so intimate,
Fostered in danger and long isolation, formed bonds

    Which would serve for a lifetime
        of memories
            secret and magical.

Kona used idle time carving a totem for me
To keep tucked in my amulet bag. Made from cedar, and tiny
Though larger than rabbit, two people he jokingly called
"The lithe beast with two backs." "Very clever," I told him. "Our children
Will find it one day, be amused to discover that youth's
Fleshly passions once burnt in their parents; old, white-haired infirmities
Masking our past from belief." "Will we live to be old?"
Kona wondered. "Oh, yes," I assured him. "Your peace-seeking wisdom
Shall guarantee that." So I tied the twined figures up tight
In my amulet bag for safekeeping. When Medicine Otter,
Returning quite late with some wood for the fire, said he'd gone
On a shape-changing visit to Long Bay where flooding
Had ruined their village, drowned many asleep one wild night,
Sent survivors in groups on the path to Red Hill for salvation.
With eyes of the raven he'd watched them limp northward in grief
And in shock. Saw an infant the others thought lost to the waters
Lodged high in an uprooted tree's branch and crying downstream.
"We must go to it quickly," urged Lame Fawn. The paddle, still dangerous,
Gave her no qualm. As the winds were abating somewhat
We were eager to travel again. We descended the hillside
To find one canoe had been crushed under huge fallen limbs.

    It was useless,
        too mashed for repair,
            so we loaded the other.

We paddled with furious energy, four of us strong
And in rhythm, mind, muscle, and bone to the task without tiring.
The plight of one infant our paramount focus. Our aim
To retrieve it before it should perish. Each sweep of our paddles
A prayer for speed and good fortune. Lame Fawn, knowing well
The great effort the birth of each baby exacted, the glory
Each little life came to fulfill, the sweet stillborns she grieved
And the frail ones she coaxed out of dying, massaging life into
Them time after time, worked her heart with her hands and her breath.
If the stranded one bore one faint flicker of spirit within its
Wee frame, she would save it I knew. Sky was dark in Long Bay
As we landed amid the sad wreckage of lodge poles, and shattered
Utensils painstakingly crafted and made to endure.
Kona's people had buried their dead before leaving the village,
One mound a mass grave elevated beyond the flood's reach.
All lay quiet and terribly empty this night. We stood hoping
To hear a weak wailing from somewhere downstream in the dark.
There was nothing. But Medicine Otter went striding and splashing
Away from the ruins along the swift outflowing stream
While a sliver of moon winked through fast-scudding clouds, gave us
            glimpses
Of firm soil for footing. We followed until Lame Fawn fell.

    "Go on! Hurry!" she cried to him.
            "Find the child.
                    Carry it to me."

"Build fire and fetch water," she ordered. "It must ingest warmth,
Overcome the wet chill of exposure, be heated from inside
To keep it from stress that can kill it if blood that is cold
Flows too fast to its organs." I did as she asked, fetching embers
The men had brought with us. I had some slight tendrils of smoke
And flames rising as Kona and Medicine Otter came crashing
Through branches and muck with a bundle of tightly wrapped skins
Otter cradled and handed to Fawn. I saw Kona was shaking
His head with a hopeless expression. No movement, no sound
From the bundle as Lame Fawn undid the wet wraps, cooing softly.
A pinched little face with blue mouth and closed eyes could be seen
As Fawn motioned to me for warmed water to drip from a finger
Inserted between tiny lips. The babe swallowed and choked
Then grew still again. Skinny and splayed it resembled a spider
Asleep on its web just awaiting an insect or breeze
To arrive and to jostle awareness. A girl, it was dying
In front of us, senseless and cold to the touch, with no lift
Of the ribs to prove breathing, no twitch of the toes or stiff fingers,
No sucking response to caress on the cheek. And yet Fawn
Never wavered. Undoing her clothing, she tucked the bare body
Inside, skin to belly, where heat was the highest, and rocked

    Back and forth singing,
        "Spider, oh Spider,
            brave Spider, awaken."

"The Earth wants your footfalls to tickle Her. Moon wants your eyes
To behold Her. Adventures await you. Your mother is crying
To hold you and feed you again. You are wanted and loved,
Little Spider, come back to us now to grow strong and be happy."
The three of us watched in a circle surrounding the fire,
Each amazed that Lame Fawn would persist past all reason, keep singing
And rocking and stroking and turning the bulge hidden limp
In her shirt. I was weary and dozing against Kona's shoulder.
And Medicine Otter lay curled around Fawn's legs and hips
So his heat might replace body warmth she was losing to baby.
Recalling again my sick, pitiful infant taboo
Dream near Long Bay, I felt, quite uneasily, stark recognition
Events here unfolding in waking suggested events
Of my dreaming, with eerie detail. Vague and shadowy preview
That lingered in memory, almost forgot, coming true
In reality, wholly surprising, unsettling, suggesting
Dimensions I visited sleeping beyond what I thought
To be all that there was to be known. "Crescent Moon," I implored Her,
"Please steady my will to accept the unknown with the known,
And to trust that my heart separates in its core the authentic
From foolishness, shuns superstition, embraces with awe

    And humility
            each new experience,
                    keeps me receptive…"

"Expansive and loving. Please free me from judgments that pinch
At my soul or that narrow awareness." Remembering Spotted
Whale's story of watching from treetops her mother prepare
For her birthing, I wondered if Spider hung watching above us
Deciding, or not, to reenter our world. The weird image, intense
And disturbing, came prickling my palms, making restlessness jiggle
My legs with anxiety. Fearing my prayer high flown
And ridiculous, I felt too young for such yearnings of spirit.
I sneered at myself in grave doubt of my reason and sense.
How precarious life was, how raw, and how rich in the living.
Exhaustion assailed me. I slept. I awoke to first light
And commotion. Thick mist, orange halo reflecting the flare-up
Of flames in the rekindled campfire, held Lame Fawn within
Its soft aura bent over me, calling my name. "Ellacoya,
We need you to travel, to run and to dance on the wind.
Your strong legs are the fastest. You know the path homeward. Wee Spider
Is hungry. Her mother despairs that her breasts, firm and full,
Will soon harden and pain her." "The Spider's alive?" I cried dumbly
And stared at small face pink and scrunched up to utter a wail.
Wrapped again in dry deerskins, the infant protested her hunger
As Medicine Otter described grieving mother, alone,

>   Off the trail, dropped back
>   hidden, refusing to walk
>   with the others...

Her grief overwhelming. "Take Spider and hurry," he said.
"You will find the lost woman halfway to your village but hiding
In bushes so no one can bother her, comfort unsought,
Inconsolable, wishing for death. As you run you must listen.
Her sobs are diminishing. Soon she will sleep and succumb
To the chill of wet garments unless you arrive with her infant.
Allow time to nurse, then encourage her onward to home
And safe dwelling place high on Red Hill with our mingling peoples."
"But where is her husband?" I asked. "Would he leave her alone?"
"He was drowned with their two older children. Their bodies lie buried.
Now stop pesky questions and go!" I felt chastised but placed
Baby Spider inside my loose blouse. As I ran I felt better
About how he spoke to me. Urgency mattered. The child's
Needs came first, curiosity second. My pride, because wounded,
Lent speed to my feet. I would prove myself fit to the task.
It was awkward to run with one hand or the other supporting
The baby against my hard belly. My strides were too short
And my rhythm uneven, my stamina weakened in idleness
Forced by wild storm and long waiting. Though Spider was slight,
Weight affected my balance. I loped on and on, well aware that
Insistent and challenging motherhood made strong demands.

    As I paused,
        repositioning Spider,
            I heard a soft sobbing…

A woman much older than I sat half hidden by brush.
Breathing hard, I stopped close to her, knelt down in front of her saying,
"Sad mother, please open your eyes, dry your tears, feed your child."
But she turned from me, keening, disconsolate, angry, untrusting,
Bereft and unwilling to heed me, or look as I thrust
Out the baby, exposing to air its small mouth and smooth forehead.
The cold woke warm Spider. She let out one squeal of surprise
And the woman responded by clutching her breasts. "I am leaking,"
She cried. "With good reason," answered. "Now open your eyes."
"I am dreaming, or dying," she muttered. "A spell has come over
Me. You are not real." "But your milk tells you otherwise, flows
At the cry of your infant. Your body knows better than you do.
So honor its wisdom and nourish your child while she lives
Or you surely shall kill her. Starvation will soon overcome her.
She's thin as a spider, lethargic, dehydrated. Feed
Her," I shouted, impatient and frightened. Hysteria gripping
Her mind shut out sense. Unresponsive and wooden, she sat
With legs folded, arms empty and useless, milk staining her dress front.
Despairing of reasoning with her, I opened her blouse,
Put the babe to her breast, let it nurse. It was eager, voracious,
Insistent, and noisily swallowing air with rich milk.

    Little Spider threw up
        without warning.
                Her mother then seized her.

"You know very little of infants," she said with a frown,
Wholly present and calm as she patted the baby to ease its
Distress while relief flooded over me, glad our eyes met.
To be scolded by someone I thought had gone mad made me happy.
A normal rebuke of my ignorance welcome in place
Of detachment and helplessness. Motherly impulse reviving
Her spirit once more made her tend to the child with the skill
Of long practice and easy assurance I envied, while hoping
One day I would do half as well. When wee Spider had burped
Only air without spitting up milk, she was put to the other
Breast briefly, her mother examining fingers and toes
And distinguishing features that only the mother would look for.
Once certain that Spider was truly her own, here alive in her arms,
She reached out to me, palm to my cheek. I could smell Spider's vomit,
Surprisingly sweet and attractive, an odor that clung
To her hand, a perfume in my nostrils, no stench, no repugnance.
She watched my reaction and laughed as I sniffed. "You do know
Very little of infants," she said, this time smiling and shaking
Her head. "For as long as they nurse they are fresh as spring dew.
A delightful, compelling aroma, incitement to bonding
Few mothers repel once they smell it, regardless of pain."

    Cradling Spider
        and rocking her gently,
                she asked how I'd saved her.

"Not I, but tall Medicine Otter and Lame Fawn," I said.
"In the shape of the raven he witnessed destruction and flooding
Had ravaged your village. He spied this small bundle caught up
In a tree fork above the receding black waters, and hearing
A cry he returned to us swiftly, recounted babe's plight.
So we paddled as hard as we could to Long Bay from High Island,
Arriving at dusk. Through the night Lame Fawn, warming your babe
In her blouse front against her bare belly kept stroking and coaxing
The child back to life. Though we thought it was futile to try,
She persisted. This morning they chose me to run with her, find you,
Expand your crushed heart, fill your arms, let your milk flow again."
"I have lost both my boys and my husband," she moaned. "She is all
I have left of the life I once loved. I'm indebted to Medicine
Otter, our shape-changing shaman. Where is he?" she asked.
"He and Kona and Lame Fawn are paddling to Red Hill, my home
And now your home," I answered. "Come. Walk with me quickly to
                welcoming
People and food and safe shelter." She stood. I could see
That some cuts on her legs were still bleeding, her moccasins missing,
Her feet bruised and bare. "Take my slippers," I offered.
"The soles of my feet are still tough to the trail. Let me carry wee Spider."
"Is that what you call her?" the mother protested, dismayed

        But amused. "She was born
            underneath a stout web
                bright with dewdrops."

"I watched them while birthing her. Glittering beads of clear dew
All reflected the early dawn sunlight. The gentle breeze rising,
Caressing the web, woke the spider above me as this
Child broke free of my womb. All long legs and thin arms, with great
        energy
Thrashing. A strong girl her brothers adored for the brief
Days they knew her. A sister at last. How they vied in deciding
A name for her. Silly names. Scuttlefish. Beady Eyes. Ant.
I am calling her Dewdrop for now," said her mother while handing
Her to me. "Perhaps you have learned of the spirit name she
May in future uncover. Until then, she's Dewdrop, no mention
Of 'Spider' to color taboo when she's ready at first
Spots of womanly blood to go forth on her trek to discover
Her nature, her purpose, her skills. You must ask that the name
Be kept secret with you four who gave it." "I promise to tell them
You've asked this," I said as we walked side by side slowly on
With wee Spider—no, Dewdrop—asleep, fed and warm in her wrappings,
So glad this sad mother was looking and planning ahead
To her daughter's eventual womanhood. Life again tempted her.
Grief a companion but never a conqueror. Grief,
Vital thorn that drives numbness away, that prompts action and struggle
And striving, this mother's strong summons to nurture her child.

        She was proof here beside me
            that women like her
                can be heroes.

"What happened with you and your Dewdrop? Why did you not drown
With the others?" "When rain stopped," she told me, "I stepped
        outside hoping
To nurse her in quiet, not waking the boys or my man.
She had just finished feeding when water came rising around me.
My screams awoke many. The boys and my husband emerged
To save others, I think. It was hard in the dark to know who had
Run where. I tried climbing steep slope but loose rocks were dislodging,
Kept striking me. Backwards I slid and the rushing black water
Ripped babe from my arms. In the dawn, those who lived searched in vain
For their loved ones. Some vanished, but most of them sprawled
        drowned or injured.
No sign of my baby although I kept searching all day
While survivors took care of the hurt ones and buried the corpses.
They forced me to leave with them, fighting, unwilling to go
Before finding her body. Convinced it was futile to look for her,
Tiny and weightless, they said she'd been carried downstream
On the current too swift to explore. Still too dangerous walking
Such weakened terrain by the riverbank slippery with silt.
She was dead, they insisted. Despairing, I followed them, witless
And numbed by my losses. We all were in shock, wet and cold,
Without food, a most pitiful band of dispirited wanderers.
Falling behind, I concealed myself, stubborn to die.

    I was giving my soul
        to the wind
            when you found me near senseless."

"I dreamt of a black bear approaching and welcomed my doom.
Nothing worse could befall me. Bear spoke. I escaped into madness
Then woke to the babe at my breast, saw your anxious young face."
"I am Laughing Bear. That is my spirit name, born Ellacoya,"
I told her. "Your dream was authentic, a vision of strength
For the future. My mother is Grey Goose who waits in our village
For news of my welfare. I'm certain she worries. The storm
Was so long and so powerful. Four, newly married, canoeing
To Long Bay before the wild weather arrived to delay
Us and pin us to ground at High Island for days." "I am Meadowlark,
Widow of Elkfoot," she said, walking faster, erect and with purpose. "Your
Mother deserves to know soon of your safety.
Well, hurry. Don't lag, child," she scolded me, striding ahead
In my moccasins. Goodness, how everyone chided me, focused
Upon their concerns and quite heedless of wounding my heart
In their haste. I had often been told I was overly sensitive,
Taking offense although none was intended. "Is this
Yet another of growth's little lessons?" I grumbled to Dewdrop,
My mouth to her ear. "What a lot you'll be learning if so."
It was one mother's care for another's distress that made Meadowlark
Order me onward so curtly, distress she well knew.

    Understanding her urgency,
        sharing it,
                crowded out childishness.

Thinking outside my own petty response made a leap
Toward maturity. Insight dawned readily as it was needed,
I found. Situations of personal stress called it forth.
Here I was, stumbling barefoot and hungry, with Meadowlark's infant
Asleep in my arms, dodging roots and sharp pebbles and washed
Away gullies, avoiding low branches entangled in blackberry
Vines, my mind fully ensnared in the physical world.
Yet my soul did its duty, and Moon up above heard my pleading
Desire so intense, fertile field for her hints to take root
In my heart and then bloom with a flourish like maypop or lily
In springtime, and just as surprising. This growing up work
Was like climbing a mountain. The more I persisted and struggled,
The higher I scrambled, the more I could see. Even more
Was expected with every attainment. Here Meadowlark, ready
To die, was recalled to her reason by life-saving care
For a child she thought lost. So much older than I yet still able
To rally, plunge on through life's thickets, respond to demands
Thrust upon her by tragedy. "Meadowlark, stop for a moment,"
I begged her. "Your Dewdrop's awakened and I need to ask you a
Question." "Your feet aren't as tough as you thought, Ellacoya.
We'll sit while I nurse her. You question, and tend to your feet."

"Does a woman your age
          reach a point
                    where life's learning's behind her?"

"Great Spirit, is this what it's like to be raising a girl?
Heavy queries and innocent thoughtless assumptions that aging
Alone confers meaning and answers, reveals with just time
One's life purpose and destiny? Boys seldom question their mothers
This deeply. Instead, they go hunting with fathers who teach
Them survival skills, fishing and fighting. Such thoughts, if they have
        them,
They keep to themselves, taking refuge in action or sleep."
She stopped speaking. Again I felt downcast, felt teased for my candor.
My simple desire to explore my insatiable mind,
To make sense of this life, know my place in it, rankled
My elders. It never occurred to me then that, perhaps
As uncertain as I was, they shunted aside the deep mysteries,
Hiding in busy work, blaming the fates when the world
Did them ill. Or, constructing a framework of logical fable
To banish anxiety, sought for control, some Great Plan
For us all, in the wind and the clouds and the slime of dead entrails
That only the chosen might know and declaim. Even young,
I had never been able to set aside reason, or swallow
As truthful pronouncements denying the world I could see,
Empty promises, glorious, never fulfilled in one's lifetime.
I knew I was different, doubting, a girl out of step.

     And yet, Meadowlark's levity
          hinted that she felt
               as I did.

"As long as you're living, life's lessons are never behind
You," she answered me. "I do not know why I'm living when Elkfoot
And both of our sons now lie buried. Yet Dewdrop survived
This most grievous calamity. I have been tugged back to caring
Again by your earnest persistence and generous gift
Of these moccasins. Questioning why these things happen is fruitless.
They happen. We grow or go under. It's simple as that."
Dewdrop burped and then grimaced to prove she was thriving, was filling
The moss in her wrappings with waste. We both laughed at her look,
Mighty efforts apparent, productive, relieving discomfort.
I sensed life's demands, all consuming, were crowding out awe.
My pursuit of deep mysteries lost out to practical searching
For suitable moss to reline Dewdrop's deerskins, safe leaves
To use wiping her bottom. No mysteries here as we tended
Her needs. "You are brave to ask questions," said Meadowlark then.
"There is great need insistent within us to know why we're here
On this earth. Many legends and myths have arisen from peoples
Who wondered as you do. I cannot believe those who threaten
Of devils and tricksters unseen, inescapable, make
Themselves seem to know things we cannot, or have power to alter
Our fates if we bribe them, pretend only their way is right.

> Circumscribing behavior
>   with many harsh rules
>   and dire penalties."

"Punishments brought on ourselves by some wickedness wrought
Long before us by deeds of our ancestors, shamed and found guilty
At birth to explain why life hurts so, implying some bleak
Unenforceable contract with masters unknowable, cruel
Or careless, judgmental and distant. Such tales I have heard
From the traveling ones who come sit at our cook fires recounting
The preaching of newcomers camped on our beaches and fields.
An unhappily rigid-jawed people, in small ragged numbers,
Still far to the south but advancing upon us with sticks
That blow flames and loud noises. They kill, from great distances, turkeys
And men as they please as though they had a right we do not
To this earth and her bountiful spaces. "But they are mistaken,"
I shouted. My rage startled Dewdrop. "I know in my heart
That this infant is faultless," I cried as she squalled with my ruckus.
My feelings of outrage consumed me. To hear of beliefs
So destructive, so crippling, so hopeless, designed to imprison
The mind and the soul in black bondage, just words on the wind,
Mere persuasions enslaving incurious, gullible numbers
Unwilling or fearing to look to their hearts, was a shock.
Such an alien way of perceiving the world and our place in it
Angered me. Meadowlark read the distress on my brow.

    Her voice softened.
        "Hard questions like yours
            are essential," she murmured.

"Not everyone growing as you are dares ask them, or thinks them
Important. Do you feel alone in your wonder?" she asked me,
"Sometimes," I responded, amazed she could know me, could see
Just how different I felt, after all she'd been forced to experience,
Able to speak with me caringly though I was young
And a bother perhaps. She was almost as old as my mother,
Could easily summon superior age to commend
Me to silence, shut down my inquiring mind with a careless
Remark on my folly, my seeking to know the unknown
And unknowable secrets of being. Could easily prattle
The usual myths of my childhood, delights that now seemed
Too fantastical. Whimsical, passionate stories describing
The start of the world. Bits and pieces of make-believe told
With an air of authority. Wholly unprovable. Fiercely
Repeated to stifle all doubts, ridicule all debate.
I had often watched elders, confounded by mystery, fearfully
Lapse into litany, muttering ritual chants,
Close their minds to a thought deemed forbidden, unwholesome, not
            fitting
Beliefs they had settled on, seeming to panic. What made
Dewdrop's mother so open, I wondered. Why didn't she cancel
My queries, resort to stale litanies, legends and myths?

    "There are some few
            who do not accept
                    entrenched fable," she said then.

"I see you are one of us. Serious, sober, alert
To complexities. You may be one of our Spotted Whale's thinkers
Who live in the present with joy and attention to what
Lies around us, content to appreciate beauty, abundance
And love as they grace us, to focus on seeing the best
In each other, which some call naive, even foolish and dangerous."
"Spotted Whale died many days ago, Meadowlark. I
Was one privileged to tend her, with Medicine Otter
And Kona and Fawn in Wiscasset, the Place-of-Tall-Trees
As she called it, the glade of her birth." "Yes, she spoke of it often,"
Said Meadowlark, "wanting to reach it, to see it again
Before death overtook her," surprised not at all at her dying.
"Suspecting the journey would end her long life, stop her heart,
We each said our goodbyes, not expecting to greet her again in
This world. So she chose you to witness her breathless escape
From that massive imprisonment. Excellent honor," said Meadowlark.
"Where is she buried?" "She isn't," I told her. "Her bones
Lying white in the glade are awaiting return to the ocean
As she has instructed." "So like her," said Meadowlark, pleased.
Up ahead on the trail I saw Little Fox trotting to meet us
To help with the baby and give us some water for thirst.

"Lame Fawn told me the story,"
        Fox grinned, adding,
                "Mornings, she vomiting..."

"Happy and queasy by turns. So we tease her distress,
Will not leave her alone, feed her greasy cold venison breakfasts
And jeer as she runs to the soil trench, hands clapped to her mouth."
"Lame Fawn runs?" I exclaimed. "This is just as important as
         pregnancy,
I think, and just as miraculous. Merry good news!"
"Yes, her ankle is strong now," said Little Fox, "needing no wrappings,
Her foot straight and slim as the other and supple again."
"Meet my sister," I then said to Meadowlark, manners remembered.
"Such energy," Meadowlark marveled. "She's bold as my boys
Were at plying some goodhearted torment on those that they envied.
Imagine what she'll offer you as you make her an aunt."
"I'm not pregnant," I protested. "Oh, yes you are," whispered
         Meadowlark.
"Signs are appearing you haven't yet noticed, but my
Practiced eye sees the tracings of darkening skin and the softening
Outline of breasts that are swelling despite lack of food.
You are young and your body is tough and athletic, well suited
To carry. You'll seldom get sick or have trouble with births."
This was news of another sort Little Fox seized on with joyful
High whistling and stomping in glee. "Little Mother," she cried,
"You shall make me an auntie. Song Maker and I will sing lullabies
Over your bellies, the two of you clumsy and fat."

     So my quest for the meaning of life
         was colliding with
            living it.

Walking together toward camp, I felt mainly unchanged
By this news. Though assessing the feel of my body, it gave me
No clue to developing life and yet Lame Fawn was sick
In the mornings already. More physically sensitive, softer
In nature and body than I, she would feel every shift
All the way to her core in the instant her body accepted
Its gift. And yet I stayed oblivious, sturdy, intent
Upon Meadowlark, urging her onward with Dewdrop to safety,
Reviewing the wisdom she'd willingly shared as we sat
At the side of the trail for a rest. She was gentle and patient,
Once sensing the strength of my impulse to ponder the fates.
Now my gaze had turned inward again. Our brief respite of inquiry
Vanished. Demands of reality pressing enough.
So when Little Fox reached out for Dewdrop, to carry her homeward,
Said "Auntie-to-be needs the practice, and you need the help,"
Girlish laughter a welcome relief, so light hearted and tuneful,
So earthbound, unquestioned acceptance of everything real,
We were glad she had come for us. Cheerful and vibrant and noisy,
Her usual liveliness lent us new energy. End
Of the journey in sight made me eager to share news with Kona
And see Lame Fawn walking with ease and lithe grace once again.

"You will find a good home
     in my village,"
          I reassured Meadowlark.

"Having met you I am certain of comfort," she said,
And the first smile I'd seen changed her face from stark grieving to beauty.
"My mother will welcome you. White Crow and Red Feather see
To your heartbreak along with the others who've come from your village
To live here among us as sisters and brothers, our tribes
Reunited." We entered the village to greetings, embraces,
And tearful relief on the faces of many who'd lost
All but hope. They surrounded their Meadowlark, peered at her baby
In wonder, believing at last her survival was real
As they touched her and marveled, "Your motherly instinct, not subtle,
Was right," said a woman. "But how did you know she still lived?"
"I don't know," answered Meadowlark. "Thinking her dead, I just needed
Her body to cancel that wisp of desire I still felt
For one child to live on, give me solace, my effortful birthing
Awarded one talisman, keepsake, a life left to care
For, to nurture and love, one remainder of Elkfoot's existence
To cherish." I listened, recalling how Spotted Whale's birth
Story echoed in Dewdrop, and hoped for her sake she'd be pardoned
From having to carry a burden like Spotted Whale's girth,
Be a substitute, standing for family lost. I just hated
The thought any child might be born with a task to fulfill

    Not its choosing,
        not be fully free
            to perfect its uniqueness.

I'd seen some friends thwarted in growth by parental demands.
The mother live not for the child but the child for the mother,
A backwards relation, lopsided, improper, unfair,
Without comfort. The child never knowing the reasons its efforts
Fell short, so downhearted and sad, or rebellious and mad.
A harsh father berating a son for no reason but secretly
Hidden beliefs, expectations, or fears—the boy dropped
In his world to be tiny solution to all father's problems.
How foolish. How wicked. How selfish the immature were,
Not deserving of children but having them anyway. Careless,
Neglectful, resentful, still childish themselves, unequipped
To give nurturance children are owed, and quite deaf to the heartsongs
Within trusting beings dependent on them. I had not
Understood what was happening, watching such parents behaving
That way. But I should have seen clearer that Lame Fawn's neglect
By her mother came from the same cause—an impossible duty
To have been born male, as if being her gender were whim
To confound expectations, deliberate waywardness, impish
Disdain for the mother's deficiencies Fawn was conceived
To erase. I was grateful my mother knew better, took action
To validate Lame Fawn's true personhood. Healed my friend's heart.

    I felt lucky to have
        such a mother
                so caring, supportive.

Here many a grandmother, aunt, or perceptive good friend,
Or a grandfather, uncle, or generous wise tribal elder
Encouraged such youngsters, dispelled their anxieties, paid
Them respectful attention, accorded them dignity, selfhood,
Acknowledged accomplishments, readily set worthy goals
For them. All of this done so routinely, so quietly, constantly,
Taken as nothing exceptional, simply the way
Care was owed to the children. Not always successful, however.
Fleeting awareness like this came flickering bright
And then vanished from mind as I went to find Lame Fawn and Kona.
I felt I was living in two worlds at once—one of flesh,
One of spirit. Reality and contemplation combining,
Enhancing new views. I was keenly alert to how home
Coming differed this time from the last, when I fell into
Mother's strong arms with a childlike dependence. But now I was wife,
Now with child, with the duty to carry Whale's bones to the ocean.
A glorious difference in so short a time. I found Fawn
Weaving baskets for backpacks we'd use on our long journey eastward
With Spotted Whale's bones. I embraced her and knelt to assist
With the weaving. "I hear you are pregnant and puking," I teased her.
"Don't even discuss it," she groaned, "or I'll prove how it's done."

But her laughter belied
a sham misery.
Joy graced her features.

"This happened so quickly, I don't understand why I could
Not give Yellow Snake children." "I think it more likely he couldn't
Give children to you," I retorted. "Just think. Would you want
Such a snake to be father to your precious children, or treat then
As he treated you?" "Oh, he wasn't that bad," Fawn exclaimed.
"Yes, he was," I insisted. "Enduring his blame and his insults
Was crushing you yet you defend hurtful memories. Please
Leave him buried. His name can stay dead as his body and conscience."
"What conscience?" Fawn spat as she threaded a slat into place
In one backpack. "Indeed!" I agreed. We collapsed into laughter
Where Kona and Medicine Otter found both of us balled
Into howling hilarity, baskets abandoned, forgotten.
We could not stop laughing. One glance at each other would seize
Us with spasms of giggles no matter how hard we attempted
To regain control. So the men simply gave up and laughed
Along with us, not knowing the reason but finding our antics
Amusement enough. It felt good to let go of old stress,
The past storm and tense rescue, relax into everyday habits
Of safety and friendship and love we four happily shared.
Just to heal and find respite from danger, enjoy lusty merriment
Gusting through woodlands, refreshing the breeze with our breath.

    At that moment
            I wanted our giddiness
                    granted forever...

Our laughter and happiness endless. Our mutual burst
Of elation persistent through time. If one instant in life could be
Chosen as perfect, then this was the moment supreme.
Nothing more can surpass this, I thought, as we lapsed into spasms
Of chuckling and gasping, embracing each other with sighs
Of exhaustion. We sprawled on the ground amid splints for the baskets,
Fawn's weaving forgotten, pure silliness rampant, all cares
Set aside. Life was good. We were young and expectant, the future
Predictable, safe, and eternal. Though others might die,
We four knew we would not. An invincible quartet of heroes
We were, at the peak of our personal prowess and skills.
What an arrogant youthful exuberance reigned with a vital
Belief in ourselves overwhelming all obstacles, sure
We could conquer the fates with a wave of the hand and the force of
Our will. In the grip of such ungrounded, grandiose spates
Of euphoria, nothing impossible threatened to smother
Our prospects. No caution assailed our bold plans, our wild schemes.
We lay dreamily talking and owning the world in sweet mania,
Fantasy ruling our high-flying chatter until
In the treetops a chill gale came screeching, sent branches to crashing,
Commanding cool reason resume. So the moment was spent.

> We soon settled to earth
>   once more, sober
>   and sensible beings...

A chuckle or two stayed alive in our ribs as we sat
In Fawn's workspace and spoke of our upcoming trek to the ocean
And Kona's desire to confirm what my sister had told
Him about my condition, "So Meadowlark says," I admitted,
"But I can sense nothing as yet. If she's right we must wait,
As for now I am starving and dirty. Let's eat and go swimming,"
I said, jumping up. So we joined all the others who ate
By the campfire. I met Kona's people surviving who greeted
Me warily, curious what kind of woman I was
Who had married the son of their chieftain late slain by her father,
A circumstance incomprehensible, even bizarre
To some warriors sitting, arms folded, reluctant and sullen,
Across from Ahanton, old training still urging revenge.
I could see Kona had much persuading to do to release them
From anger. Despite their agreement to merge with our tribe,
If disaster had not forced them northward to gain a safe haven,
They might have remained renegade, unconvinced. Kona's plan
For a peaceful solution to hardship and weakening numbers
Was tentative given long enmity, brief bloody raids,
Grim fatalities suffered on both sides. Hot anguish still written
In crippled old limbs, jagged scars, blinded eyes, missing ears.

How I loved these old warriors,
        stoic and stern
                in their dignity…

They were the trees of our forest. The men were the trees
And we women the water. A fanciful image, for certain,
But I rather liked it, decided to dance it for them
To distract from the tension. So, rising, I gestured to Sister
And Song Maker. "Water-and-Trees is the dance I shall do
Celebrating our coming together," I said. "A reunion
Of peoples once driven apart by rebellion and strife
That was none of our making, inherited, not of our choosing,
So harmful and hurtful, divisive and wasteful of life.
Now the killing is recently ended by Kona, my husband,
The son of your chief so lamented, respected, and mourned
On both sides of this campfire." Then Little Fox whistled a ripple
Of flowing swift brook sounds and Song Maker sang of the oak
And the cedar while I stood as tall as the aspen, leaves drinking
Soft rain, fingers fluttering lightly, accepting each drop
As do leaves or green needles. Then, settling toward ground, I embodied
The twirling winged seed of the maple, dropped acorn, the cone
Full of nuts from the pine. Plunging hands into soil, strong roots
          burrowing
Deeply, unfurled my lithe body with careful control
To rise balanced on hands, bare feet treetops, strong legs sturdy branches,
I held until murmurers sighed, comprehending the pose.

     Then I danced to each warrior,
          watered each wound
               with tears falling…

Emotion so strong and so sudden seduced me. I wept
Uncontrollably, moving among all the maimed and disfigured
Across the wide circle. Survivors of skirmishes. Blood
Lost so needlessly. Letting this girl of their enemy dance in
Among them, come close to them, rain on them tears of respect,
Was forbearance indeed for these stalwart, untouchable heroes
Who suffered no sentiments tender or gentle to melt
Their reserve, to relax their stiff hardened demeanor, impassive
Habitual posture of calm, while the scars on the heart
Burned the skin of their souls without end, and their howls in the
          nighttime
Embarrassed their mornings. Those true cries of war that escaped
All unbidden and hideous, rent the dark silence, went streaking
Through sky, screaming comets that spoilt sleeping children's good
          dreams.
"You are brave and enduring" my dance and my tears full of gratitude
Told them as, leaping the fire, I flew over to our
Side and moving among all our maimed and disfigured we honored
As well, did the same for their wounds in my passion for peace.
In my dance I became someone else—Ellacoya transported
To some perfect world where no killing occurred and no battles
Were fought. Where our boys were each granted the promise of growth
Into men, mild of heart, whole of limb, and where women could dare

     To believe in long life
          for each infant,
               birth agony worth it…

And never undone by the violent evils of war.
There was accident, illness, disaster enough to contend with.
I felt overwhelmed by new grief, by ecstatic deep love,
And hot pity for all of us living confused or mistaken
Or bumbling, both sad and enraged, so uncertain, cocksure
In our ignorant hopefulness. Mixtures of feeling all roiling
My blood sent me racing and twirling in frenzy around
The enlarged tribal circle while heads turned to follow my progress.
But then I calmed slowly and stood once again as begun,
The tall aspen accepting the rain on its leaves of my fingers
While Little Fox whistled a last falling droplet and Song
Maker hummed the sly whisper of one brown pine needle's dry tumble
To ground. In the silence that followed I gazed through the high
Enlaced branches to stars in the sky just emerging to sparkle,
And then to the faces all lit by the fire. A small nod
From my mother released me from fretting I may have exceeded
Commendable figures of dance, gone too far, leapt too high,
Lost my reason in excess emotions much stronger than any
Before had assailed me. Approaching, my mother spoke low
In my ear, "Do not fear your more heightened sensations of loving
And grieving. You're pregnant, your body creating new life.

    This expands your awareness,
        enlivens, intensifies
            every occurrence."

"Though new, it is normal for women, but hard on the men
Who suspect no least hint of our bodily changes and turmoil
The power developing life brews within. We become
Inward focused and outwardly volatile, edgy, contented
By turns in the long months of work we perform without choice.
A full womb guards its treasure against all foreseeable hazard,
A proud and yet challenging siege to embrace and endure,
Like taboo. This is your task alone to be suffered and relished,
Fulfilled in good season with painful delight and great fear
For the fragile dependent wee creature who bursts into being
So helpless and beautiful, bloody and slippery, caked
With its newborn's white coating of skin balm protecting its passage.
You've helped with the bathing of one or two infants, have seen
What they look like. In time you shall feel all the perils and pleasures
Of birthing your own. You shall do so with grace and good heart,
Ellacoya, my daughter. Your husband will be a fine father,
His character solid and loving. I watch him and like
What I see. Take his hand and encourage his sharing this venture.
Describe for him what you experience. Teach. Place his palm
On your vigorous belly, then dance and make love without caution.
No harm is inflicted when joy rules the mother-to-be."

    "Thank you, Grey Goose!
        If that is the case
                then I think I'll go swimming."

With Kona beside me I ran to the water. We plunged
In together, both whooping at cold. Our wet clothing was heavy
And dragging us down as we waded ashore and collapsed
In the sand celebrating our blessing with carefree high humor.
We knelt with our foreheads together, inhaling the breath
From each other, the odors of skin, the rich taste of wet shoulders,
The scent of damp hair in a tangle of fingers and lips.
When we later crawled into our bedding, all naked and chilly,
The press of his silken-skinned body on mine was caress
I would hold in my physical memory, often reliving
The feel of it even as age made skin rippled and rough
As dry hide, and bad hips and bent backs left us separate, groaning,
And children, concerned we were dying, aroused us from sleep.
I imagined our futures that way at this moment so pleasant
And comfortable, warming and sleepy in private and dark.
Free to pleasure each other again, after brief separation,
Sweet Kona seemed hesitant, cautious and gently restrained.
When I told him how Mother assured me no harm would be visited
On our wee seedling, his passion rekindled. Restraint
Was abandoned. My body more sensitive, flesh more acquisitive,
Heightened my eagerness. Startled him. Gone, the shy pair

    We had formerly been.
        No more coaxing, slow climb
           to responsiveness...

Fully alive to this moment of bliss, we let go
Of the pull of the world and relaxed into utter contentment,
Then slept, limbs entwined and hearts slowing to restful calm beats,
Our sweat drying, our breathing returning to normal, our dreaming
Suspended, no tasks to perform until waking at dawn.
In the dark toward morning, first snow of the season fell muffling
All sounds. Not a rustle of chipmunk, a scurry of mouse,
Not a crow's caw or owl hoot or hawk's piercing cry in the distance
To rouse us, no sunlight to signal arrival of day.
The camp slept, fires extinguished, not even the usual snoring
Of elders could carry from shelter to shelter through flakes
Falling thickly. I woke and smelled winter's crisp crackling odor
Come tickling my nostrils. I crept out and stood in the cloak
Snow provided, unseen and still hot from our bed. Snowflakes sizzled
Upon my warm skin as they melted. A magical cloak
Hiding tree trunk from boulder, entrancing the eye with white motion,
Excited ecstatic quick rush in my heart once again
At first snowfall. I crept back inside. My cold body against him
Woke Kona with protests. "Great Spirit, you're icy," he gasped
As he pushed me away. "It is snowing," I said and went burrowing
Under his arm while he struggled, recoiled and then laughed.

"It's too early for snow.
        You've been swimming,"
                he guessed, incorrectly.

"Just listen," I said, "to the silence of snow on the world."
"I hear hissing, not silence," he answered. And then I, too, heard it,
Snow changing to pellets, then rain, as the air up above
Received heat from the late-rising sunlight, compressed the white magic
To clots of wet snow slipping free of the evergreen tips,
The clumps plopping and smacking to ground in thumps sudden and
        random.
Rain stopped. Clouds dispersed and the people of camp all emerged
Unaware of the flurries they'd missed, only feeling the dampness.
I loved secret moments like mine when out early, alert
And receptive to beauty, when no one was using the world but
Myself, no one spoiling pure glory with comments to call
My attention with words to what needn't be talked about anyway.
Obvious, candid, impulsive and talkative folk
I avoided while guarding my solitude, often dismaying
Good people who craved only company, others surrounding
Them, always uneasy alone. They accomplished together
With friends of like character many astonishing feats
Of great kindness and charity. Love for us all fed their efforts.
Their hearts were as open as smiles, and their energies great
As their cooperation was seamless, effective, and genuine.
Kona and Otter and Fawn moved among them with ease

    Never minding their bustle
        and busyness.
                Yet I retreated…

My differentness causing me worry quite often, that I,
So unlike all the others, was curious, questing, reflective
Intense, solitary, too sensitive, keenly aware
That I baffled my friends at times seeming to live in a universe
Outside their own. And yet Kona and Otter and Fawn
Each accepted my dreaminess, absence of mind, inattentive
Brief preoccupations. Amused and indulgent they'd wait
My return. And I noticed that each of them drifted in spirit
To other realms also. Perhaps I was not as unlike
As I thought. How could anyone know what another was thinking
What secrets were harbored, what wishes unspoken lay hot
In wild hearts. What the fears, what the passions, the questions
            unanswered
Bedeviled cold nights and bleak days while the world made demands
Of a physical nature, immediate, vital, imperative,
Voiding calm reverie, forcing quick action or slow
Patient labor, survival the only concern of the moment.
I needed to fuse my two worlds, of the spirit and flesh,
Into one. To feel unified, whole, and untroubled by oddities
Felt, more imagined than real perhaps. People seemed flat
Uninspiring, both boring and bored, very often appearing to sleepwalk
Through life, superficial or silly, more chatter than sense.

     I found speaking with Mother
          or Meadowlark
                privileged and solid…

Their words going right to the heart of an issue, their thoughts
Sympathetic with mine as I struggled from girlhood to woman,
My body so often ahead of my brain. And they seemed
To remember themselves at my age, gave me gentle encouragement,
Models to emulate in my own personal style
Admiration my stimulus, wanting to be like them driving
My growth work. Contented I nestled in Kona's warm arms
For a few minutes longer before we arose to the morning's
Harsh challenges, finishing packing our baskets, prepared
To return to The Place of Tall Trees for collection of Spotted
Whale's bones. A sad task. One I dreaded. To see scattered bones
Where once reigned an enormous, expansive, imperious presence
Was eerie to contemplate. Kona's face mirrored this, too,
In his furrow of brow and the clench of his jaw. He was bracing
Himself to confront what we must. I wondered if Whale
Could have known just how hard this would be on great-grandsons
Who loved her, had learned so much from her, revered her, enhanced
By her wisdom and guidance in all they had chosen to make of
Themselves. As we worked I spoke softly to Kona, aside,
"I am feeling uncertain of courage, and sad to be doing
This gathering up of dear Spotted Whale's bones. How are you?"

   "I am glad you have said that,"
          breathed Kona.
                 "I, too, am uncertain..."

"My feelings a mixture of pride and great heaviness deep
In my heart. Until now I could think of her otherwise occupied,
Simply away. Now this proves her death final and true."
We stood shoulder to shoulder, looked down at our feet in shared anguish.
Then Medicine Otter and Lame Fawn approached, hand in hand,
Their expressions as solemn as ours, footsteps slow and reluctant.
We took up our backpacks and food, said goodbye to the tribe,
And set out on the path to The Place of Tall Trees without hurry,
No one of us wishing to lead or be first in the glade.
My mind reeled with the horror imagined of wolves in a frenzy
Voracious and vicious and bloodied, all tearing her flesh
From her skeleton, scattering bones, even gnawing and cracking
Them loudly to get at the marrow, then rancid remains
Left to summon black bears and rude ravens completing the clean-up.
I shuddered, these vivid imaginings tainted by fears
She could feel what was happening to her. A dread superstition
That lurked in dark corners of mystery, strangled good sense
With foreboding of what might become of our own precious bodies
In death, of what really would happen. Although I had been
There alone in the glade with her, sensing a subtle departure
Of energy, knew her bright spirit was gone from that place

     I expected encountering
         some kind of presence
            there waiting …

As if at a grave where one spoke to the dead with fond hope
Of awareness, though ground never trembled nor breeze ever tumbled
A single red leaf from its tree in response to one's pleas.
How uneasy we felt was borne out when Lame Fawn and brave Medicine
Otter stopped short of the glade and both set down their packs
At the spot on the trail where the men had awaited our whistle
Returning from bathing and tending to Spotted Whale's rites.
"We shall rest here a moment," said Otter, "assemble our prayer.
One purpose uniting our will, to obey this last wish
Of beloved great-grandmother, Spotted Whale, honoring destiny."
Quietly seated we calmed apprehensions with love
Thoughts, remembering Spotted Whale's wisdom and kindness and jollity,
Knowing her spirit could bring us no evil, no ill,
Yet we needed an anthem of sorts to embolden our spirits,
A chant regulating our footsteps, our rhythm of march
For the journey ahead, a bracing of will for confronting
The wreckage and mayhem just short steps beyond where we sat.
Then the words and the rhythm took form as we shared our desires.

> *Great Spirit, be with four frail youth*
> *Collecting death with grief and fear.*
> *We pray for strength to see us through*

> *This burden promised*
>   *we*
>   *must bear...*

With heads bowed and hands clasped in our circle we chanted these words,
Simple innocent prayer invented to carry us forward,
Repeating these phrases in unison softly until we were calm.
We fell silent at last, hearing only the hiss of our breath
Among trees standing airless and still. It was time to proceed.
We rose slowly and sighed as we shouldered our backpacks embracing
Each other for solace, resolved to do well at our task
Never flinching nor faltering. Reaching the glade we four halted
And gazed at white bones in the clearing reflecting pale light
From a bleak peering sun slanting weakly through evergreen branches.
The weather was changing again. I could sense coming snow.
As I stepped around Kona to enter the glade, begin gathering
Bones, his hand clutched at my arm and he whispered, "Stand still."
Then I saw what the others had already seen. A gray timber wolf
Female stood stocky and heavily pregnant, on guard.
Eyes unblinking she studied us, muzzle immobile, ears forward,
Alert. Unperturbed by our presence she yawned and then sat
On her haunches. Tongue lolling, she panted and groaned as she shifted
Her bulk to ease pressures within. She was mightily round
In her belly and beautifully furred for arrival of winter.
"Unusual season for pregnancy now," said Lame Fawn.

    "She's not pregnant, she's fat,"
        I said laughing.
            "She's Spotted Whale's joke for us."

Timber wolf yawned once again at us, stood up and stretched
Then retreated with dignified bearing, composed and disdainful
Of humans so cautious and hesitant. When she had gone
We advanced and began our sad duty of gathering skeleton
Fragments in four equal piles to distribute the weight
Of them fairly among us. We worried aloud about failing
To find pieces carried away and dropped elsewhere in bits
Very small or concealed under leaves. I determined to locate
Each segment right down to the least tip of finger and toe.
I searched deeper and deeper, past bushes and tree trunks and deadfalls
In forest surrounding the glade. My gaze focused on things
At my feet. Scuffing leafy ground cover, intent and oblivious
As I kept going, I came upon animal lair
And saw she-wolf's eyes sleepily lidded, half closing and languid
Accepting my presence as proper. She showed no alarm.
So I spoke to her, voice a scared quaver, stiff body a totem
Carved rigid with fear. But I swear she was grinning at my
Trepidation, not showing her teeth, just black lips drawing backward
All shiny with moisture, eyes meeting and holding. Again
I absorbed that same sting of intelligence shared with the otter
That swam alongside me in Long Bay when I did taboo.

> I assumed she was Otter
>   shape-changing
>   and went on with gleaning…

Ignoring the prickle of skin and the flutter of pulse
That was making me shaky. Intent, I forgot her while picking
Up delicate bones of Whale's fingers and wrist carried far
From the glade by small varmints or dropped from the treetops by ravens.
Each find led me farther away from my husband and friends.
I had never been lost in deep woods, had no worry of losing
My bearings, could trace my way homeward no matter how far
I had wandered. With sky clouding over and sunset streaks dimming
Pale greenish behind the bare trees on the southwestern ridge,
I returned to the glade with my bundle of bones as the darkness
Arose from the ground to envelop us. "Welcome," said Fawn
As she hugged me. "I feared you were lost." "Oh, but Otter knew better,"
I answered. "I thank you for caring to see I was safe
And for visiting, using the body and eyes of gray timber wolf
There by her lair," I said knowingly. "Ah, but I did
Not change shape, nor go find you," he said, "for I never sensed danger.
I felt you were able to make your way back without harm."
Their three faces were puzzled. And one look at Kona's expressive
Dismay was temptation to keep my encounter with wolf
To myself. But I wanted no secrets between us to compromise
Trust. And the story was wonderful, magical, true.

> "I met wolf and she offered
>   no threat to me,
>   simply sat watching."

"I swear she was grinning," I added, aware they might mock
My fantastical tale. But they listened and nodded acceptance.
We started a cook fire preparing to eat here and sleep
Through the night, make protection from snowfall with baskets and
        branches.
I worked alongside them still seeing wolf's eyes in my mind,
How she caused a connection between us benign and appealing.
A wordless intention of amity flowing across
The short bridging of her gaze with mine. Could she truly be Spotted
Whale's messenger come to encourage, or maybe just check
That the promise we made to her as she lay dying was being
Fulfilled? Superstition and eeriness pecked at my soul.
When we sat down to eat I decided to voice my imaginings,
Risk what derision the three might well heap on my thoughts.
"This gray timber wolf tugs at my feelings," I said to them softly.
"She seemed to be willing connections I cannot explain."
"This is dangerous business," said Otter. "Well fed and so
        cumbersome,
Wolf is complacent. But hungry, she poses great threat
To your safety. I urge you, use caution. Stay close, keep together
With us from now on." He was right. I supposed when we left
She-wolf's home territory behind we would see nothing further
Of her or her hypnotic gaze that still burned in my brain.

    As we settled to sleep
        Kona held me
            and whispered, "Dream sweetly."

"And you," I responded, exhausted and grateful to be
In his arms. We awoke to the cold and the silence and brilliance
Of sunup on new fallen snow, a thin layer of white.
At the edge of the clearing sat she-wolf, her breath curling visibly
Upward in puffs of pale mist catching sunglow all pink,
Dissipating, reforming, as calmly she waited and guarded
The stacks of Whale's bones we had piled in the Place of Tall Trees.
Fat as ever, she watched us emerge from our makeshift low shelter.
"Good morning," I said to her, feeling quite foolish and yet
Unafraid. If she'd wanted to feast on us helpless in slumber
She'd had the whole night to dismember us. This was the place
Of a glorious meal she'd remember, an opportune setting
For more of the same. As the four of us stood, close and awed
By her sentinel presence, Fawn pointed and asked, "Am I seeing
More bones at her forepaws?" "You are," agreed Otter. " They were
Not there yesterday. Wolf must have dropped them." Now this was
       a happening
None of us credited, could not accept though we saw
The same vision. Then she-wolf retreated to forest but left us
The bones. They were human. Two shin bones, picked clean, to complete
Our collection. Astonished, wolf proving our mission most sacred,
We packed up the bones in our backpacks, set forth on our trek.

    For days followed faint trails
        leading eastward,
            and chanted our prayer.

The going was easy downhill toward the coastline and sea.
We were tracing the very same journey the half tribe had taken
So long in the past when they split from our people then turned
Once again to the mountains and lakeside at Long Bay.
Our lake drew them back. She was bred in their nature. Their source
And their comfort. The sole place on Earth to call home. Not resisting
The lure of the waters that nourished their blood, washed their souls,
Fed their hopes, they returned to their origins not understanding
The power, perhaps, that her purity had to compel
Their allegiance. Misguided and angry and seeking secession
They still felt uprooted until they returned to lake's shore.
I could well understand how our lake drew them homeward. Departing
On this sacred journey, though knowing I soon could go home,
I felt sad as we widened the distance from place so familiar
As Red Hill, my birthplace. The rhythms of Earth there combined
With my own and I flourished in harmony with them. Now leaving,
I sensed with each new scene we passed a distressing hard jar
To my marrow, discomforting atmosphere, alien, subtle
Vibrations, disharmony deep in my nerves, up my spine.
It was merely a sense of displacement I thought, so I buried
Uneasiness, walked with bold steps, tried to relish the strange

    Changing landscape
        enjoy low terrain
            breathe in new briny odors.

I never had scented the smell of the ocean, the rank
Reeking odor of mud flats and seaweed, nor tasted the tangy
Salt air blowing landward, all heavy with moisture, exotic,
Alluring. The sight of the sea as we reached the last bluff top
Made everyone gasp. An horizon so flat and so far
In the distance, so limitless in its wide sweep seemed impossible.
Stories of strangers who'd come from beyond the far edge
Of that water seemed fables all falsified, tales too fantastic
To credit as likely. Not yet on the beachfront, we chose
To make camp on the bluff for the night and descend in full daylight
When sun would be rising from out of the ocean itself,
An event we expected would thrill us with newness and splendor.
Each morning of our lives the sun had arisen to shine
From behind eastern mountains and trees, partly hidden 'til midday
And high overhead. So the four of us sat by the fire
After eating. As evening was coaxing our thoughts toward dreaming
A rustle of undergrowth caught our attention. We looked
To see timber wolf standing and watching us, almost invisibly
Blending with bushes surrounding the rock where she stood.
She had followed us noiselessly all the long days of our journey
It seemed, having given no hint of her presence. But now,

    With one rustle emerging,
        had signaled
            she meant us to notice …

And notice we did. Strange behavior for such a wild beast
Of the forest to seek out and follow us, openly letting
Us know she was here with us on the same journey as we.
Explanations eluded us as we sat talking and watching
Her. Fear was no longer the paramount feeling. A keen
And most curious interest melted our attitudes, wary
At first but just pondering only now what this might mean.
"Is she Spotted Whale's ghost in the form of the she-wolf?" I wondered
Aloud. "I believe not," said Medicine Otter. "I'd feel
Her around us. Her spirit is gone to the whales in the ocean.
Her job here is done." To which Kona agreed with a grunt.
"This is something quite different, new to us, novel but natural,"
Added Lame Fawn. "I have heard an occasional tale
Of a wolf that befriended a human, approaching and touching.
A kind of affection developing, lasting through life,
Although rare. As I said, I have only heard tales, sweat lodge gossip."
Her hesitant tone might have prompted denials except
For magnificent she-wolf still standing alert and observant.
"The wolf is the one who decides that relationship then,"
Offered Kona," not likely are humans attempting such closeness."
"Well, not with a grown wolf," I said, "but perhaps with a pup."

    "But the mother would never
        allow it
                unless she were stricken…"

Said Lame Fawn. So, having no answers, we settled to sleep.
But my mind entertained in my dreaming a she-wolf, enormous
Yet docile, who lay by my side keeping watch through the night.
We arose before dawning, saw clouds glowing orange, horizon
Alive with the tip of the sun just appearing to breach
From the depths of the sea, growing larger, unbearably brighter
Until we could no longer look at it, blinding and full.
Then the surface of ocean untroubled changed color from blackish
To green, and the breezes bestirred themselves rippling the sea
Surface, skipping in patches across its expanse like the footprints
Invisible giants might leave as they hop at their games.
My eyes ached with absorbing such spaciousness uninterrupted.
No islands, no trees out there, nothing but ocean and sky.
All seemed sterile until one whale breached and then sprayed a white
        plumage
Of droplets above its huge head. Then another appeared,
And another, their spouts catching rainbows, entrapping, dissolving
The various colors so briefly, the visible tints
Hardly real. What was real was the stink of the puffed exhalations
That drifted our way, much diluted yet pungent and stale
On the air. Then my stomach rebelled at the odor. I vomited,
Certain at last of my pregnancy, proof against doubt.

    Lame Fawn came to me offering water,
        "Just rinse.
            Do not swallow…"

She said to me, smiling in sympathy. "Well, this is new,
And unpleasant," I said after rinsing and spitting and gagging
Once more. "It won't last," Fawn assured me, "I'm over it now."
"There's a promise I'll hold you to." Retching and gasping and wiping
My mouth with the back of my hand, I said "Being with child
Is becoming a full occupation, I think." "It may seem so
At times," Fawn said soberly. "Nothing we do else can be
More of value than this in our lives." We embraced. I felt better,
My nausea quelled. Then we laughed as we whispered a few
Of our benefits. "No monthly bleeding," she said. "And we cannot
Get pregnant right now," I put in as my joke on our state.
Just then Kona approached, so Fawn left us to speak our thoughts privately
There on the bluff staring out at the ocean. His arm
Linked with mine, his voice filled with concern. "Can you travel?" he
                    asked me.
"Of course," I replied. "This is only a short-lived distress."
I was pleased he would notice the changes that pregnancy brought me,
Did not turn away in disgust or embarrassment, came
To my side in support. I felt vulnerable, hostage
To internal forces beyond my control. This new joy
Had its drawbacks we both were discovering. Vigor, diverted
From cooperation in everyday chores, drawn inside

    By demands of digestion.
        A tyranny
            rather revolting.

I wanted my mother right then with an ache that surprised
Me. Though Kona still held me, he'd never experience feelings
Of utter dependence like mine at this moment. I felt
A great distance between us, a sense of aloneness that Mother
Had warned of. Not even my best friend Lame Fawn understood
Me I feared. Although pregnant herself she seemed buoyant, lighthearted
And outwardly fearless. Perhaps being older and skilled
As a midwife, experience bolstered her confidence, gave her
A strength that I felt I was lacking for what was to come.
My old arrogant attitude, thinking that I ruled my body,
Flip-flopped in the instant that nausea spasm took hold.
I was frightened and feeling too young for this coming production
Of new life depending on Kona and me for its birth.
With a shuddering sigh I leaned closer, my head on his shoulder.
He rested his free hand upon my flat belly and left
It there, warming me, calming me. Touch so important, so comforting,
Letting me know without saying a word he was with
Me and loved what was happening for us, a true caring partner.
I felt our connection grow stronger than ever. He knew
That so simple a gesture went straight to my body's disquiet
And needed no talk. Sometimes touching was language enough.

His best gift to his infant
within me
was loving its mother.

Absorbing his nearness, the warmth of his hand where it pressed
On my belly, I let myself relish the deepening bonds of
Affection and trust we were forming in such simple ways.
"I am happy," I murmured. He grunted, as usual, making
Me burst into laughter, eyes blurring with tears as I gagged
Once again, dryly retching. He never let go, just supported
My doubling cramped body until the wave passed and I stood
Straight and strong breathing deeply the tangy salt air off the ocean.
"Great Spirit your moods are so changeful," he marveled, "I can
Not predict them." "My sympathies, Kona," I answered him, "neither
Can I." Then remembering Mother's encouragement said,
"Though appearing now different, I'm still Ellacoya, the woman
Who married you not long ago. I see Otter and Fawn,
Though they're older, seem somewhat off balance and strange to each
          other
At times just as we do, or haven't you noticed?" "They do
Act distracted," he commented wryly. We stood many minutes
In thought, calm and quiet together, observing the tide
Creeping high up the beach toward rocks, rounded pebbles and seaweed
That lay at the base of the bluff. Kona suddenly grabbed
Me and pulled me to earth, made me crawl in a scramble to Otter
And Fawn, barely mewling the cry of the gull in his throat.

    They both heeded the signal
        and crouched out of view
           from the water.

"What is it?" I whispered. "Strange people," he said, "in a boat
Just off shore. Using paddles a way I've not seen. Stroking sideways
Instead of upright. Both hands touching at only one end,
And the shank stuck between two stout pegs on the boat's upper edges."
I had to see that. So I crept to a rock and peered 'round it to look.
True enough. A small boat with two men in it seated and sweeping
And dipping the paddle-things, backs to direction of thrust.
The boat lurching along with their efforts in spurts as their pulling
Strokes, working together in cadence, propelled them along
To the north, past our hiding place. Bird skimming low over water
They looked to me, wingtips just splashing, preparing for flight
Like the loon or brown osprey. Then one of them shouted and pointed.
They rested and studied the bluff where we crouched. I then feared
I'd been seen, drawn attention unwanted, endangered us, stupidly
Careless and curious. Noise, like the crack of an oak
Split apart by a wind gust, came echoing up from the water.
The yelp of an animal sounded close by. Timber wolf
Scurried past us, ear bleeding. We grabbed up our packs and retreated
Away from the shoreline and shunning the path we had used.
We went southward where tree growth was taller, concealment was better.
Wolf's blood trail lay readily telltale. We covered her drops,

    Overturning stained leaves
            as we went,
                    feeling oddly protective.

We came to a stand of tall conifers, dense growth and green,
The light dim in among them, their needles a mat lying thickly
To cushion the ground and to muffle the sounds of our steps.
Otter stopped, looked around, pointed upward, said, "Climb," as he boosted
First Fawn and then me to the nearest strong branches above
Him while Kona stood watch. "Now stay close to the trunks and go higher,"
He ordered. We scrambled, still holding our packs, a tough trick
Not to tangle or topple them, losing our grip. Fawn in one tree
And I in another beside hers went high as we dared.
Not the height but the frail top growth branches were what gave us caution.
We broke off some well-needled branch tips and plaited small nests
For soft seats to conceal us from casual upward quick glances,
Sat cross-legged close to the trunks and then waited to see
If the strangers were chasing. I lost sight of Kona and Otter.
They vanished, no movement or sound to expose where they'd gone.
Like obedient bear cubs we two remained high on our perches,
An image delighting my mind. Laughing Bear was my name.
I could practically feel black fur sprouting to warm us and color
Us shadowy, shapeless, invisible to an unskilled
Interloper. A hunter pursuing some beast he had wounded
Would never look up, merely scour the ground for fresh blood.

A slight tremble of bush
revealed she-wolf below,
crouched and bloody...

Not far from the base of my perch. It was almost as if
She were guarding our hiding place, offering herself as distraction
Should anyone come. Her behavior seemed purposeful, hurt
Though she was. Not a whimper escaped her, no sign of self-pity.
Accepting her injury, bothered but silent, alert,
She crouched hidden and watchful, becoming as one with surroundings.
I copied her mood, listened carefully, waited, kept still.
Nothing stirred. Even natural sounds of the creatures of daylight
Were absent, sure sign of disturbances more than our own
Would have caused. Enough time had elapsed since we settled in
        hiding
For life to resume its small busywork, birds to return,
Squirrels leap branch to branch, shiny beetles crunch bark, ants start
        hauling
The fragments of ripe vegetation they fancied was good
For the needs of their colony. Often in childhood my wonder
Was captured while watching the lines of those laboring crews
As they struggled with loads twice their size, going somewhere from
        nowhere
And back without pause. It's amazing how quickly thoughts dart
As new dangers intrude, I was thinking. My reverie rising
To occupy idleness served its intention, made sharp
My awareness of every least quiver of atmosphere. Calling
To memory old agitations, as when on taboo

    That hunt party's approach
       irritated
          the wily old she-bear.

We waited. The sun crawling higher brought warmth and more light
Penetrating the evergreens, patching with shadow and flicker
The floor of brown needles below. Looking eastward I saw
Through the treetops sun sparkling and winking and dancing on wavelets
And wanted to move my cramped limbs, do a dance of my own.
I grew restless, believing the strangers we'd seen had gone northward
Lost interest in killing a wolf for its stringy tough meat.
Lame Fawn frowned from her perch at me signaling me to be quiet,
Stop fidgeting, listen. I heard them, men's voices from near
By the cook fire we'd not had the time to extinguish or scatter
Sufficiently. Loud and high pitched were their voices. No skill
At concealment or stealth in these men. Just all blither and bluster
Their style, as though owning whole earth and the creatures upon
It. I guessed they'd brought firesticks (described in the tale told by
            Meadowlark).
Feeling invincible, killing both wild things and men
As they pleased, unafraid of a people like us, only arrows
And knives for our weapons. My anger was building, my fear
Disappearing in fury. My Kona and Medicine Otter
Were down there. And she-wolf was hurt by this arrogant pair.
Just a target, a thing, to them. They hadn't seen the intelligence
Burning behind the keen eyes that had looked into mine,

> Did not honor the spirit
>   of wolf
>   nor apologize to it.

They came into sight looking down at the ground for a trace
Of wolf's bleeding. Their footsteps were clumsy, dislodging and snapping
Dried twigs as they clumped along heavily booted, kicked stones
From their path. Haughty progress, assaulting Earth's innocent surface
Ignoring the fact she would feel them, recoil from their heels.
I had never seen movements like theirs as they stomped our way stiffly
Upright, overdressed in dark garments which hampered the swing
Of their arms by the belts and the strapping of gear to their bodies.
No chance they could run in a chase, and that heartened me some.
Even Fawn might outrun them if need be, despite her old injury.
None could outrun harmful reach of their firesticks, since wolf
Had been hurt from the distance of shore, I assumed. And I wondered
If Otter and Kona had known of such weapons, would keep
Them in mind should a fight be provoked. We had only directed
Our talks toward peaceful endeavors, had never discussed
What we'd do when encountering enemies threatening conflict.
Remembering Kona's suggestion of fading ourselves
Out of sight and then living the woodlands invisibly, secret
And peaceful, I hoped that perhaps we'd succeed at that now,
Could avoid outright fighting, remain undetected, well hidden.
The strangers paused under my tree perch and scanned soil for blood

While wolf, flowing like water
around an obstruction,
slunk sideways...

Not making a sound, not disturbing a leaf, bunched and low
Behind roots of an upended hemlock, avoided detection.
Wound blood had stopped seeping, no trail left to prove where she'd gone.
From above I could smell the foul stench unwashed bodies exuded
And wanted to vomit again. They stood scratching. One peed
On my tree trunk. The reek of hot urine at least masked what odors
That she-wolf and we might contribute, despoiling cool air.
As the strangers moved on I saw Kona behind them and trailing
Them skillfully quite unobserved, making sure we stayed safe
And unseen. He had circled around them, while Medicine Otter,
I saw, had created false trail leading off to the south
And away from our hiding place, fooling the strangers who followed
It easily, jabbering, wasting what chances they had
Of discovering anything useful. Insensitive, loutish,
And deaf to the messages nature might yield, they tramped on
Out of sight. Gliding under my tree Kona never glanced upward,
Intent on his quarry. I knew then the men would be led
Into ambush of Otter's and Kona's design with those obvious
Tracks. There would surely be fighting, I felt. So did Fawn
As she looked at me, worried yet certain, she signaled, we needn't
Be fearful. Our men knew their way around weapons and war.

Though they'd rather have peace,
    do no killing,
        they'd kill if they had to.

We sat and heard nothing except voices fading afar
As the strangers, still talking, went over a rise, disappearing.
The silence returned and we waited. I burned to climb down
And go after them, see what would happen, assist in the fighting.
The best I could do would be throwing my basket of bones
At them. Futile to hope bones would do any good against firesticks.
I yearned for a weapon, impatient with helplessness, fired
By a drive to act boldly, could hardly sit still doing nothing.
My instinct for action was hasty, misguided, I knew.
Lame Fawn saw my impatient distress, so she patted her belly
Then pointed at mine. With the smallest of gestures she signed
Our true duties were not prosecution of battle but tranquil
Gestation. Protection of lives yet to come was our task.
I relaxed then, accepting the truth of her warning that more than
My own life at risk to consider must govern my will.
I had so much to learn, and this infant was growing regardless
Of wisdom or ignorance, patience or impulse the stuff
Of my character. Learning to think outside personal limits,
Take into account how my conduct affected a life
That was barely beginning, was lesson enough to be pondering
Perched as I was in a tree feeling hungry and chilled.

    Then below appeared Kona
        and Otter.
            "Come down," they were gesturing…

Fingers to lips for full silence. We slithered down, glad
To be moving, and followed the men as they trotted ahead of us
Back to our campsite. I saw that each carried a gun
As they called it, a firestick each took from the blustering strangers,
Though how they obtained them they'd yet to explain. We went past
Our old campsite down over the bluff to the shore and found, floating,
The boat that the strangers had left loosely tied to a rock.
Without speaking we knew what great luck this was bringing to Spotted
Whale's wishes, a means of transporting her bones out to sea.
I had pictured the four of us standing on shore as we mightily
Hurled her bones singly as far as we could, nowhere near
Where the whales breached and spouted. A pitiful effort, no grandeur
Of homecoming, plunked in the shallows, exposed by low tide,
Rolled about with the pebbles and seaweed and shells of dead creatures.
But now we would borrow the boat made of wood with its long
Heavy paddles and try to propel it the way I had witnessed
It done. So we loaded our packs in, released line to wade
Alongside until water came up to our kneecaps, then boarded
And fumbled with paddles too long and too awkward for use
In our usual style. "Let me show what I saw," I said, placing
One paddle between the two pins on the rim. I then pulled.

We spun 'round in a circle.
The paddle jumped free
of the rim pins...

I almost lost hold of it. Drifting, we studied the boat.
Short and wide, much more stable afloat then our long and more narrow
Canoes, it was also less lively, more clumsy to move.
I recalled the position the strangers had taken to manage
Its progress. And Kona had seen them as well, side by side
On one seat, each one sweeping his paddle in time with the other.
So, shifting to sit down beside me, put shoulder to mine
And together as one we tried dipping these paddles and pulling.
It worked. I let Medicine Otter take my place. We skimmed
Out to sea as the men soon perfected their rhythm, adjusting
The strength of one's stroke or the other's, controlling our aim.
I sat facing direction of travel to guide with hand signals
Corrections of course. We soon reached the deep playground of great
Spouting whales all around us, exuberant beasts of the ocean,
Enormous and agile and barnacled, powerful, sleek,
Truly frightening, close as they came to us, able to capsize
And drown us all easily. Surfacing under our boat
They might carelessly toss it and spill us like corn or ripe berries
From basket upended, no malice intended, benign
But gigantic and needing more room than one ocean provided.
We floated among them and marveled. Then flinging white bones

    In great arcs to her sisters
        we cried to them,
           "Here is your namesake" …

A calm settled down as the whales, diving deep, disappeared,
Left the surface untroubled except for the circles of ripples
Bones made as they splashed before sinking. We, vying to see
Which of us could throw farthest, made Spotted Whale's bones fly a
    skipping
Dance over the glossy green waters. An irreverent child's
Game, solemnity utterly lacking. The weather too beautiful,
Day too magnificent, perfectly brilliant, too clear
For a sadness to stifle our mood. Celebrations of jollity
Spotted Whale always engendered in life rose again in our hearts.
As the last bone sailed farthest to spin and then splatter,
The honor of winning the contest was Otter's. The end.
Thus our promise completed gave great satisfaction, communion.
We sat a while, leaving the boat to drift slowly along,
Looked to shore and saw timber wolf wading in shallows, immersing
Her head, raising up with great shaking, immersing again.
"The salt water is cleansing her wound," exclaimed Lame Fawn, delighted,
"She knows how to heal herself." "Maybe she's fishing." The quip
Came from Kona. "This wolf is too smart," added Otter, "she's shaman
And next she will walk on hind legs like a man, I suppose."
They made sport of her frolic as she-wolf ran splashing and snapping
At bubbles kicked up by her feet, seeming playful, bemused.

    Just then Kona grabbed one gun
        to raise it
           and Otter, the other.

I feared for the wolf but I should have known better. The men
Simply dropped both the guns in the ocean to sink to the bottom.
"No harm from them now," muttered Kona. "But what have you done
With the strangers?" asked Lame Fawn. "They're hurt but alive,"
                    answered Otter.
"We'll go to them now and decide what to do. To release
Them or leave them to make their escape on their own, if they're able."
Though eager to meet these invaders up close, my desire
To remain in the boat, to float dreamily out on the waters
So level, to bask in a sun soon to sacrifice heat
To the onset of winter, a last idle respite in comfort and
Peace, was seductive. I wanted the world to retreat
For a while. Leave us be: confrontations with strangers avoided.
We landed the boat, disembarked, and then watched as the men
Overturned it, broke paddles on rocks and then shoved the boat seaward,
It looking to be the result of an accident caused
By rough waves should a search party come, find remains all in pieces.
Our wolf went to woods as we readied ourselves for the walk
To the place where the strangers were left. It surprised me that Otter
Would have us accompany them, would not keep us away
Out of sight as before. As we traveled we covered our traces
Behind us, thus leaving no marks climbing down might have made
Where they'd paused underneath us before marching into the ambush.
Their tracks were too obvious, easily seen. We erased

    Them as well to delay
        any rapid return
                to their landing place...

Hide any story the ground might in future reveal.
We eventually came to a hollow where earth had subsided
As though long ago something deep had refused its support.
The collapse of a cave might have caused it, or underground river.
Clear water emerged from one rocky steep side, a cascade
To a shallow stone basin before overflowing and seeping
Away. Such a spring was a gift that we welcomed, in need
Of fresh water, all sticky with salt. As we drank, the men guarded
From high on the rim, let us rinse off the salt. Feeling safe
And refreshed, we changed places to stand in their stead and give signal
If threat were perceived. I admit my attention was drawn
From my duty as lookout to brief stolen glances at Kona's
Nude body below at the spring. He was beautiful, lithe
And well muscled. He moved with sure grace in the smallest of actions.
Delightful to watch and admire. A whole army of men
Might encroach without notice unless I looked elsewhere, recaptured
My dutiful first obligation to be on my guard.
Such distractions were dangerous. He had no right to be handsome
As this, to our peril. Instead of chastising myself
I just blamed my besotted fool senses on him and the maleness
So natural, real, that I treasured. He lived with an air
Of assurance innate and well founded. Abilities, talents
And purpose, affections and energies all in command.

> Mother Earth was inspired
>   when she gave to her daughters
>   such creatures.

I thanked Her for such generosity. Deep in my heart
Great joy bubbled. To feel so alive, to be glad to be woman,
To relish existence in this time and place was enough.
And whatever might come, I'd have this to remember, to cherish,
Recall in harsh moments; the sight of my lover, the feel
Of his skin next to mine, smell of smoke in his hair, his voice resonant
Low in my ear as we privately shared deepest thoughts
Before sleeping. This pause at the spring let me crystallize images
Sorrows or losses, so certain to sober our years,
Could not shatter. My mind would be amulet bag, hold sweet memories
Solid as pink crystal rabbit that Kona once carved
For me, durable nuggets of feeling to take out and offer
To light again, clasp to an aching old faltering heart
At the end of my days, and say "These I have known. These my blessings."
This somehow seemed vital, important to feed to my soul
On the day of fulfilling our promise to Spotted Whale. Endings,
Beginnings, were everywhere, cycling, recycling. Our lives
But brief whispers of ecstasy tossed to the clouds and the mountains,
Impermanent. "Timeless somewhere beyond mystery's thrall,
Where no life can be lost nor forgotten, our energies vibrate,
Collapse, re-emerge," so our channeler, Star Seed, has said.

    I again heard her words,
        felt my body respond,
            comprehending…

In muscle and nerve's agitation my state on taboo
When no boundaries pinched my awareness. I felt universal,
Connected to planets and stars, an unbearable state
To sustain without madness. These throes of expansion in consciousness
Terrified me. Otherworldly and sudden they came,
This the second one now, in a place and a time all unsuited
For bolts of enlightenment coursing right through my small frame.
Every particle in me alive, independently tingling
While I was supposed to be grounded, alert and on guard.
As the men both climbed up from the hollow, tall Otter was studying
Me with a grin. "I can see Star Seed's minions are with
You," he said. "I am fearful, disturbed and unsettled," I answered him,
Glad to be recognized mere Ellacoya once more,
My familiar and natural state re-assumed and most welcome.
"You'll learn to invite and enjoy these far visitors, trust
That they mean you no harm. You can trust who you are. Don't feel crazy,"
He said as he touched me in passing, "Just get past your fears."
We're so very much more than we know, I was thinking, astonished
To hear him predict future visits, to find that he knew
All about this experience, sensed my distress. As a novice
In wanting to know so insistently all that I could

    I'd invited assistance
        from sources unknown
            but available…

Willing to teach me. I wondered if Kona knew, too,
Of these visiting energies. Or, so well grounded, would think me
Demented if told what I felt. All my earlier sense
Of my differentness now was explained. Though contained in a physical
Body at present, my mind could be anywhere, merge
Like a bird with the wind and be borne to far reaches of nowhere
Where everything is. Strange elation perfused my whole view
Of existence, exalted my spirit. I followed with light step
Behind the three others and wanted to dance on the path
As we walked. In the distance hurt she-wolf was howling. An answering
Chorus, far off, lent the air her pack's music, their cue
To return to them sounding. They'd tend to the wound her ear suffered.
If ever we saw her again we would know it was she
By the notch in her ear and the scar on her jaw, and her curious
Interest in human companions. If lost from the pack
Then we people would do. Lame Fawn's tale of the overheard gossip
In sweat lodge was probably based on encounters like ours,
Rare and brief, but amazing enough for retelling, significant.
Wolf was revered forest creature, admired for its care
Of its young, for its swiftness, its loyalty, cooperation
In hunting, formation of family, peacekeeping ways.

    So the structure of wolf's
        social order and ours
            was quite similar.

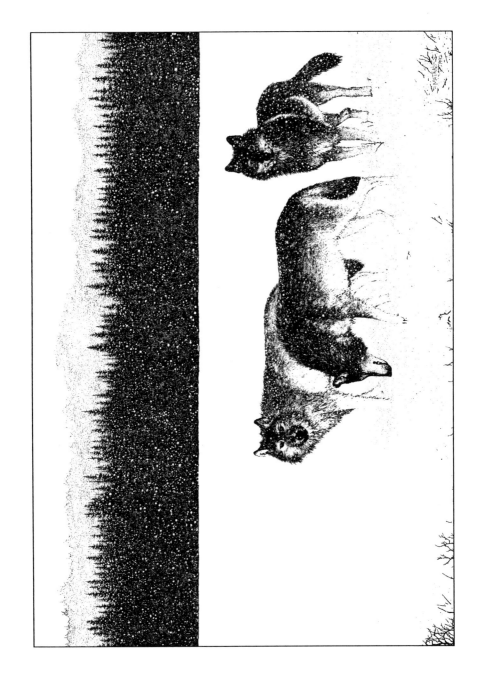

Many a prayer to wolf's spirit was uttered around
The night's campfire, as howls from the mountaintops solemnly echoed
And faded, gave woodlands melodious lullaby airs.
We slept soundly on those nights, the forest untroubled, wolves' singing
Untroubled as well. I would always remember wolf's eyes
Looking out from beneath sleepy lids as I garnered those pieces,
All scattered, of skeletal bones near her lair, remember
That eerie intelligent sharing of mutual glances
In reverie, often, while falling asleep to wolves songs.
We had reached where the strangers sat back-to-back tied to a sapling
Surprising them both, I could see, with our soundless approach.
Though their faces were hidden by hair, wide blue eyes appeared startled
And gave them away as afraid of us. Well they might be.
They had hunted us, finding our cook fire, pursuing wolf's bloody
Escape after harming her needlessly, not for the meat,
But because she was there, and they could, with their treacherous firesticks.
I disliked with intensity how they'd behaved in our woods.
Now their noisy aggression was tamed as they shrank from us, wary,
Defiance lamentably lacking. No fire in their stares.
These were men? Not the bravest. One, we could see, was a youngster
Years younger than Kona had been when first met at Long Bay.

Lame Fawn touched the boy,
smoothed back his hair.
Then we saw he was bleeding.

She bathed away blood as she uttered soft cluckings to soothe
His great fear, while the older man struggled and twisted and shouted
Some guttural threatening words we could not understand.
It was obvious these two were father and son by their similar
Features revealed as Fawn moved to the shouter to look
At his wound. Superficial but bloody, his scalp cut was oozing
Blood still, and lay open above his right ear. As she cleansed
It she motioned me over to hold back his hair, red and wiry.
As soon as I touched him my hatred dissolved. Though he stank
Just as bad, all unwashed as he was, his clothes rancid, scalp greasy,
He was, after everything, only a man in distress
And was probably frantic to see his son safely delivered
From capture. His fear no doubt more for the boy than himself.
By allowing two women to care for these strangers, both Otter
And Kona, though fierce in their manner, impassive in stance,
On their guard against any attempt to abuse our skilled kindnesses,
Signaled intent to inflict no more harm. Lame Fawn closed
The long scalp gash by knotting together hairs lining its edges,
A row of small snarls that would hold until healing was done,
We stepped back then, rejoining our husbands, then watched them retying
The strangers more cleverly, using the knots of a child's game

That taught patience—
The harder the struggle,
the tighter the binding.

We loved to snare two squabbling youngsters and see just how long
It would take them to figure it out, come to peaceful solution
And free themselves easily once they relaxed and moved close
To cooperate, loosen the tension, let knots slowly separate.
Quickly we left the two strangers who tugged at their bonds
Loudly arguing, frustrated, bold again now we had tended
Their wounds, given water, and gone. Out of earshot, I said
"I give boy the advantage. He'll figure it out." Lame Fawn chuckled,
"If father will listen to him, which I very much doubt."
"Then they'll be there a long time," said Kona, "but we'd better hurry
In case they are smarter than proven by actions so far."
So we ran single file, heading northward, misleading direction
In case they could follow. With Otter in front running fast
We had covered much distance, uphill all the way, before turning
Southwestward toward home and Red Hill. With less weight in our packs
We could travel more swiftly. I noticed, however, my energy
Flagging, my breath feeling labored, a pain in my side
Burning sharply. Ashamed of my weakness I strove to keep running
To stay with the others, but soon I was grunting aloud
With each jolt, growing clumsy and faint. Lame Fawn, too, began
          faltering,
Slowing ahead of me, walking at last. When she stopped

    Then the four of us rested.
       "Well done, little mothers,"
        cheered Otter.

"I thought you'd both tire long before we reached here. In a while
If you'll walk a bit farther, you'll see we've arrived at the campsite
We used on our way to the ocean." I noticed that he,
Even he, the tall Medicine Otter, was breathing hard, panting.
And Kona was, too. "I just guess we did well enough, Fawn,"
I gasped into her ear, "Both our husbands lie flopped with chests heaving,
Pretend only we are exhausted." She grinned at the men.
"You were glad to stop, too. Now admit it," Fawn said to them, teasing.
Though Kona reflexively tried for denial, one look
At me stopped him. He laughed in agreement. Once more we were merry
And this time we all knew the reason, no secrets, no false
Roles to play. So, refreshed by good humor, we stood and proceeded
As dusk filled the woods, masked the trail, cooled the air, lured the moon
To her great orange rising behind us. We soon reached the campsite,
Well rid of the signs we had been there before. But we knew
It familiar, though no passing stranger would find any traces
Of use of the space. Only trees and the rocks underneath
Them remembered our ghosts. They accepted our presence, the welcoming
Atmosphere palpable. Good place to stay for the night.
As we finally settled for sleep, Moon encouraged wolves' howling.
Night air, crisp and windless, enhanced every glorious note.

> She-wolf came to my dreaming.
>   She stared
>   as if bearing a message.

Uneasy at waking, I pondered the dream as we ate,
Cleaned the campsite, prepared to move on. Kona noticed distraction
Had hold of me. "How are you feeling?" he asked. "Are you well?"
"Wolf appeared in my dream last night trying to send me some message,"
I told him. "It troubles me still. I could not understand."
"Dreams are like that," he said as he hoisted his pack to his shoulder,
"Dream images puzzle me often." An answer would come
When I least was expecting receipt of one. Something in future
Would happen to nudge recollection of dreams I'd forgot.
Like the rescue of Dewdrop. She was the sick pitiful infant
That squalled in my vision dream so long ago on taboo.
I just had to be patient, not tug at the knots of my physical
Being so fiercely. As Otter had urged me, get past
My own fears. "You remember your dreams?" I asked Kona, delighted
He'd mentioned them readily. Many men wouldn't admit
To a dream, much less think it could be something worthy of puzzling
Over at waking. "Some mornings I certainly do,"
He said, handing my pack to me, hugging me briefly. Then whispered,
So shy, "Just the ones that are vivid. They linger in mind."
"And the ones that are scary," I prompted. But he merely grunted,
Got busy adjusting the straps of my pack. Kona scared?

  It was not to be thought.
    But fears may be felt
      without showing.

How often a boy believed natural fears made him weak
And unmanly, mistaking felt fear for a flaw in his character.
Kona appeared to have hardened his view of himself
Since our meeting much younger at Long Bay. Emotions then rampant
Now guarded, concealed, as if others might judge him as less
Than he was. More than once he had jostled me free of a nightmare
With sympathy, proving he knew some black terror had built
Me a scene insurmountable, panic infesting interior
Struggles that made me cry out, so afraid, in my sleep.
His concern when I woke and wept onto his chest was a comfort.
I knew by his thrashing he sometimes had dreams that upset
And awakened him, too, with sweat pouring, breath short, and heart
        pounding.
Together we'd lie awake, mentally flensing the dream
From the real in relief without speaking, each sensing some turmoil
The other was battling. In darkness we understood well
How the dreaming mind practiced its infinite, volatile choices.
But dawning and daylight demanded he put on the mask
Of a stolid, heroic demeanor. I loved this about him
So long as it offered no bar to our intimate times.
So I said it again, "And the dreams that are scary, remember?"
"Great Spirit," he hissed at the forest, "she pushes me, hard."

    Then relenting,
        he whispered for my ear alone,
            "And the scary ones."

"You had a dream that affected you last night," he said.
"It was Little Fox singing," I said, "a magnificent melody,
Making me want to be home again, praise her rich voice."
"You dream music?" he marveled. "Amazing." The four of us finished
Restoring the campsite to undisturbed nature. Our Earth
Was a sentient being and did not take kindly to careless
Disruptions, abuse, or neglect. Every hurt left upon
Her would give us away as unthinking, destructive and selfish.
We stood in a circle, eyes closed and hands clasped, in that place
Where we'd slept the night safely and sent through the soles of our
         moccasins
Gratitude, worship and awe. The forbearance Earth showed
For our puny existence deserved to be honored, acknowledged
With love. Earth allowed us to cling to her surface, mere nits
In the hairs of her woodlands, gave food and warm sunlight and water
Abundantly. Strangers had seen what we had and would want
It themselves, I was certain. A sadness for what might be coming
Lent urgency to my desire to be home. No delay
Was acceptable now we had sampled displays of the arrogant
Ways of the pair we had dealt with. Our story would need
To be told, wise decisions be made, actions taken to safeguard
Survival. That sparing their lives, cleansing wounds bore no weight

     With those two was apparent.
         Restraint merely fed
            their disdain for us.

Boy might have learned gentler ways if encountered alone,
I thought sadly. No friendship was possible now. The men's scalp wounds
Were proof we were savages, once their wild stories were told,
Overlooking their actions attacking and tracking us started
The incident. Knowing how tales were embellished by some
Less than brave ones to cast them as heroes if witness were lacking
To tailor their exploits reported more closely to fact—
The lone fisherman's arms were too short to describe his catch eaten
Before it was seen, for example—I had little hope
What we'd done out of mercy would benefit us in retelling.
I wanted to hear from my husband exactly the way
They'd subdued the two strangers, and how the decision to spare them
Was made. I intended to ask him about this tonight
As we sat after eating, while talking and watching flames dying,
Our last night alone on the trail before reaching Red Hill.
As we walked at a comfortable pace I kept hearing the melody
Little Fox sang to my dream in my mind with the beat
Of my footsteps, her song staying with me for hours all the morning.
At noon when we rested I hummed it aloud as we fixed
A scant meal without cooking. "How pretty that tune is," said Lame Fawn,
And hummed along with me, well able to mimic the notes.

> A shared song, a best friend,
> two fine men we adored,
> life was perfect…

The air was so fresh, the weather so clear, and the smell
Of the sun-heated balsam so tasting of seasons remembered
In sequence since birth, all seduced me, reduced me to one
Keen receptor absorbing the physical world all around me
And banishing any ethereal haunts left from dreams.
I was fully awake, my mood greedy for every thing natural,
Avid to cherish the beauty in every least twig
At eye level as onward we walked again homeward together.
Toward evening the weather turned chill. We made camp, built a fire,
Huddled close as we stared at the flames. Then I asked them my question.
"How did you subdue the two strangers, decide they should live?"
Both men thought a long while before answering. Medicine Otter
Spoke first. "It was easy to stalk them, they made so much noise,
Never knew we were there until one blow apiece stole their senses,
Made binding them simple." He paused then, recalling the scene
Of the capture. I saw by the flush in their faces, their mutual
Glances, their restlessness, they were reliving the deed
In recounting it. Violence, however minor, distasteful
To both of them. Kona spoke next. "We examined them, limp
As dead fish as we tied them, and guessed they were boy and his father,
Alike as they looked in hair color, each stocky and short."

    "Took their guns,"
        added Medicine Otter,
            "to render them harmless."

"But when did you talk about letting them live?" "We did not,"
Answered Kona, "No need to discuss it. A boy needs his father
At that age." A pain pierced my heart. I remembered how he
Had lost his in the skirmish with mine just before our first meeting.
Heartbroken and angry he was then, prepared to dislike
Even hate me on hearing my name. But we talked and he peeled away
Fury from what lay beneath it, deep grief, profound loss.
Not concealing his agony, sickness of spirit, his restlessness
Driving his body to run, and to climb, and take risks,
He allowed me to know him completely, so open, unguarded,
His sorrow revealing the strength and the depth of his love
For his own vanquished father. How like him to want to be sparing
Another young lad from such grievous despair, if he could.
"They do not know our ways. They are not of the woods or the
      mountains,"
Said Medicine Otter. "Their lives, come the cold, will be hard.
We pray nature herself can defeat them, can drive them to southward,
Can keep them away." "It depends," added Kona, "how large
Are their numbers." I shivered then, thinking how awful a woods full
Of strangers like those two would be, with their shouting and stench.
Where we glided as soundless as shadows, they trampled and blundered.
We signaled with birdcalls. They bellowed. We hunted with stealth.

> They exploded the air,
>   scattered birds far and wide
>   with their blastings…

I saw how gray gulls all took flight when they wounded our wolf,
Whereas birds when we hunted just watched from their branches our
        passing
Below as we tracked and then soundlessly loosed a swift clot
Of our arrows to bring down the deer or the moose, after thanking
Its spirit for sacrifice given. We killed for our food,
Not for sport. Though the hunters, successful, came homeward
        triumphant
Elated and eager to go out again on the trail
Of large game, though their hunt formed strong bonds, was exciting,
        they never
Killed wantonly, never left game they had wounded to die
In the woods, never wasted an arrow or spear on some varmint
Inedible crossing their path. I had often been sent
To track blood spoor and locate an animal, wounded and hunkered,
To signal a hunter to come and dispatch it, to end
Its calm helplessness. Thanking it. Telling it what was to happen
Before death arrived with a merciful knife in the neck.
I could skin and dismember and cook any creature, but killing
I left to the ones who would do it far better than I.
My reluctance no prompt for derision but understood, honored
By memories each hunter held of his very first kill,
Of the moment of brief hesitation, of pondering whether
He wanted to bring a magnificent creature its end

        Or relinquish his power
            and watch it march off
                in full majesty.

Loon Diver, fresh and agog from his very first hunt,
Told me what he had felt upon aiming at ugly old turkey
Too stupid to know it was doomed. But it wasn't, he said,
Because Loon Diver, youth who had practiced his aiming at targets
Inanimate, sand piles and fluttering skins hung on trees,
Had allowed himself time to consider results of his actions
And turkey had vanished. Returning first hunt with three birds,
Each one stuck with his arrows, did nothing to quell his anxiety
Over that brief hesitation that cost him a bird.
So he told me his feelings and, younger than he by eight seasons,
I still understood. I had often refused to reveal
Where I'd seen nearby turkeys or rabbits which had my affections,
My sympathies, pleasure in prowling the woods within sight
Of them keeping me silent. Yet fishing required of me killing
Green frogs to supply them as bait for the fishermen's hooks
Made of bone. But I never could kill them, just whacked them with
         branches
To stun them, delivered their limp slimy bodies, and ran
Away hoping my duty was done for the morning. No breakfast
Smelled good to me after those pre-dawn demands on a child.
I retched then as I now retched some mornings, upset in my stomach
With far different reason. I thought of these things before sleep,

     Childhood scenes and activities
          tumbling through drowsiness,
               fading...

Awakening earliest, Fawn roused us, eager for home.
As I lay there and watched her so bustling and busy, her belly
Beginning its first sign of bulging, I smiled to myself.
Soon we both would be awkward, off balance, slow moving and clumsy.
At home was the best place for us now. Tonight we'd be there.
It was time to arrange camp for winter, retreat to the south-facing
Slope where strong winds seldom reached us, where rivulets flowed
Without freezing, where snows melted fast and ran off without flooding.
Then days would again become longer, bring rains that would wash
Away hillsides, fill valleys, turn soil into mudslides and bury
Whole campsites abandoned 'til springtime had ended its romp.
When the weather once more brought us peaceful bright days and
           black insects
We both would deliver our infants, be mothers at last.
A whole winter to wait and prepare seemed forever. My birthday
Would come and be gone before then. As we started for home
On this last day, my happiness swelled. I refused to consider
That anything dire could arise, make the future turn dark.
A complacency sturdy replaced the emotions so tricky
That earlier ruled me. My passions converted themselves
Into shaping a new tiny being, enriching my body
And calming my energies, sending them inward with love.

       How I relished these mental
          and physical workings
             within me!

A private intense way of being had almost shut out
Any other concerns or affections, so focused, consuming
It was. My desire to wrap Kona's experience in
With my own, so include him in everything joyous or painful,
He'd never feel distant, forgotten, not needed, alone,
Became uppermost. Many new mother I'd watched in her pleasure
Ignore the child's father, irrelevant render his role.
She would coo and then cuddle and nurse their production, excluding
Her husband's first tentative efforts to share his child's care,
Drive him off to conclude in dejection that children were women's
Work only. But instincts protective, maternal in this
Way proved very unwise. Understandable though, they were foolish,
Shortsighted, unfair. I resolved that the joy of a child
Would be Kona's as well as my own, an endeavor shared equally.
Clearly, by actions so far, he had shown keen desire
To participate fully. I wondered if Lame Fawn considered
Such things. I determined to talk with her once we were home.
For right now our attentions were drawn to concluding the journey,
Reach home before darkness might tangle our steps, blur the path.
A long trek lay ahead of us, mostly uphill, the trail winding
To skirt craggy peaks, no direct route unless we would climb

> And descend again, wasting
> good energy
> over and over.

We entered the village at sunset. Our welcome was sweet
But subdued for Red Feather had died in our absence, was buried
Three days ago. Gone were the stories and legends he told,
Delightful to listen to, all the while teaching our history
To us and shaping the ways of our thinking about
Ourselves. Ancient and proud was our heritage. Who would be telling
Our children his stories, I wondered, and whom had he trained
To remember them. This was a loss we felt keenly, well knowing
His tales were essential, the framework our values relied
Upon. Doing without them unthinkable. Knowing them fabulous,
Fanciful, still we adhered to the truths in them, bright
As the stars and as numerous, lights poking holes through black ignorance,
Guidance delivered amusingly, never forgot.
His life talent stupendous, delivery riveting, memory
Flawless. The circle of children he taught often joined
By adults drawn to seat themselves, happily letting his spellbinding
Voice seize imaginings, challenge grown minds, cause their thoughts
To range freely through exploits of old, entertaining, provocative.
Snagged by details of a story, perhaps, a new scheme
More efficient than habit had proved might devise itself brilliantly,
Vividly clear in a flash of invention unsought

That came crashing, full formed,
in the mind
of one transported listener.

Minds, idly toying with images teased up from deep
By a gripping old story familiar and often recited,
Hear different things. Richer meanings emergent and sharp
Make a point never grasped when heard younger. The beauty of legend!
The more it was told, the more the retelling revealed.
Now how often a tale I had thought to be simply of slaughter
Enlarged as I heard it recited again and again
Into struggles of conscience, ambition and jealousy raging
Within a young warrior's soul, unresolved before death
Cut him down. As a child I felt justice was done with his dying,
Relieved, avenging of crime satisfactory end.
Growing older my interest lingered much more on the battle
Of personal traits the young felon was wrestling, fell prey
To, selecting the worst of his nature to govern his actions.
He only regretted his choices in failure, when once
His bad act brought him censure. Betrayal, disloyalty, murder
His legacy only. No glory in that, despite all
He had plotted to gain. Not his crime, nor his end, but the viciousness
Tainting the soul of the person and driving his deeds
Was what gnawed at my thoughts. How did people do evil so easily?
Why no internal aversion to wrongdoing prick?

>   Why no check on foul passions?
>   What vital ingredient
>   lacking?

Remembering Yellow Snake's treatment of Fawn, and his scheme
Of revenge, it was obvious to me that something was missing
Within him. Some emptiness flawed him. It made him unable
To think beyond wants of his own. His effect upon Lame Fawn
Escaped his awareness, so callous and blind to the hurts
He inflicted. She always forgave him. Whenever I asked her,
"How could he do that to you?" she simply answered, "Dear, how
Could he not? Nothing personal. He'd do the same to a tent flap
That blew in the wind." These thoughts rose for an instant and sank
Again. Mourning the passing of Red Feather made me reflective.
For now my big question was not how we got here but how
Do we live here without these old legends and old storytellers
Recounting our history, placing our present small lives
In the center of who came before us and who we'd send after.
The mood in the village was somber. Reports we soon made
Of the strangers encountered did nothing to lighten the atmosphere.
Worries consumed us all. Only the children could sleep
Without cares. And as trying as blending two villages into
One grouping was proving to be, as the balancing roles
Were revised with reluctance, the shifting of dominance patterns
Achieved somewhat grudgingly, wisdom and patience prevailed

> When the news of how close
> were the strangers
> united our reasoning.

Stay here and welcome them. Fight and repel them. Or live
All around them invisibly deep in the woodlands and mountains
As Kona suggested, were tactics considered in turn.
No decisions were reached. "It depends on the strangers' behavior,"
My father said. Forceful and ready to fight to expel
Them if possible, he had the warrior spirit his training
Demanded. Not hasty but adamant, purposeful, skilled
In the art of war strategy. When he was needed his leadership
Proved him the best and most clever in planning repulse.
Slow to go on attack, if provoked he would study the enemy,
Plan a swift raid and prevail with our men. That was how
He'd responded when Kona's brash father had led a rash foray
Which needed a stiff opposition as check on his reach.
I remembered Ahanton's distress when he killed Kona's father.
Unusual agonized weeping in secret that I
Overheard in the night. Had he slain his own brother, emotions
Would not have been harder to bear. I did not understand
Why no victory lifted his spirit then. No celebrations
Were held on return. Now I saw he'd grown tired of the fights,
Had been sickened by endlessly battling our own dwindling peoples
While foreigners threatened encroachment, endangered our lives.

   Even then dire reports
         were beginning,
               although I'd not heard them...

Too young then to listen to whispers we children were barred
From exposure to. Meadowlark first gave some substance to White Crow's
Remarks by repeating the tales fleeing Sagamores told
When she spoke with me kindly, expanding my knowledge while rescuing
Dewdrop. I now had the sense that we lived on the rim
Of destruction. I feared for my baby and Lame Fawn's. The future's
Uncertainties plagued me. That night as I slept, the same dream
Of bold she-wolf recurred. Head held proudly, erect ear tips flicking
Attuned to the sounds of the world, yellow eyes fixed upon
Me with interest, no wariness evident, nothing to indicate
Harmful intentions. Her presence alone filled the scene
Of the dream and then vanished. Although in my dream I went searching
To find her, to ask why she'd come to me, she-wolf was gone.
I awoke disappointed and baffled, with no explanation
For what the dream meant. As we worked to move camp up the slope
For the winter I asked Little Fox about Red Feather's dying.
"So peaceful," she said. "His last words were a sigh of relief.
We all heard him say, 'Death is no punishment. Death is no penalty.'
Later he added a whisper, 'Here's Death, my reward.'
He did not live much longer. He said nothing further. No struggle
Disturbed his last hour so I stayed by his side to the end.

> I shall make him a song
>   with sweet words
>   so we all may remember."

"But who is to tell all the legends as he did?" I asked.
"He was training young Weasel, the boy with the leg that is withered,"
Said Little Fox, shrugging, "But Heron is better. Her words
Are precise and her memory flawless. Red Feather ignored her.
She hung in the shadow of Weasel, attentive and rapt,
Often quietly cueing the boy, at his lessons forgetting
The words, or so full of himself he would draw out a tale
Into tedious droning, thus boring us all with additions
Irrelevant simply to keep the attention on him."
Disappointed to hear this, I worked with the others establishing
Winter camp's shelters, and communal areas clean
And protected with room for our gathering times and discussions.
It was the same site we had used many years but too small
For the people of Long Bay until we enlarged to accommodate
Them. So we worked a bit harder this year to expand
All along the high ridge, interspersing our private small shelters
With theirs so as not to divide ourselves into two camps.
Placed to blend our most intimate interests, mundane occupations
With theirs every day was the plan introduced by White Crow
And accepted with willingness. Happy, I'd live next to Meadowlark,
Tending to Dewdrop at times, and learn much by her side.

> In the spring when my baby came
> she'd not accuse me
> of ignorance.

Winter came early with powerful winds and deep snow.
We spent many a day at our crafts, stitching deerskins, men knapping
Flint arrowheads, spear tips, and slicing raw hides into strips
For the lacings of boots and the webbing of footgear snow-walking
Required when they went out for hunting. On days when the sun
Sparkled crystals of snow into icicles hanging from cliffside
We relished the brilliance and warmth and the respite from dark
Huddled hours of fierce weather. My belly grew rounder, and Kona
Delighted in feeling his growing child kicking inside.
With his ear to my belly he'd tell me of hearing wild stories
The baby was telling him, just to amuse me. "And now,"
He would whisper, "she says we shall call her our Snow Owl in secret"
"We're having a daughter?" I'd ask him, excited. A girl
Was my hope. He was teasing, I knew, but his face was so serious,
Words so enchanting, he made me believe that she spoke
To him somehow. One calm day Lame Fawn and tall Medicine Otter
Came visiting, Lame Fawn supporting her bulk using sticks
As she carefully slogged through deep snow to our shelter and breathless
Reported their news. In her womb were two babies alive
And both vigorous, growing and swelling her belly enormously.
"White Crow detected two separate infants," Fawn laughed.

> "She examined me
>   at my insistence,
>   confirmed my suspicions."

"So much for you thinking you'd never have children," I teased
Her, remembering how she had sadly remarked she was barren
While bathing together dear Spotted Whale's corpse in the glade
Just before we were wed. "Now at once you have doubled your chances.
Good fortune, my friend," I said happily, glad for them both
As the two of them sat with us grinning, so pleased with each other.
I saw the same shyly shared glances of mutual joy
First exchanged when they'd met and her ankle required his attention
So skillfully given. Regard for each other was quick
To take root and then flourish in love neither one had expected.
Lame Fawn newly widowed and Medicine Otter resigned
To his gift as shape-changer, believing his lot to be single,
His life solitary, most women afraid of the height
Of the powers that set him apart, made him awesome, commanding,
At times unapproachable. Fawn had been schooled by the whims
Of a merciless man, hardly husband in substance, feared no one,
Was match for the talented character traits so austere
Which tall Otter possessed. She was tiny but mighty. Intelligence,
Warm understanding of everything human her strengths.
They were perfectly paired, my best friend and the uncle of Kona.
I wondered if children would alter the oneness they shared.

    When the men moved aside
        to talk hunting
            I asked her my question.

"Won't children divert your attention from Otter?" I asked.
"Something troubles you," Fawn then replied, looking thoughtfully at me,
Her hands spread protectively over her belly, concerned
And yet calm, focused inward as I was. "I worry the baby's
Arrival will change the way Kona and I will behave
With each other," I said, "Come between us in ways unexpected,
Divide us somehow. We're so close that perhaps there's no room
For another." Ashamed that I sounded all selfish and shallow,
I gazed at my knees seeing nothing and feeling exposed,
A bad mother already. "We need a good talk with your mother,"
Said Lame Fawn. "Grey Goose has the wisdom of partnership, child
After child notwithstanding. Ahanton and she have a marriage
Enduring and close that we want for ourselves. I confess
The same worries," she said in a soft, sad admission. "So many
New parents distract themselves, carelessly losing their bond
To demands of the infant, grow separate, even competing
Against one another in wooing the children. The girl
Is the mother's, the boy is the father's, ignoring the child's need
For each parent's talents and strengths to be offered, absorbed
And reflected." We'd seen such things happen around us, not thinking
Until we were mothers-to-be that we might fail the same.

My father, as much in my life
    as my mother,
        shared equally.

Discipline, humor, affections from each felt the same.
Both involved in my learning, developing skills, my behaviors
Encouraged toward growth, self-reliance, integrity, joy.
I was often admonished and guided but never insulted,
Ignored, or belittled as too young to join in the work
Of the village. With great satisfaction I fetched and I carried
As soon as I walked, understanding my efforts were part
Of my family's welfare, were needed, expected and valued.
We knew what to teach to our children, but what to expect
Of ourselves was less clear when it came to enhancing each marriage
So treasured. Afraid we might lose the sweet magic, divert
Our affections, demands of the babies compelling distraction.
We needed advice and examples from women who'd been
Through the shifting relationships children brought into a family
Unit. When Meadowlark stepped from her shelter, we called
Out our greetings, inviting her over to share our excitement
At Lame Fawn's good news, and to play with her Dewdrop a while.
She was happy to sit with us, bask in the sunlight of winter's
Rare blessing, and answer our questions with patience, amused
At our innocent earnestness. Mention of Elkfoot was painful,
Recalling his drowning, the loss of her boys. But she spoke
To us gladly describing the earlier days of her marriage,
Arrival of babies, delights to them both, and their pride.

> "The love only increases,
>   grows deeper
>   with each child delivered."

"You'll see," she assured us. "Love simply expands, cannot shrink
Or go elsewhere." Then, thoughtful, she sat and looked inward
As Dewdrop crawled happily over one lap and then on
To another while babbling and laughing and cooing and drooling,
A package of singular energy, knowing her mind
And determined to sample this world she had entered, surviving
Despite its disinterest regarding her safety in flood.
She was fearless, bore watching, with constant exploring made peril
Her plaything. Broke twigs with her four tiny teeth and then spit
Out wet pieces of bark, left them dribbling, a chin decoration
Enhancing her satisfied grin as she pulled herself up
To stand wobbly and proud a short moment, then thump on her bottom,
Brief triumph enjoyed and repeated until she grew tired, fell asleep
In an instant wherever she landed, all limp and oblivious
Of her surroundings, not waking as one of us gathered her up
In a lap and then cradled her wrapped in strong arms and a deerskin
To give us some peace. When awake she demanded all eyes
Track her actions, distraction unsafe, inattention impossible.
Sleeping adorably, Dewdrop made bother all worth it.
Relaxing we gazed at her, smiling, admiring the miracle
Medicine Otter and Lame Fawn had worked for her life.

> Would she ever remember
>   disaster
>   and frigid swift waters,

Long hours in the tree as the torrent boiled wildly beneath,
Barely sparing the sagging great oak branch her wrappings had caught in
To keep her from drowning? Red Feather in stories had told
Us our bodies stored memories, finger or elbow or ribcage
Absorbing each trauma, each bruising, each comfort, caress,
Which the mind could call up as it needed for reference. Instruction
From old situations embedded in sinew and bone
From the day of our birth, no experience wasted, forgotten.
If true, little Dewdrop knew somewhere in body and mind
Of her near fatal escapade, whether or not she would ever
Be able to tell it. Her recklessness now presumed faith
In her destiny, thinking herself indestructible, mortal
No more than the mountains or ocean or air of the sky.
Though some infants were fearful of falling, or bawled at loud noises,
This Dewdrop accepted as wondrous and proper events
That occurred as she watched and reacted, amused and enchanted
By every least thing, as though all were created to please.
It felt right then when Meadowlark added, "Believe that each infant
Arrives fully gifted, brings with it the love its own life
Shall evoke and give back without limit. A child just increases
The joys of your union. Relax. Do not fret. You'll do well."

> Reassurance so solid,
>   so readily given,
>   was welcome.

My gratitude swirled through my heart as wise Meadowlark spoke
To us warmly. Her words a soft blanket of comfort wove 'round us
A sense of new confidence. Altered completely was she
From the woman half mad and too willing to die in the bushes
Alone by the pathway, believing all lost she held dear
Until Dewdrop, voracious, insistent, and greedily suckling
Recalled her to sense. Now she smiled, bore more weight, seemed content
To let memories serve her, enjoy little Dewdrop, and counsel
The two of us, graciously sharing the things she had learned.
What I learned from her then at that moment came not from her speaking.
I felt in that wordless space deep where I dwell a brief jolt,
Comprehending how marvelous, stalwart, resilient we humans
Are made. When life hurts so, we suffer, then rally, press on
With compassion embedded more firmly than ever, refusing
Defeat. Her example would stay with me always. My life
Had known little of pain or of loss, and what little I did know
Was one step removed from myself. My own family lived
In sound health and safe village. No danger immediate threatened.
The deaths of the old were expected and properly mourned
In their sequence. The foolishness Yellow Snake's nature exhibited
Killed him, but few of us wept for his passing, once gone.

    This was callous
        but born of his failings
            unlovable, venomous.

I felt no guilt from not mourning his death. It set free
My best friend for real happiness, children, a husband devoted,
Well worthy of love and of trust, admiration, respect,
All the qualities Yellow Snake proved he was lacking. No matter
How often her brothers had shown by example the ways
A true man would behave, something missing inside kept him shallow
And selfish and ignorant all of his life. Early charm
Soon succumbed to his habits of laziness, falsehood and slipshod
Performance. We called him The Actor and saw through his roles;
The charmer, the suitor, the false sympathizer, cajoler,
The liar, the braggart, the petulant pouter who sulked
When his acts were exposed. His foul temper played tyrant to Lame Fawn's
Sweet nature. Resisting his tactics, she quietly kept
Up her friendships, persisted as midwife and nurse for new mothers,
Stayed sociable, stouthearted, busy, refused to withdraw
Though he viciously strove to impose isolation, subdue her
With critical comments, belittling her work and her worth.
A few times I had seen him watch carefully actions of others
He saw bring responses he sought for himself and then try
Them for similar benefit. They were mere aping and mimicry,
Genuine caring all absent, his skits insincere,

    Transparent and jarring,
        no substance,
            seductive but soulless.

Too handsome by far, he lured many a female to swoon
At his looks, envy Lame Fawn, be flattered he paid them attention.
They thought him so nice, such a gentle man, never aware
At first meeting how damaged he was. It took time to uncover
His cruelties. Lame Fawn and I were both fooled by his charm
'Til he married her quickly, and quickly changed tactics, dividing
The two of us, spurning my visits and hurting my heart
With his words of impatience. To him I was merely annoying,
A buzzing green bug at his tent flap, a fly to be slapped
Into flight. His complete transformation, as soon as his capture
Of Lame Fawn perfected his scheme, was a shock to us all.
Only White Crow had seen through his blandishments, given Fawn
          warnings
She chose ignore, so afraid no one else would take on
As a wife one so crippled. He came to our camp as a stranger
From no one knew where, bearing tales of long journey, great loss,
Built our sympathy for him so skillfully, lulling suspicions
So brilliantly no one but White Crow had wondered at charm
So relentlessly slathered around, quite unlike our own menfolk
Who failed very soon to accept him as brother or man
Of the tribe. Next to Meadowlark, feeling her kindness, her caring,
I wondered just why I still suffered from Yellow Snake's spite.

        True forgiveness was absent
              from my wounded heart.
                I still loathed him.

How Lame Fawn had given him endless forbearance, excused
His behavior as thoughtlessness merely, accorded him dignity
Quite undeserved, was a mystery yet to my untutored
Mind. Why I dwelt on old hurts he was no longer causing
Was also a puzzle. "Fawn, how can it be I resent
With a passion dead Yellow Snake's memory? Plagued by disquiet
I'm left with hot anger, yet mournful. His evil rebounds
In my thoughts all unwanted." The two women studied
My strong agitation in wonder. "Now, where does this come
From today?" queried Meadowlark. She knew so little of Yellow
Snake's history. Knew of his fall at Long Bay and his death
But knew nothing of what came before, of how Lame Fawn had suffered
Abuse and neglect at his hands, or of why I still seethed
While recalling unbidden his outrageous ghost. "Your forgiveness
Will free you," said Lame Fawn. "He'll haunt you until you forgive."
"Not forgiveness again," I howled angrily. "Always forgiveness."
I wept with frustration. The thought that I could not endure
Was that what he had done was not wrong, was all right, was acceptable.
That was the path to forgiveness, I felt. I did yearn
To be free of such poisonous energy eating serenity.
Didn't know what I could do for it. How to forget.

> "But behavior so awful.
> How can you forget
> or condone it?"

"I do not forget and I do not condone," answered Fawn
In a voice full of tenderness, seeing my total bewilderment.
Meadowlark sighed and leaned forward to speak but Fawn stopped
Her by laying a hand on her knee. "Ellacoya, my Laughing Bear
Friend, feel along with me here as I open my heart
To you, sharing my path to forgiveness, inviting indulgence.
Try stifling your protesting thoughts, put your anger aside
For some moments. We've talked thus before. Comprehension comes
Slowly when hearts have been broken, when trust is betrayed, when old
        wounds
Scar the soul though the body seems whole." Her soft voice
        and her gentleness
Calmed me. Her earnest demeanor was proof that she cared,
That she knew he had hurt me as well as herself by his meanness.
Knew also temptations to wallow in wrongs of the past
Rose at times, overwhelming good sense and beclouding an otherwise
Perfect clear day. How a chance observation might pull
Up from seemingly nowhere reminders uncomfortable, anger
Surprising and bitter, believed long forgotten, to sting
Like a thorn prick, invade without warning, replay in sharp memory
Scenes of weak helplessness, fury, of feeling at fault,
Or unjustly accused, or not worthy of decent, kind treatment,
Defective somehow. Only Yellow Snake ever had caused

    Me to shrivel so.
        Salmon hung drying
            seemed livelier, smarter...

More valued than I. "I am feeling unsure of myself
To be mother, " I said. "Doubting festers. It rakes up old miseries
Yellow Snake's meanness imposed. I relive the old fears.
On this beautiful day, in fine company, feeling diminished,
I worry and rage." Lame Fawn nodded agreement. She knew
What I felt. "Feelings lace themselves one to another in sequence,"
She said to me, "old ones connecting with present events
Come alive in our hearts again whether or not we invite them
Until understanding deprives them of heat and of harm."
I sat motionless, listening. Dewdrop asleep sweetly dreaming
And heavy upon my crossed legs kept me grounded and warm.
I was glad of her absolute trust that my lap was safe haven.
Then Meadowlark spoke. "When a person is nasty or mean
Without cause, then the fault is not yours but a defect that person
Possesses. An internal character flaw bedded deep,
So entrenched and habitual nothing will cure it and nothing
You do either change or provoke it. It can't be your fault."
But it felt like it still, although reason was telling me otherwise.
This was a wounding, hard earned, mere words seldom erased.
"Think how different Yellow Snake was from the men of this village,"
Said Lame Fawn. "A man who could not tell the truth, felt no shame,

> Only blathered and blamed.
> Simply seized what he wanted
> by trickery…"

"Devious, hostile so others would not get too close,
Not uncover his secret." "What secret?" At this, Lame Fawn, blushing,
Looked back into time with eyes blind to day's beauty and peace
To before, when entrapment prevailed, and her own pain was hidden
In keeping his secret, preserving his semblance of man.
"No one knew what I really went through with him, while I was with
       him,"
She said. "I pretended the marriage was valid, ideal,
So important to him to appear a good husband though everyone
Saw he was not." Again lost in the past she withdrew
Into memory. "Secret? What secret?" I wanted to hear it
No matter how weird. "He is dead," I near shouted. "You owe
The man nothing now. Tell us." But shame overcame her. Embarrassment
Flooded her features. She sat with head hanging, and mute.
"Without conscience?" guessed Meadowlark, putting together our
       comments
And hoping to help us work through to completion this rift
In our pleasure. Experience told her disclosure we needed
Was thinly restrained now and ready for bringing to light.
"That and more," agreed Fawn. "He had three separate problems
All woven together. No conscience. Unstoppable needs
To perform senseless actions repeatedly. And, the conviction
He really was woman. He copied my manner, wore dress

       In our shelter.
              He hated and envied
                     my nature, resented me...

"Thought that a woman had life a lot easier, soft
And excused from hard duties expected of warriors, hunters
And husbands. Not seeing the truth of our bodies and lives
He soon gutted the stomach of promises made to be husband,
Confused me lamentably, squashed my identity, made
Himself wife in the shadows. His pretense, his mimicry, mockery,
Made his enactments of femaleness travesty. 'Just
A poor girl who is trying to make it,' he whined to me privately.
Pity took over. I stayed and felt somehow to blame
For not being the wife who could cure his illusions."
Well outraged at this, I cried, "You didn't cause it. You could
Not have cured it." I then understood what she meant when she'd
        answered
My question of "How could he do that?" with "How could he not?"
With three traits interwoven of tragic dimension, his struggle
To emulate others, seem outwardly like them, had failed
Every time. His frustrations, I saw then, could only be constant.
No wonder his temper was vicious. With this in my thoughts
Understanding replaced old resentments. My hatred just vanished.
Relaxing, I smoothed Dewdrop's hair from her forehead and smiled.
Lame Fawn laughed with a lightness not shown since her walkabout injury
Crippled her playfulness so long ago. She was back.

    Even Meadowlark noticed
        her brightness,
            her new carefree manner.

She barely had time to remark on it, saying, "You see
How the keeping of secrets can stunt your true nature? Revealing them
Free you?" when Kona and Otter returned and sat down.
Fawn looked young as the girl she had been when we played and discovered
Our powers in innocent youth. Otter stared at her, stunned.
Transformation of spirit reflected in flesh was amazing.
Her face was aglow with relief and release. Even she
Recognized she was never to blame, was unfairly conscripted
To cover for Yellow Snake, living a double life not of her choosing.
"Now what has been happening here?" asked tall Otter.
"They've worked on forgiveness together," said Meadowlark, pleased.
"On forgiveness?" moaned Kona, "What have we done now?" but his
        wide grin
Betrayed him. We all collapsed laughing, awakening pert
Little Dewdrop who instantly burbled and babbled in tune with us,
Then filled her wrappings explosively, making me wince
And the men look alarmed. Quickly Meadowlark took her, remarking,
"Enough of life's lessons for one day. You men can learn this
With your own little ones." So we said our goodbyes as she left us
And then Fawn explained what had troubled us ever so long
About Yellow Snake's conduct, the secret Lame Fawn so well managed
To keep though it mangled her spirit. "I've sensed you were sad.

    Your heart hurt.
        I could not find the reason,"
           sighed Otter. "It troubled me."

"Now you are open and free of the malice he bore."
"So am I." I explained to them how he had treated me badly
As well, in his efforts to isolate Lame Fawn, prevent
Her from challenging him or comparing his pose to reality.
"We have been living with poisonous memories, bound
Like those captives we left near the ocean." "How apt a comparison!"
Medicine Otter exclaimed. "Just as soon as those two understood
How we tied them they loosened the bindings and freed themselves
Easily. Hope they were able to do so at least."
Once I saw that forgiveness had nothing to do with excusing
The wrongs and required no forgetting, I no longer ached
Or felt scorched in my soul. It might take me more time to feel neutral
Toward Snake but the hatred was gone. Yet I still had to ask,
"Gentle Blue Jay, our woman/man here from your village harms no one.
We know and all love him, respect him, admire his great skill
With his artistry. What is the difference?" "He has no secrets
To burden another," said Lame Fawn. "I often had hoped
Yellow Snake could be brave, as is Blue Jay, accept his own nature,
Live honestly, openly. But he would not. Dishonesty
Ruled." "Just all form and no substance," spat Otter, irate.
"It can run in some families, parents to children in line."

　　"Oh, how sad for a babe
　　　　so affected,"
　　　　　　cried Lame Fawn with sorrow.

"It's rare. Can be beautifully brought into harmony, used
To enhance the wide range of our talented peoples. Our Blue Jay
Is proof that our differences serve to enrich us. Expand
Understanding of how many ways we contrive to be human,"
Said Medicine Otter, his voice low and thoughtful, his face
A reflection of myriad feelings internally flowing.
From sorrow for Lame Fawn's past misery, anger at Snake's
Harmful legacy, weary acceptance of life and its colors,
And, lastly, a slow blooming happiness, smiling at Fawn
With her belly so full of the fruits of a promising future.
At least, I imagined those feelings supplying the face
That he showed to us, open, unguarded, reflective and tender.
The sunlight of short winter's day had grown weaker. The cold
Was returning. So Otter and Fawn said goodbye and toiled homeward,
While Kona and I sat a few moments more in the last
Of the light before entering shelter to eat and prepare for
Our usual sharing and talk of events from a day
When we worked or relaxed at our separate chores, or chance meetings
Conversing with others. I asked him what Otter and he
Had discussed while apart from us that afternoon. "Was it hunting?"
"I wish." He said ruefully. "Fatherhood troubles us both.

    We have doubts of our patience,
        sense jealousy
            may rise unbidden."

"A terrible thing to feel jealous of one's coming babe.
But our lives are so perfect like this we are wary of changing
The balance." He seemed so ashamed to be voicing such doubts
That I hugged him until his resistance was melted. His physical
Tension relaxed, and he looked at me, stricken with guilt
Yet relieved to have spoken aloud such uncomfortable feelings.
They fought with his sense of himself as a right-thinking man
And he said so. "I shouldn't feel that way," he whispered, unhappy.
"And how did your uncle respond to those fears?" I then asked
Him, still holding him close. "He's as worried as I am. Confessed to
His own apprehensions. Not liking them much." "Let me tell
You what Meadowlark said as we uttered our own selfsame turmoil,
Asked her to advise us. I'm certain Lame Fawn will assure
Troubled Otter with these very words about children I'm saying
To you." Then with lips to his ear as we lay side by side
I repeated the day's conversation with Meadowlark, sharing
Her warm reassurances, easing his mind and my own
Until sleep took us over and trust in ourselves and our future
Wove bliss once again. In my dream then calm she-wolf appeared
To me, lazily grooming her forepaws, no message remaining,
No urgency in her apparent. My dream brought sweet peace.

She-wolf settled down satisfied,
eyes slowly blinking
then closing.

We waked to the sound of our Little Fox singing, a song
Very much like the one from my dream on the trail after flinging
Whale's bones in the ocean last Fall. She put words to her tune
That seemed wise well beyond what her few sheltered years could have
      taught her
I thought. Perhaps Song Maker lent the idea for her use.
She was standing outside our dark shelter, to rouse us politely
And pleasantly, certain we'd not be annoyed by a voice
So melodic, with phrasing embroidered so richly, so rhythmic,
So true and low-pitched no one else was disturbed by the sound.
Kona yawned and untangled himself from my arms as he wakened.
"What's this serenade?" He called softly, "Come in, Little Fox."
I adored his sweet nature, accepting and gentle and welcoming.
Even just roused from deep sleep he showed no trace of ire.
I hoped that would hold true when our infant might wake us repeatedly
During the nights after birth soon to come in the Spring.
Little Fox crept inside all excited and bursting with gossip
Of how we were all to be summoned to council because
Of an argument simmering over the choice of our myth-telling
Person succeeding Red Feather. "But Weasel, you told
Me, was trained for it. Wasn't he?" "Yes. But he fails to remember
Whole chunks of some legends, and Heron is always his prompt.

    Many say she is better,
        although a young girl,
           and deserves recognition."

Now this was some gossip worth checking. A custom upset
After eons, it seemed. Only men had been bearers of legends
Our village revered as the guide to the world as we knew
It. Could Heron fulfill such a role without someone's objection?
"So tell us," said Kona with interest, "what have you heard?"
"There is argument brewing," said Little Fox. " Some say no young girl
Is fit for that duty, while others insist that our lore's
Preservation and faithful rendition is much more important
Than shape of the vessel that keeps and delivers it true.
It is said that young Weasel makes up what he doesn't remember,
Grows fanciful, misses the point, gives the elders offense
By not seeming to care. When a tale wanders too far astray for
Their patience, they look to young Heron to set Weasel straight.
Which he doesn't take well. Though she whispers corrections in ever
So kindly a manner, he bristles. He once even said
He did not want the task." To reject such an honor was shocking.
I gasped when I heard this. But Kona thought different. "Perhaps
He was chosen for all the wrong reasons," he said. "What does Weasel
Himself wish to be? Or has no one attentive paid heed?"
It occurred to me then that Red Feather assumed Weasels' withered
Left leg had disqualified him from his place with the men.

> Was it pity that made him
>> choose Weasel,
>>> persist with him fruitlessly?

Weasel had troubles enough with infirmities birth
Had inflicted without the great insult of pity to nip at
His essence. He ran like a crab. But he ran with a will.
His left arm flopped a bit, and his hand curled up oddly, an angle
He used to advantage when needed. He also could fight
Off a bully convincingly, seldom required to repel an attacker
A second time. Passion for physical prowess had ruled
Him since crawling had challenged his infancy. That as a young one
He sat for Red Feather's instruction was rather a feat
Of obedience, given his natural restlessness. Eager
To help with construction of shelters and bridges and weirs,
He would speak when he pictured in mind a much easier method.
This often might shorten the time for a project, improve
The result. Always watching and thinking and trying the novel
Approach, he impressed us. His knowledge of how things could work
Was original, clever, surprising. He sometimes would harness
The wind in his shirt to propel a canoe when no one
Would go with him to play on the water. This frightened his mother
But furnished his father with rich satisfaction and pride.
No allowances needed, no granting of Red Feather's favors
Excusing the boy from demanding pursuits was required.

    Kona's comment gave pause.
        So we urged him to speak
           at the meeting,

Lend Weasel support in his right to make choices, make clear
To the rest of us what he preferred. "I would hate being made to
Be something I'm not," I said, feeling strong sympathy rise
On behalf of young Weasel. The longer I thought him ill-chosen,
The more I did wonder at Red Feather's judgmental lapse.
He did not make mistakes in his reading of people and talent.
So why had he done so with Weasel? We rose and prepared
For attending the meeting, sent Little Fox off on ahead to
Tell Meadowlark of it, explain, and invite her as well,
Then tell all we'd be coming along. I was slow in my walking
Through snow now, and Meadowlark carrying Dewdrop took time
To step carefully, too. It was hard to believe that my body
Could change so completely, so quickly, and still be my own.
I was home to another small being, a bulging container
Both awkward and happy, a bit apprehensive of how
It would feel to give birth. We sent Kona on forward. Though willing
To plod with us, carry young Dewdrop, and see us there, safe
And well seated, his manner revealed his thoughts elsewhere, distracted,
Composing apt phrases intended on Weasel's behalf.
For myself, I supported young Heron's abilities Little Fox
Praised. Yet I wanted to hear her recite for herself.

> Would a contest be ordered
>   I wondered,
>   enjoying the prospect.

The council lodge hummed like a beehive we heard on approach.
Much excitement enlivened a dull winter's otherwise tedious
Grayness and frigid damp atmosphere. Odors of breath
And the warmth of packed bodies inside became almost unpleasant
Compared to the purity winter air granted our lungs
During walking. We soon found a place at the wall next to Mother
Where I could lean back yet hear everything that might be said.
I saw Heron, a girl who had just done taboo under difficult
Weather conditions. She looked quite well fed and robust.
She seemed up to the challenge this meeting might offer, a confidence
Furnished her quiet demeanor. I hoped she'd prevail.
Then the murmuring paused as young Weasel lurched in through the
        entrance
And folded himself in an awkward collapse at the front
Of encircling rows. I saw Kona had made him a welcoming
Space by his side, and felt glad as I watched while the two
Of them bent to each other, conferring and nodding agreement.
It seemed to me Medicine Otter and Father were not in attendance.
"Where's Father?" I whispered to Mother. "He's coming,"
She answered. "This has to be done in a delicate way
Or tradition, though foolish in this case, may threaten to smother
The gifts of two talented young ones." So that's where she stood.

    Just then Father and Otter
        made entrance.
            The people fell silent.

The two stood together and beckoned the boy and the girl
To come forward. Strong Heron delayed until Weasel had risen
Before moving next to him, always supportive yet shy
Of appearing a challenger, confident, though, in her manner
When facing us. Weasel stood tall on his good leg with poise
And sure balance much effort and practice had earned him, deservedly.
Otter spoke first, which surprised me. Ahanton was Chief,
But deferred in this instance so Otter could outline the problem
We'd met to explore. I saw wisdom his reticence lent.
His selection of Otter prevented soliciting favor
By anyone trying to guess how he felt toward one side
Or the other in this. There were always some few who endeavored
To trim their opinions to what they thought he'd want instead
Of providing him well-reasoned arguments which were more useful
In reaching decisions regarding what's best for us all.
With this tactic, they'd have to rely on themselves, find good reasons
For choosing of Heron or Weasel to be the next honored
Historian, teller of legend and myth and tradition
So vital in shaping our values, in binding the tribe
To the principles long held so dear, weaving unity in with
Diversity, building tribe's spirit, true, upright and fine.

Otter finished explaining
the choices
then nodded to Weasel...

Who said. "You may pull up a fish, but you can't make it breathe.
You may capture a bird, but you can't make it sing." He reseated
Himself with more physical grace than I dreamed he possessed.
It was Heron's turn next. She looked first to the elders, gave Weasel
A grimace, apparent apology, then looked to each
Of us, slowly surveying the multitude crowding the meeting.
She spoke in a voice deeply resonant, soft, plain and clear
To the farthest dim reaches where we sat, absorbing her message
As though she were next to us seated. "A fish in its lake
Can swim freely. A bird on its branch sends its song to the mountains."
Chin tucked, she sat down again. Father then spoke. "You have heard
These two young ones. Their voices, their thoughts they have offered
        you bravely.
Discuss with each other now soberly how each has touched
Your fine minds. We shall send them outside to await your decision."
The buzzing around us became quite intense. Voices rose.
Some were angry and harsh. Some were soothing, placating.
Persuasive, dismissive by turns. The great clamor unbearably swelled
Until no one could think or be heard. It was chaos incarnate.
I covered my ears, felt my Snow Owl rebel with a kick
Even Mother could feel as I snuggled within her encircling
Arms 'round my middle. Protectively, proudly she grinned,

    Stroking Snow Owl's meandering
        elbows and knees
            rippling belly.

Provocative as the brief adages offered had been,
And as much as I wanted to think on them, draw some comparisons,
Pregnancy, always insistent now, coaxed warm caress
From my mother, distracting my mind from the meeting's true purpose
And making me wish I could concentrate better, keep hold
Of a thought long enough to discuss it, without the diversions
My stomach so fondly elicited at every turn.
For there still was a head on these shoulders I planned to keep using,
If anyone cared. I was nothing but chamber for child,
So it seemed. I felt almost impatient with so much affection
Refocused, my personhood swamped by this process in play.
How I wanted to dance, to reclaim my agility, blissful
On tiptoe go leaping and twirling with arms wide outspread
Like the wings of the red tail that soars overhead on air currents.
Yet here I was, earthbound and heavy and hampered by bulk
I'd begun to resent. Though I wanted this child, I was edgy
And weary. "This phase is the last and the hardest endured,"
Whispered Mother, so close in my ear I had no trouble hearing.
"At your stage I mentally willed every one of you out.
'Out, out, out,' I would hiss as I puffed and I panted my way
Through those last days before every birth. Mothers know how it feels."

Yes, they did. The words helped.
        She was proof she'd survived us all
                handsomely.

Words of the song Little Fox had been singing at dawn
Came to mind. "It is easy to follow a path where there is one.
But lost in a thicket, each breaks his own branches alone."
Drumming ordered us silent, the only successful sure method
Commanding attention when feelings were running so high
And loud voices impassioned were screeching and whining and
    thundering,
Causing the rooftop to shudder, shed trickles of dirt
From dried mud that dislodged from the rafters and sifted upon us,
Rebuking our riot. We brushed at our shoulders and sleeves
And grew quieter slowly. Then Little Fox joining with Song Maker
Lulled the commotion by singing the very same song
With the words she had sung us that morning, so strange and so sensible.
We were "in thicket" for certain. Required to adhere
To tradition, we'd sacrifice quality. Flouting tradition,
We'd risk the displeasure in people change always aroused.
When the singing had brought us to thoughtful repose and attention,
Ahanton, my father, arose and took charge of the scene.
"Of those favoring Weasel, choose one who will speak on his merits.
For Heron, choose someone the same. We shall listen to each
With minds open to reason alone. Set aside any bias
Before your decision." My brother spoke first, saying, "One

        At a time, and apart,
            should young Weasel,
                then Heron recite for us.

"Thus we can judge of superior fitness, or not,
For the honor." He sat amid murmurs approving suggestion
The two should compete. "Do you speak for the girl or the boy?"
Father asked him. "For good of the tribe," Diver answered. "We're taking
No side at this time." Then the eldest, most crippled of all
The old warriors spoke without rising. "The boy must be chosen
If skills should prove equal," he said. "But Loon Diver speaks well
To propose a small contest. Besides," he said, chuckling, "some stories
Well told pass the time, make this morning's derangement worthwhile."
So agreement seemed easily reached until Grey Hawk objected.
"My Chieftain, you asked for spokespersons from each of the sides
To make argument. No one has done so, for these two were neutral.
Now I speak for Heron, whose words amply prove her well fit.
She has shown by her sayings intuitive knowledge of being
In harmony with her true nature when called to recite.
As the fish and the bird in their elements thrive, so does Heron.
Her voice is well pitched, words pronounced with a clarity most
Of us envy, and emphasis coupled with great understanding
Give freshness to stories that otherwise might well grow stale."
Then spoke Red Elk, quite angry, "But Weasel was rightfully chosen.
He must be the one. Our traditions cannot be defiled.

    Sacred stories are never
        entrusted
            to mouths of young girls."

At this a new furor erupted. Positions entrenched
And not open to reason were shouted once more with a vengeance.
Red faces, raised fists, and the baring of teeth all around
Made the people seem ready for war party's foray, the tension
Too high for discussion to prosper. I feared that today
Was a waste, resolution impossible. Heated exchanges
Could soon become physical, bloody, if nothing was done.
I expected that Father would send us all home, and assemble
Us later, to try this again, when emotions had cooled.
A slow beat of the low drum began to be felt in the ribcage,
Deep sounds all but drowned in the shouting. Vibration alone
Penetrated our bodies. It mimicked the rate of a calm resting
Heart. Even Snow Owl inside me stopped kicking, grew still.
One by one angry voices diminished. The drum's subtle power
Prevailed. It restored us to sensible beings, at ease
In soothed bodies. We calmed with the drumbeat, then slowly and gently
We swayed all together in rhythm 'til only the drum
Could be heard. Father stood in the center and held up the talking
Stick, signal that his was the only voice proper to speak.
Many sighs were exhaled as the people relaxed, freed of tensions.
"Bring Weasel," said Father. He entered, respectful, at ease.

"Tell a legend you heard from Red Feather,"
said Father. "Speak
faithfully."

Young Weasel's legend was this:

On First Morning, First Boy ran to Grandfather's knee
And demanded a story, but Grandfather said,
"Not today, for a tragedy struck in the night.
I am blind. I must borrow your eyes for my own."
Now First Boy knew great fear. He would have to give up
His sharp eyes, pluck them out of his head. Make a gift
Of them. Though his grandfather he loved, he did love
His eyes more. Not to see would be worse than to die.
So he ran away quickly and hid in the woods
Weeping loudly. First Uncle then heard First Boy's sobs
And approached him with pity, asked "Why do you cry?"
"I must pluck out my eyes so Grandfather may see.
He is blind now and wanting to borrow my eyes."
Uncle laughed. He knew Grandfather's scheme for the young.
So he cleverly said, "Give but one. Then you both
Will see more with one eye than can be understood."
Then First Boy, on returning to Grandfather's knee
Proposed giving him only one eye so that each
Could see something. "Well, I have an easier plan,"
Said Grandfather. "Just stand here beside me. Report
What you see all around us. Describe each thing well.
Then I'll know you deserve those bright eyes in your head."

So First Boy spent the day in describing the things
That he saw; the black coals and gray ashes, birch bark
For canoes, and the sticks for the fire, drying fish
Hung in lines on slim poles, mended arrows, stout bows,
And stone axes, flint knives. In their workplace, the men
At their tasks. And the women with baskets in arms
Coming back from their patches of garden with beans,
Squash and herbs for the dinner that night. A few pots
Made from clay, or a cup carved from burl, or a pipe
For tobacco. All these he described as his eyes
Fell upon them. Just when he was sure nothing else
Could be seen, he would spy something more, very small
And unnoticed before, like a rip in a shirt,
Or a moccasin lacing that broke lying frayed
Where it snagged on a root in the path. Or a doll
Dressed in cornhusks, forgotten, abandoned in dirt.
First Boy, tired of his task as the time for last meal
Was approaching, announced there was nothing to see
Left remaining. "You see nothing more in this world?"
Asked Grandfather, dismayed. "Nothing more," said First Boy,
Irritated. "You see what you *can* see, I see,"
Sighed Grandfather. "Tomorrow come back. I'll be deaf."

So young Weasel
     with these words
         made end of his tale.

There were murmurs approving the tale he had chosen to tell
And the way he had spoken it. Some thought his phrasing was awkward
In places but true to the meaning, forgivable lapse.
Others fussed he'd forgotten to mention enough of the items
First Boy should have listed, the paddles, the spears, and the nets,
For example, but they missed the point of the story completely.
"His heart wasn't in it," said Mother. "I thought he did well,"
I responded. "My interest was held well enough to the ending."
"Some people seemed bored," answered Mother, "and nary a child
Appeared scared at the prospect of plucking out eyes. Thought it silly,
I sensed by their giggles." I wondered how Heron would do
When her turn came. Watched Weasel and Kona sit, heads bent together
And talking once more as before, when this meeting began.
I knew Father would call for one person to speak for the favor
Of Weasel and one for the favor of Heron as choice
When the contest was over. How Kona would manage to balance
His comments in favor of Weasel's performance and skill
With support for the freedom of Weasel from tribal historian
Duties, I could not imagine. The voices then hushed
As Ahanton and Otter stood shoulder to shoulder, arms folded.
"Bring Heron," said Father. She entered, respectful, at ease.

> "Tell a legend you heard
>   from Red Feather," said Father.
>   "Speak faithfully."

Young Heron's tale began with sacred words:

Before our Earth was made, dark waters covered all—

She was halted by protesting bellows from Red Elk, who cried,
"Sacred stories are never entrusted to tongues of young girls."
Then Meadowlark rose from the place she'd been seated beside
Me and said, "In Long Bay Spotted Whale told this legend most sacred."
Her words were confirmed by the people who came from Long Bay.
Otter nodded agreement as well, and said firmly, "There's precedent."
Father then handed young Heron the talking stick. I couldn't
Breathe with excitement. This Heron was bold, risking everything.

> Before our Earth was made, dark waters covered all.
> No tree, no rock, no valley deep, no mountain tall,
> No man, no woman, squirrel, bird or waterfall.
> Just mist and wave and nighted sky was all.

> Great Spirit summoned energies from Star Seed Race
> To come create, for peoples new, a living space.

> So mud was dredged from far below the waters deep,
> One fistful at a time, and piled in mounting heap
> To form one slender spit of land, a place to keep
> Them dry, and building up a sandy place to sleep.

> Great Spirit blessed the energies of Star Seed Race
> Come to create, for peoples new, a living space.

When mountain peaks were raised and valleys dug to hold
The waters in their basins, Star Seed Race was done, and told
Their work was good, that they could go back home, behold
The Earth from far above, and watch events unfold.

Great Spirit called The Many from their secret place
To decorate, for peoples new, their living space.

The Many varied energies surrounding Earth
Then visited and saw but mud and dirt, a dearth
Of living things. They scattered seeds for all their worth.
Then tree and fern and squash and bean erupted forth.

Great Spirit blessed The Many and their bounty placed
Upon the Earth to decorate the peoples' space.

A great supply, but almost dead from lack of light
Until The Many pooled one thought with all their might
And, in the space 'twixt Earth and Star, a sun so bright
They hurled to sky. It traveled high, made day and night.

Great Spirit, rousing Earth awake to light and space,
Commanded Her take care, for living things make place.

Earth then prepared Herself for woman, man, and bird,
For creature great and small to live, let song be heard
To ripple in the air, teach fish to swim, great herd
Of deer and moose let roam. She was The Earth—The Word.

Great Spirit praised The Many and the Star Seed Race
And urged them to admire the Earth they set in place.

The Star Seed Race looked down and marveled at the way
The Many had improved upon their work. How day
Gave light and warmth for Earth's new creatures' work and play.
How night gave time for rest and sleeping cares away.

Great Spirit and The Many and the Star Seed Race
Agreed their work was good, and sanctified the place.

So woman came, and man, and beast and butterfly
And bird and snail and snake. And all did multiply.
They pulled from Earth more than She had for their supply.
So, one by one, both great and small began to die.

Great Spirit wept. This cannot be. I must not waste
These creatures or this beautiful and holy place.

A balance must be struck so Earth might always thrive
And living things come visiting, be flesh alive
A while then travel on in spirit, not deprived
Of self, be beings still, in blessedness survive.
I'll go to enter Earth and live in every thing,
Each rock, each tree, each wavelet, cloud, and misty ring
Of moon. You, Star Seed Race, rebirth our Earth each Spring.
You, Many, gather souls who go—and babies bring.

And so it was.
And so it is.
And so endures.

Heron stood straight and sturdy, her gaze seeing no one, her face
Still aglow with the magic the myth of Creation
Infused in her spirit. The people were silent, seduced
And transported to mystical realms, contemplating the privilege
Of wonder and awe this Creation myth always inspired.
No one moved. Not a rustle of clothing, no throat-clearing gurgle,
No restless relieving of stiffness of joints. Not a sigh
Could be heard in this place that had earlier thundered with argument.
Heron was true storyteller. All during the tale
She assumed with her movements and voice every character's essence.
Great Spirit spoke deep-voiced, commanding. The Star Seed Race dove
And returned to the surface, with industry smacking and shaping
Our home. And The Many were everywhere busy with seed
And with sun, guarding souls who departed, companioning infants
Just coming to Earth. Witless boulders themselves received sense.
It had been a long time since a spell had been plaited like this one.
Young Heron became what the story demanded she be;
Was dramatic, intuitive, subtly inventive in manner.
Delivery, flawless from memory, clear and precise.
If the people were fair, I was sure she would be the one chosen.
Transported myself, I had almost forgotten my state.

Then, as Heron was seated,
the people recaptured
their senses.

Some whispers were quietly shared, no one wanting to speak
At full volume, offensive to moods of reflection still keeping
Most silently drifting in thought. Not since Red Feather's time
Had a teller had power to captivate minds and emotions
Completely. The lilt of the meter, the punch of the rhyme
Wrapped ideas of mystic dimension in packages simple
And pleasing. A number had not heard this tale since their youth,
Knew it once but forgotten its details, its powerful images.
Weasel's brief episode couldn't compare in effect
On his listeners. Heron's selection seemed almost unfairly
Presented. Then, all of a sudden, I caught on to Red
Feather's ploy. If he hadn't meant Heron to be storyteller
He would have just sent her away. Since our custom might not
Accept the girl he truly preferred, he taught Weasel, whose talents
Were good if rejection of Heron occurred, let her skill
Be persuasion enough. He had never appointed young Weasel
Successor in so many words, had left open the choice.
Clever fellow, I thought to myself. From the grave you are having
Your way after all. I then prayed that the people would see
Whom he wanted—young Heron. Perhaps now the people
Of Long Bay might exercise sway with their customs more free.

    Just then Kona arose
        to speak out
            on behalf of young Weasel...

Went right to the point. "You have heard how our Weasel can tell
A tale well. He stays true to the meaning, each word recites clearly.
And yet, though his manner is proper, sincere, there is lack
Of enjoyment quite evident. Somber of mood in this duty,
His heart wanders elsewhere. Red Feather soon saw this in him
And was faced with a problem that custom imposed on this village,
A custom not found at Long Bay, he soon learned. So he let
Heron sit at his feet during lessons, ignoring her avid
Absorption and perfect remembrance of every detail.
Never once giving sign that her talents were pleasing, deserving
Of praise. Her persistent desire that integrity rule
In each telling, that passion invest recitation with vigorous
Joy or black sorrow when called for, impressed him. He spoke
With the Council about his concerns; but, soon after, the illness
That took him prevented disclosure from reaching the rest
Of us. Now we have met to engage in this open discussion
And here we are left to decide Weasel's fate. He's prepared,
He assures me, to be storyteller if Heron will cue him
As needed. He'd rather, however, do what he does best
With great pleasure. You know he is skillful devising constructions.
Old cumbersome tasks he makes easier, swifter to do.

> His nature is one
> > of a builder, prefers that,
> > > he tells me."

The people sat thinking. Then Meadowlark spoke as she stood.
"You have put the case ably," she said, thanking Kona, then added,
"I had the intention to speak out on Heron's behalf
But you've done so with eloquence I am unable to equal.
Your comments intended for Weasel make Heron's case clear.
I believe that allowing each young one to follow with blissful
Expression the talent that Spirit has granted will best
Serve the village. I urge we discard artificial distinctions."
With that she was seated again, somewhat nervous, but proud.
Mother nodded approval of Meadowlark's words, handing Dewdrop,
Asleep once more, back to her mother. We waited to hear
How Ahanton and Otter would handle the rest of the meeting.
"The time for decision has come now," said Otter. "Your choice
Will be made as you leave. We have placed by the circle two baskets
Outside—round for Heron and square for young Weasel. Break one
Twig to drop in the basket you choose, then depart. Final counting
Of twigs will be done by the Council. Results be made known
To you all in the morning by drumbeat. A seven for Weasel,
A ten if for Heron." Outside, as I stooped for a branch,
Kona broke twigs for us, then another for Mother, then Meadowlark.
Each dropped a twig in the basket for Heron and left.

> The suspense would be keeping me
> wakeful all night
> I suspected.

Once home and well fed I dropped instantly into deep sleep.
Never woke until Kona returned from the soil trench and touched me
To say that the drumbeats were ten. It was Heron the choice.
"By how many?" I wondered aloud, for the people seemed evenly
Split between Weasel and Heron. "Was probably close,"
He said, laughing. "We set a big change before folks of your village.
The number from Long Bay too few to have carried the day."
"I am glad it is Heron," I said, and collapsed into satisfied slumber,
Exhausted from yesterday's slog through the snow and the noise
Of so many when life here in shelter was quiet and peaceful
For day after day of long winter. With Lame Fawn now near
To her time, as was I, we no longer would visit each other
From opposite ends of the ridge where our shelters were placed.
I was longing for snow melt, and springtime, and coming of babies,
And sharing our friendship again face to face with delight.
As the winter dragged on, seemed reluctant to leave us, kept snowing,
Refilling the trails between shelters, I fretted and fumed
At imprisonment too long imposed and extremely oppressive.
My restlessness simmered. The weather stayed fickle, some warm
Days but freezing cold nights, then snow coating whatever rough pathways
Were packed down for walking, concealing bad stretches of ice.

But one morning, the day
dawning sunlit and warm,
I went walking.

Without telling anyone where I would go, I hiked down
To the glade where we'd tended to Spotted Whale's dying
And where I had promised myself I would birth my first child.
For I wanted to sit all alone and feel restful recalling
How Spotted Whale told us her earliest memory there.
How she watched from above, before entering body, her laboring
Mother awaiting her birth. I was hoping my Snow
Owl, so soon to be born, would be hovering, listening, watching
Me too. I intended to sing to her welcoming songs,
Make her promises we would be good to her. Guarantee safety.
For I was afraid for her, deep in my heart, with an ache
Lodged elusive and shadowy, fleeting, unspeakable, wordless.
A dread hardly credible, kept to myself, it was faint
But persistent, recurring in moments unguarded, disturbing.
No reason to feel such fear offered itself to my mind.
I was healthy and young. So was Kona. No mention had ever
Been made in my hearing such fears harried others this way.
And besides, this strong wriggler within me could well be a boy child.
If so, it was silly of us to have given a name
To it early, not knowing what name would befit it, be suitable.
Sitting and singing my promises, safe in the glade,

    I remained until cold
        stalked my bones
           and spring snow began falling.

I shook off my unfounded, nagging and foolish distress
And dismissed it. A mere superstition I'd better abandon.
The glade filled with beauty. The snow thickly swirling and white
Shrouded all but the nearest of tree trunks from sight. Somewhere deeper
In woods a weak branch, overburdened, came down with a whump.
Which reminded me no one would know where I was. Even Kona
Had not been informed that I'd left. He'd have probably stopped
Me from going alone. Had he known my intention to venture
So far he'd have offered to walk along with me, assist
With his usual caring concern that I sometimes found tiresome,
So headstrong, impatient and stubborn as I had become
In these last trying days. Soon he'd enter our shelter, find emptiness
Greeting him. Then he would fret 'til he found where I was.
Climbing slowly I scaled the steep route to the ridge of our winter
Camp's site never losing my way. I could find home eyes closed,
Which was fairly the case as the snow was so dense and so blinding.
I hauled myself up grabbing saplings for balance and hoist
For my cumbersome bulk. I felt happier, struggling and panting,
Than I had for days. I was energized, careless and free
In my mind. I had banished my fears by exerting my body
Again with the finest of outings. But on the high ridge,

> Close to home, hidden ice
> > tricked my feet.
> > > I rolled tumbling and bouncing…

A snowball of merriment. Nothing to do but to ride
The slope down, then begin ascent over again, feeling silly
For being undone by conditions I should have foreseen.
It was dark when I entered our shelter. Both Kona and Meadowlark
Stared. I was covered in snow clots and laughing in spite
Of my looks. "I fell down in the snow," I said. "No need for worry.
I'm fine." "Thno, thno, thno," blurted Dewdrop, her very first words.
Which set all of us cheering and praising her, taking the focus
From my little escapade. Grateful I needn't explain
Where I'd been, for the moment at least, I brought food and invited
Our guest to be seated and eat with us. Meadowlark saw
Through my ruse and excused herself, saying her own meal was ready
At home, she had dropped by to visit and see how I was.
"As you see, I am fine," I said, thanking her, kissing sweet Dewdrop
Goodbye. Then I busied myself with the food, knelt to eat
Beside Kona, who chewed with deliberate slowness, and waited.
I saw he was angered by worry but would not speak first.
My behavior had caused his concern. It was my obligation
To set the mood right again. "Kona, I needed to walk,"
I said. "Winter and idleness making me restless, I went to
The glade where dear Spotted Whale died. There I sat a long while

Simply thinking of her.
      Sensed no passage of time
         with my musings.

"The snow brought me back to my senses." I had no desire
To report on my fears for the child that I carried. Mere vapors
The anticipation of labor had likely brought on,
I kept telling myself. When we finished our meal, I shed clothing
And hung the wet items to dry. Kona, shaking his head,
Still annoyed, watched my nakedness moving about our small shelter
And mellowed a bit with relief. I had been so unfair
To him, trekking about without telling him that I was going,
Then coming back late and snow covered to worsen his woe.
"I am sorry I caused you to worry," I said in apology.
"Foolish to go so far, woman," he grumbled, both hands
On my belly. "Lie down, cover up, and let's hear what our Snow Owl
Will tell me about her adventurous, crazy fat Ma."
With his ear at my hip he pretended to listen intently.
Then mockingly scolded me, ridding himself of the last
Of his anxious dismay with complaints of rough ride from the baby,
He claimed. And so I was forgiven, and peace was restored.
Three days later my back began aching down deep where no rubbing
Relieved it. I couldn't get comfortable. Sleep wouldn't come.
I was anxious, unhappy, unable to sit still or concentrate.
Meadowlark thought me beginning my labor too soon.

> She sent Kona for Mother.
>> While waiting
>>> we played with sweet Dewdrop.

I tried for amusement by teaching new words, "nose" and "chin,"
For example, but waves of discomfort distracted my efforts
And nothing outside my own body compelled my regard.
With each easing of pressure I though the worst over, kept hoping
The process would halt, give the baby more time to mature.
Soon fatigue overwhelmed me. The aches grew increasingly frequent.
When Kona and Mother arrived I was lying down, sad.
All my promises made to this infant were broken by stubborn
And willful departure from sensible caution. My hike
Had proved selfish, endangered my Snow Owl, dependent and precious.
"Prepare for one tiny new baby," said Mother, voice calm,
Reassuring, while checking conditions. Just then a great gushing
Of water came forth and the birthing began to feel real.
Kona cradled my head and my shoulders, and kneeling behind me
Supported me firmly while Mother and Meadowlark cleaned
The space under me, readying for tiny infant's emergence.
But everything stopped. I grew restive. We waited. Too still,
Never moving inside me, my Snow Owl felt lumpy and lifeless.
I started to cry, feeling guilty, so certain I'd killed
Her before she had even the chance to be born, have adventures,
Or know her dear father. "My baby is dead," I then howled.

> Quickly Mother laid ear
> to my belly.
> "I hear a good heartbeat."

"Be calm, dear. The infant is resting, as you are, right now.
My first child was an early one also. Your brother, Loon Diver,
Was small but you'd never believe it to see him today.
I was frightened, as you are. This soon will be over and baby
Lie safe in your arms." She spoke softly to Kona as well.
I felt sure he was inwardly blaming my stupid and stubborn
Adventure for starting this, making events go awry.
"Please don't blame me," I begged him. "I never expected that anything
Harmful would come of a walk through the woods to the glade."
"Useless blame fixes nothing," he said his rough palm gently warming
My cheek. "Bring your thoughts here for now." But I felt so alone.
Though surrounded by people who loved me, I sensed a vast distance.
Remembered the words that my mother had said, "This is your
Task alone to be suffered and relished, fulfilled in good season
With painful delight," understanding now what she had meant.
Then my body took over with powerful spasms, expected
Yet sudden. I never had felt such great forces at work
On their own, no decision on my part involved until Mother
Instructed me when to relax, when to breathe, when to push.
I was actively busy at birthing, and thrilled to feel kicking
Up under my ribs, though one nerve was set stinging like fire.

> Just as long as my infant
>   was lively,
>   I'd willingly labor.

I laughed and I groaned and I panted and pushed and I cried,
So bewildering Kona that Meadowlark, seeing anxiety
Crumple his features, assured him that this was the way
Many women enjoyed the whole process. "Enjoyed?" I protested
As night turned to day again. "Soon now," she comforted. "Soon."
But it wasn't. The morning wore on. I despaired I would ever
Deliver, assaulted and pummeled and writhing for days.
Afternoon brought a visit from Medicine Otter whom Lame Fawn
Had sent, when she heard of events here, to see and report
What was happening. Mother and he stepped outside, out of hearing,
And I felt my panic explode, fearing something was wrong.
This was taking too long I thought wildly, unnerved and exhausted,
Too weakened to bellow my fears. Kona sagged with fatigue
As he held me, but wouldn't let go until Mother, returning,
Sent Kona outside to see Otter, to stretch and to talk
For a while. "I wish I were excused for a little while, also."
Attempting a joke, I was trying to seem to be brave.
Then contractions resumed, quick and hard. "I see black hair," cried
        Mother
"Now push." And I did. "One more time," she encouraged me. "Now!"
And with that I was empty. My belly collapsing. My comfort
Restored. Calling Kona she told him to look and be proud.

> "Tell your wife who the child is
>   she's given you."
>   "Snow Owl," breathed Kona.

Warm weight on my belly gave out a faint squeal. One raised foot
Curled wee toes as I reached down to touch it in wonder, the smallest
I ever had seen. "You will have a few cramps," Mother warned
Me just as they began, but soon ended. "Now watch," she said holding
A glistening packet connected like braiding to Owl's
Tiny stomach. A surge of dark fluid pulsed through it, to nourish
Her one final time from my body's supply. From now on
She would feed by her own suckling efforts. I slept all night gratefully.
Let busy murmurs of cleaning and cooing go on
All about me. Was hardly aware of them bathing my body,
Massaging my belly and combing my hair. Breathy squeaks
From the baby were music of dreams as I drifted so peacefully.
Comfortable, slender, again my own self. Once more me.
I awoke as tall Medicine Otter bent over me, saying,
"I'll go to tell Fawn of your news now. The baby is strong.
Very tiny but healthy. You did a fine job." "I feel guilty,"
I wept with a whimper. "I made her come early." "From what
I can see, it was probably best. She was born facing upward,
Her little nose mashed to one side a long time against bone.
She was craving escape." But one glance at my face made him hurry
To add, "Do not worry. Her nose will grow straight. It is flesh."

"Let me see her," I ordered.
All frightened once more
I sat upright.

So Kona brought Snow Owl to lie in my lap. We unwrapped
Her, examining fingers and toes and a nose rather flattened,
Endearing reminder her journey, though short, was a squeeze.
She was tiny. A rabbit was bigger, I thought, and much heavier.
Hair, black and long, almost dry now, was thick on her head.
And she never stopped moving her legs and her arms, blissful freedom.
Her limbs seemed exploring new space and her eyes opened wide
To our faces so close and adoring. A surge of great tenderness
Flooded me. Nothing prepared me for feelings so strong
And so fierce. I would willingly kill to protect her, my peace-loving
Ways all forgotten, so gripped by an instinct unknown
To my nature 'til now. Mother, watching the two of us smitten
With Snow Owl's hypnotic effect on us, took her and wrapped
Her again, saying, "Now you must put her to breast for a feeding."
I thought I had nothing. But clear liquid oozed as her mouth
Sought my nipple as soon as her cheek touched my breast. Then she
          suckled
With vigor in bursts, stopping only to breathe through her mouth
On account of blocked nostrils, until, with the tip of my finger,
I teased up the tip of her nose to let air in. She sneezed.
We all laughed and my fears were abandoned. Though small, she
          completely
Embodied full personhood. Separate, singular girl.

          From the start
               she belonged to herself,
                    this wee infant, our daughter.

She suckled. I cramped. Mother tended to cooking a meal
Which I ate with a ravenous appetite, greedy, one-handed,
Unwilling to set down the baby. Then Kona went out
And came back with a gift for our infant from Meadowlark—
      Dewdrop's
Small basket for sleeping that she had outgrown a long time
Ago. "Lovely," said Mother, "It's just what we needed, and skillfully
Woven to guard against drafts." So she lined it and put
Snow Owl in it to sleep, sent me outside to walk off my stiffness.
With Kona I went to thank Meadowlark. Shaky but happy
To breathe in the odors of spring vegetation commencing
To sprout at last, subtle, elusive, and welcome. We soon
Would move down to the summer site next to the lakeshore. Start planting
Again. I was already thinking ahead, pictured scenes
Of us teaching our Snow Owl to swim, see her play with the children
Of Lame Fawn and Medicine Otter, watch Dewdrop guide games,
Come to act as big sister to all of them. Such was the future
I hoped for, believed in, and wanted. So standing outside
Next to Kona, I spoke of my dreams, and my love, and my happiness,
Making him smile. He was shaky as well, having held
Me and seen the long struggle preceding the baby's emergence,
Felt helpless to hush my hysterical cries or give ease.

> It was all over now.
>   "Would you do that again?"
>   Kona asked me.

"I probably shall. And less fearfully next time, I'm sure,"
I responded with confidence, quickly forgetting the pain
And the fears that so recently plagued me. "It wasn't so bad,"
I assured him. The days that ensued brought a glorious springtime.
I carried the baby to visit with Lame Fawn before
She gave birth and then after, admiring the size of her babies,
A girl and a boy. Lark and Hawk were their names, each one born
So much larger than Snow Owl had been although Lame Fawn was smaller
Than I. Then we moved to the summer site, made the repairs
To our shelters, and planted our gardens. The fishing and hunting
Were excellent. Weather was perfect, with just enough rain
To make carrying water to gardens a chore seldom needed,
I noticed concern on the faces of people who came
From Long Bay when the rain became heavy, their memories haunted
By floods of last year. But when Weasel, surveying the land
That surrounded our site, proved no possible rising of rivers
Could reach us because we were not in a valley as their
Homes had been, we lay upstream of any potential disaster
From flooding, they settled their doubting and blended as one
With us. So much alike with shared values they were that I marveled
The old separation had ever occurred or caused strife.

 "There is one who still harbors
  a hatred inside,"
   Kona warned me.

"He covers it well. But his father was killed in the last
Fatal skirmish our village engaged in with yours, when my father
Was also defeated and slain. He is bitter. Revenge
Fires his fantasies still. It is said that his mother has managed
To poison his heart with her simmering foul discontent."
"Is he likely to act on it, Kona?" I asked, greatly worried.
"He's young and may yet learn to think for himself, it is hoped,"
Kona answered. "We work with him daily, encourage developing
Skills. In the hunt he appears to possess a good aim.
And his stealth in the forest surpasses the best of his fellows.
He stalks skittish game with a pace undetected, a ghost
Among trees, never seeming to move as he flows to his quarry,
Invisible, soundless. I think I can see him and then
He's moved on, disappeared. He can hide anywhere that he chooses,
Sometimes within sight but unmoving. Amuses himself
With our blindness. He startles us, taking great pleasure in making
Us jump when we're think we're alone." I was shocked. "That explains
The weird sense that I've had on the path on my way home from visiting
Lame Fawn," I said, "an odd feeling that someone was there
In the woods." I remembered a crawly sensation, an eeriness
New to me, prickling my skin as I hurried for home.

I was daughter of Chieftain Ahanton,
    considered
        blood enemy.

Quickly I stifled the thought. The young man was no threat.
He was carefully watched by adults quite aware of his enmity,
Working to guide him through grief to acceptance and strength.
I determined to call on friend Meadowlark, talking together
To learn what she knew of the boy and his mother before
They'd arrived in our village. Perhaps by befriending the mother
I'd lessen whatever old angers she nurtured. At least
I expected to try. But when Meadowlark earnestly cautioned
Me not to attempt my plan, good but naive, as she called
It, she told me the mother had always been mean, discontented
And fomenting trouble wherever she went. "She's not grieving
The death of her husband," she said, "for she hated his heart.
A good man, fairly beaten by constant harassment, he put
Himself into harm's way in that battle, not fighting but recklessly
Courting his death." But why hadn't he lived for his son,
For his duty to him, I was thinking as Meadowlark added,
"The mother, Sweet Fern," at this name for the woman she shrugged
With a grimace, "had poisoned the boy with contempt for his father
From earliest days. People think the boy, Black Hornet, grieves
For his father. He doesn't. He just hates the world and scorns everyone
In it. True son of his mother. Beware of his sting."

    In our shelter that night,
        I told Kona
           of Meadowlark's caution.

"This drops rotted meat in the stew," he said, shaking his head
As he thought about what I discovered from talking with Meadowlark.
"Medicine Otter has sensed the boy's malice entrenched,
But he never suspected that loss of this father had nothing
To do with it." Thinking a few moments longer, he said,
"It takes woman to know woman truly, see traits that are hidden
By guile from an unseeing man. I'll explore this real cause
For the boy's sullen mood with the others. The mother's behavior
Must alter. Deprived of her constant derision and hate
This grown boy called Black Hornet might yet shape his life to a happier
Vision." "Begin with a name change," I urged him, with heat.
"I am serious. Hornet's no better than calling him 'Trouble'
Or 'Discord'. I'm guessing his mother resented his birth
To have given that name." Kona stared at me, mulling my tactical
Shift in approach to the problem. "Perhaps if he felt
Himself other than insect with stinger, he'd view his worth differently."
How to accomplish a name change at his age required,
In itself, a ruse clever enough to seem sound on its merits
In everyone's eyes. Such a challenge delighted my mind,
Not above playing tricks for good cause, and enjoying some plotting.
"We'll think up a new name that honors what skill he has shown.

    Call him Wind Walker, Woods Ghost,
        a dignified name
            to live up to."

"But what of the mother?" asked Kona. "We women shall deal
With her. Pluck out the turd in her heart that has curdled her spirit,"
I answered. "Be careful," he said. "Take advice as it comes.
You are often too trusting. Don't try this alone. Don't be hasty."
I promised consulting with Mother and Meadowlark, Fawn
And White Crow would come first. No doubt Sweet Fern's foul temper
          already
Was obvious to them, unpleasant, distressing. No friend,
No companion seeks out such a woman who darkens the daylight
With clouds of ill temper, who mumbles and grumbles away
Her short time on this earth, and whose son has a poor reputation
As well. They'd have been left alone, been avoided by most,
Only strengthening their low opinions, confirming suspicions
We people were not worth the trouble of knowing. I met
Little Fox on my way to see Mother. "Give baby to Auntie,"
She cried with delight, was soon off, singing silly-word songs,
Doing jounce steps ahead of me, swaying with Snow Owl in rhythm,
The pair of them giggling, inspiring each other's high glee.
Such a morning this was, meant for dancing and singing and pleasure,
With sunlight and warmth, loving families sharing the day.
When she heard why I wanted to speak with the other good women,
My sister watched Snow Owl and Dewdrop and twins Lark and Hawk.

     While the four I had promised
          to talk with
               sat down for discussion,

White Crow was consulted for signs what the future might hold
For Sweet Fern. But she said after sitting, eyes closed, half the morning,
"Too murky to see what shall happen. Her form moves in mist
And in shadow before me. She glides with sure step but her purpose
Stays hidden." "A powerful warning?" I wondered aloud.
"Or a woman so troubled she lives without vision," said Mother,
Her voice hushed with pity. "She's driven so many away
With her anger, it's hard to be near her," said Meadowlark, "Hopeless
To try." "Never hopeless, just painful and difficult," Fawn
Said, unwilling to yield to discouragement. "Tell us, dear Meadowlark,
What do you know of her past?" "Very little," she said.
"Sweet Fern came to us, bloody and bruised from the south,
        undernourished
And terrified, barely a woman just out of taboo
And not speaking, except for her name. She'd no medicine animal.
No spirit name was revealed on her journey. She'd fled
Her own village. Vowed not to return. Begged to stay there among us
And live with us. Spotted Whale saw how distrustful she was,
Incomplete in her growth work and needing much care and much nurture.
We rallied to heal her hurt body, and lessen her fears.
She resisted our efforts and married soon after arrival
A widower, older than she by her lifetime, and mild.

        I suspect she'd been raped on taboo,
                for Black Hornet
                        came early."

"She never warmed up to him, hating the fact he was boy."
"He's near man, now," I said, "and embodies her scornful rejection
As part of his nature, so Kona believes, once he heard
What I told him of Meadowlark's cautions. I urged a suggestion
The men might pursue with him—change to a name better fit
To his talents." Lame Fawn caught her breath with excitement. "Exactly
The thing for the both of them, surely," she said, face aglow.
"Neither one has been recognized fully adult, nor accomplished
Taboo in traditional fashion. Both must feel that lack,
Must feel less than acceptable in their own eyes. Their own personhood
Maimed, too diminished for positive relish of life."
White Crow spoke again, thinking aloud while exploring ideas.
"Missed steps in the process of growing can keep someone mired
In the shortsighted choices of youth's limitations, persistent,
Inflexible, sad," she sighed. Fawn turned to Mother and said,
"I remember your loving attentions that finally nurtured
My faltering spirit from girlhood to woman. Perhaps
All together for Sweet Fern we may do the same?" "That way no one
Is burdened for long with her bitter rejection and spleen,"
Chuckled Meadowlark. "Sharing the hatred dilutes it?" I commented
Wryly. "The question to ponder is whether or not

It is worth it to try."
"For the good of the village,
it's worth it."

White Crow's words were forceful, convincing us each of the need
To combine to encourage Sweet Fern to explore gentler habits
Of outlook. We worked out a plan that was wily; to meet
Sweet Fern briefly, alone, always seeming by chance. Pleasant greetings
Repeatedly offered despite her downcast, sullen mien.
We would teach her her moods were not catching. Our bearing
Appearing impervious to her dejection, we'd pass
Her on by with a smile and a wave 'til she came to expect them.
"We've tried this before, But she drove us away in the end."
Such was Meadowlark's protest. "This time there's no end to the effort,"
Urged White Crow. "No one is to press her or try to get close.
Nothing obvious hinting campaign underway. Our persistence
So random and subtle she cannot detect it's a plot."
Lame Fawn grinned as she added, "Besides, if her mood never brightens
At least we'll stay happy. So, who's to be first in our scheme?"
We decided that White Crow would start, be the only one meeting
Sweet Fern "accidentally" with a quick nod, a brief smile
As they passed, while the rest of us acted indifferent as ever,
The way she had taught us to be toward her since she arrived.
By midsummer, White Crow could report a small symbol of progress.
"Sweet Fern is now meeting my eyes as we pass on the path.

> It will be a long slog
>> through a bog of dismay
>>> with this woman."

The season brought gardens to crops ripe and early and full.
And the babies grew happy and strong, their affectionate babble
At play proving bonds for their lifetimes were forming. We, one
By one, added ourselves to the wooing of Sweet Fern. Salvation
Of spirit our aim. We would water her soul. Heal its drought
If we could. On occasion a wave of a hand would be answered,
A greeting elicit a murmur, embarrassed and low.
It was wondrous how happy we felt sharing news of such minor
Improvements, no hint of a softening nature too slight
To report. "She may come around yet," muttered Mother one evening
While she and my father were visiting. Kona agreed.
"We are noticing Hornet less hostile," he said. "Something's changing.
Not much," added Father, "but something. A flicker of pride.
When we call a performance at lessons well done, he stands straighter."
"Has anyone thought of renaming him yet?" I then asked.
"He'll discover a name on his walkabout soon," answered Father.
I thought it unlikely the boy had enough self-regard
To divine from a dream or a vision an enhancing spirit.
He'd go for aggressiveness surely, his habit still bent.
To find fault with perfection, his usual impulse. And often
He followed me still in the woods when I carried Snow Owl.

"There's a Guardian Ghost
        in the woods walking with us,"
                I'd sing to her.

Knowing he heard me, I'd make it a game, hide dislike
Of his stalking behavior. Apparently calm and light-hearted
I'd talk to my Snow Owl of Wind Walkers, Ghosts-in-the-Mist
Who protected young girls and their mothers, of Magical Beings
Whose footfalls were very near soundless, whose breath was unheard
And whose souls were devoted to kindness. I once heard a chuckle
Behind me. Another time, Hornet jumped out of the woods
To the path right in front of me, blocking my progress and grinning.
A youth playing tricks he had no business playing. His grin
Was triumphant, not merry. He searched for some flicker of startled
Expression from me, but I gave him no sign of distress.
I stood tall and immobile, my Laughing Bear totem investing
My stance with her powerful spirit. I felt unafraid
For myself at that instant. I watched in his eyes a crude contest
Of innocence struggling with evil intent—battlefield
Of a spirit in conflict, a mutiny under black lashes.
We stood face-to-face many moments in silence. My child
Never stirred in my arms. Wide awake and alert to the tension,
Kept watching my face for her cue as to how to react.
I spoke evenly then to Black Hornet. "You'll be good at scouting
Some day when it's needed," I told him, and smiled. "You have skill."

But he slithered aside
        into woods again,
            wordless, invisible.

Furious, trembling, relieved, I walked on, clutching Snow
Owl too tight to my chest for her comfort but feeling protective,
Unwilling to loosen my grip. Unafraid for myself
But uneasy for her. The old twinges and hints of foreboding
I'd sensed long ago came again with a rush and a strength
Undeniable. Then they were gone. What a worrisome challenge
This motherhood was for me. Love so astoundingly strong
For this child of my body consumed me, at times made me crazy,
See threat where there was none. A boy merely playing a game
Did no harm. While it never occurred to me then I should wonder
Why Hornet was not with his fellows at lessons that day,
It occurred seasons later I ought to have questioned his absence more
Closely. As autumn wore on into winter's approach
We continued our steady attentions to Sweet Fern's unhappy
Condition of mood. She had taken a liking to Fawn,
Which was easy to do. But her liking converted to clinging
And Fawn needed help setting limits. This time as we moved
To the ridge for the winter, wise Meadowlark traded her shelter
For Medicine Otter's and Fawn's, "So the children may play,"
She explained her decision. She really established some distance
Between Fern and Fawn, with both Mother and Crow in the way.

> We all sensed that Sweet Fern
> hid unbearable knowledge
> that plagued her.

I thought it had something to do with Black Hornet, her son.
Though he always came with her to visit, she left him unsheltered,
Outside, while we talked, his dark presence unwanted. "I wish
He would form his own friendships," she'd mutter, "not follow me
Here." "Does he go to White Crow's and my mother's as well
When you visit?" I asked her. "Oh, no. Only here does he follow.
He says to protect me because of the distance from home,
But that's foolish. I frequently walk very far, return safely
Alone. It's annoying." She shrugged as she said this, her face
Drawn and wan. She appeared to exert no control over Hornet.
He did as he wanted despite her objections. She left
Us soon after she said this, and close by the entrance loomed Hornet,
A sentinel, ominous, sullen and silently grim.
He had grown very big since the day he had jumped on the pathway
In front of me. "Body of man but impulsive as boy,"
I confided to Lame Fawn beside me. She'd joined me when Sweet Fern
Arrived and had seen Hornet lurking. "A sad child," she said
As she signaled by smiling and nodding to Hawk and the girls
That their playtime was over. "An angry young man, to my thinking,"
I answered. "There's something about him, a frightening air."
"Don't be silly," she scolded. The twins toddled over to hug her
And crawl on her lap with affection. Snow Owl crawled to me.

>She was very much smaller
>>than Lark, just as smart
>>>but more delicate.

Both of them chattered away in their own special talk
While Hawk waited for language to come to him later, amusing
Himself with activities physically playful, all boy.
Both our shelters were almost too small for his antics, his energies.
Toddling in circles around Owl and sister, he tramped
With his feet a smooth ring the three used as their special arena
Apart from four parents. A place independent of us
Though right next to us. No supervision, no brief interventions
Were needed. Well loved, happy children, they played with much joy
As we visited, talking and watching them—three little beings
Who didn't exist just last winter. A magical turn
Of events for us all. On dark evenings together, snow falling
Outside, and the cook fire aglow with low light, welcome warmth,
We shared life that provided the best for our families' comforts.
The girls curled asleep in the arms of each other, and Hawk,
Fighting sleep unsuccessfully, leaned on the knees of his father,
Head wobbly, then bobbing upright. With a mischievous grin
He would check to see who might be watching until, with lids drooping,
His sturdy young body succumbed. Very often we sat
Then in quiet complete satisfaction, just watching them sleeping.
Their trust and their innocent beauty bemused everyone.

    No one willing to spoil
        the enchantment
            by voicing the obvious.

Evenings like this, when we'd wordlessly gather up babes
And then part for the night, brought a peace and a sense of fulfillment
I'd never thought possible. Happy and loved as I'd been
All my life, I had never known richness in soul and in spirit
Bloom so overwhelming, profound. Before sleep I would vow
To remember for always this moment no grief could diminish,
To build the bright niche in my heart nothing evil could touch.
A calm glade of remembrance to visit by choice in the future
Should trouble invade equanimity. Nothing so pure
Could endure. I was old enough now to know well, to see clearly,
How fickle experience changed from the best to the worst
In an instant. So, warm in our shelter at night, next to Kona
And Snow Owl, I slept without dreaming, my world all serene.
In the mornings, the two of us wakened by Snow Owl's bright chatter,
Would laugh and adore her, this sprite, tiny elf of our hearts,
Whose small stature belied her maturing intelligence. Everyone
Found her delightful, surprisingly pert. No one blamed
Us for lavishing love on her, showing our pride in her openly.
Even Grandfather Ahanton, not given to laughter, would coax
Her to come to his knee and then roar with abandoned amusement
At stories she made for him, songs she would sing out of tune.

In the spring when we moved
from the ridge,
she was the pride of the village.

Indulgent adults could have easily made her a brat
If we'd let them. Sweet Fern took a special delight in Owl's eager
Affections. She tended her often unasked. I was not
Always pleased when Fern took her, but recognized how it was helping
To soften Fern's heart, trying mothering gestures so new
For her. Snow Owl, of course, was convinced her sole purpose for being
Was piling great heaps of pure love upon anyone who
Seemed to need it. "Too trusting," said Kona while watching his daughter
Unsteadily toddle to even the surly and old.
She would melt them by patting a leathery cheek or a wrinkled
Old hand, or by wiping a tear from a milky old eye.
Not a one ever brushed her away. Not one grumbled or scolded.
She never mistrusted. She never showed caution, unease.
She went off on a regular route every morning that summer,
Assured everyone she was up, going 'round there to check
On the state of their hearts. Her impatience to start on her circle
Each morning was comical, frequently causing a firm
Admonition from Kona or me to eat breakfast, drink water.
The summer was hot. We swam often. The three learned to swim
Underwater as well as they could on the surface. Loon Diver,
Their teacher, took care at their lessons to help them be fish.

"Little minnows," he called them.
Dewdrop and the bigger ones,
"Salmon."

When winter returned, Snow Owl fretted as snowfall and cold
Windy weather curtailed her adventures. I didn't allow her
To wander the ridge, out of sight, hut to hut, all alone.
Lark and Hawk were her winter companions again. And some visiting
Children were brought by their mothers, expanding the group
Until Fawn took the boys to her shelter and I kept girls playing
In mine. So that winter passed quickly. The weather stayed mild
For the most part. The children grew hardy, and I became pregnant
Again. By the time we moved down to the camp by the shore,
Early Spring had made everything lush and the undergrowth vine-filled,
So dense that the children could hide themselves, standing unseen
While their playmates went seeking them, practicing hunting.
Black Hornet had gone on his walkabout, keeping his name
On return. He said, "Ground hornets stung both my legs, called me
        'Brother'
In dreams. I am one with them. Venom of stingers now flows
Through my body and gives me my strengths both abundant and special."
The rest of us shuddered, regretting we hadn't been swift
With our plan to rename him when chances were better for coaxing
A nature more gentle to surface, a temperament mild
To take hold. He was glad of the name his sad mother had given,
He told her. It made him feel dangerous, competent, strong.

    But Sweet Fern, then confessing
            her secret,
                    became Crying Woman...

A pitiful figure of grief without solace. No end
To her tears. Even Snow Owl, unable to cheer her, caught sadness
Herself, was subdued on return from her regular rounds.
I'd see tears in enormous brown eyes as she came to me slowly,
Embracing my neck as I sat with hands busy at work
On a basket or birch bark container with no way to tell her
What caused Sweet Fern's earlier anger and now her despair.
Such abuse as she suffered the whole of her childhood, its poison
Affecting her still, was not fit for the ears of a child.
White Crow hoped Fern's confession might free her, relieve her of sorrow,
But that had not happened. Black Hornet was constantly there
As reminder, the product of incest long-standing from earliest
Years. Once taboo journey offered escape, she had faked
Telltale signs and run swiftly as far as she could, not suspecting
She already carried the child of her uncle, her dead
Mother's brother who'd brutally fathered Sweet Fern by this sister.
Her story lay gruesome upon us, we women who'd heard
Sweet Fern gaspingly tell it. Each halting detail was fresh horror
Revealed. Early loss of her mother had left the young girl
Unprotected. Not learning for years that her father was uncle—
Disgraced and reviled by her village. "I didn't know why,"

Sobbed, " I see in Black Hornet
what evil this uncle
has fathered."

"An evil so awful," she wailed, "that I wish I had killed
Him at birth." "You did not have that right," chided White Crow, but
          gently,
Acknowledging impulses born of Fern's helplessness, pain,
Righteous fury, and present deep agony drowning what spirit
Was left in cascades of unstoppable, free flowing tears.
Crying Woman she certainly was and I sometimes preferred her old
Anger to this damp dismay. She'd had backbone back then.
Only Snow Owl could coax an occasional lull, pause a crying
Spell now. This I felt was too much for a sensitive child
To confront every day. She would visit Sweet Fern at the finish,
Not first on her rounds. Her persistence was stubborn and strong.
Owl assured herself daily that everyone in the whole village
Expected and cherished her visits. Made certain each one
Said her name. "She behaves as if fearful we might not remember
Her bright little butterfly self from one day to the next,"
Chuckled Heron one evening at campfire. "She's always so earnest,
So serious for one so young." And I sometimes saw White
Crow look soft at my growing young girl as if seeing her future
Would not be an easy one. Stories of strangers too near
And too hostile had everyone worried. Our lives, I suspected,
Would undergo changes we could not escape, would be hard.

      When I queried White Crow
           about Snow Owl,
                she gave me no answers.

"Her future has not been revealed to me. She is too young
Yet for patterns to form," she said. Time for the birth of my second
Was coming. My belly was huge. I had carried beyond
The time Snow Owl had taken, was careful to shun any urges
To hike out alone. Even dancing impossible now.
But my joy in my drumming grew full for my fingers were dancing
In place of my feet. One thing troubled me still about Fern
And Black Hornet, and even dead Yellow snake's treatment of Lame Fawn.
The men of our village and also of Long Bay behaved
As was proper. They honored the women, our rights to choose husband,
Have wealth of our own, voice opinions, hold up half the sky.
But the men from away behaved differently, wantonly cruel.
It seemed they saw little to value in women; respect
For our wisdom and healing and childbearing willingness lacking.
A grave oversight to ignore or belittle, abuse,
Or mistake our forbearance for weakness. Foolhardy to posture
Aggressive as masters when one tiny root ground to bits
In a meal had the power to render them helpless, well-disciplined,
Nursed back to health from dependence with loving concern,
New respect swelling stout in their marrow. A humbling expedient
Taught to our girls before marriage in case we had need.

But we didn't.
     Our lives were so free,
          satisfying, productive...

Our marriages mutual, solid, respectful. As friends
With our husbands our loves only grew with the passing of seasons,
No cause for complaint between husbands and wives on account
Of mistreatment. Though snoring or laziness, gossip or cooking
Misfortunes, were often the subject of good-natured jibes
That would prompt rounds of ribbing and banter and laughter at
     campfires
On long summer evenings while waiting for Heron to tell
Us a cherished old story: How Crow lost his song, for example,
Or how far off mountains and streams had been given their shapes
By Great Giant relentlessly beating them, tumbling them, breaking
Them through so the rivers might flow again rapid and clear
For our ancestors benefit, also for ours down the passage
Of time to the present. In travels we knew where we were
Though away many days from our village. Because of the stories,
We recognized where Mighty Beaver lay slain, broken-necked,
At the wide-flowing river, where fish again spawned for the people.
We knew Great Grey Giant had once stalked the land. From the North
He came grumbling and rumbling, his bitter cold breath blowing everyone
Southward until Mother Sunlight persuaded his heart
To relent, his fierce brow to sweat tears, the great stones in his bowels
To drop and release him from agony, hurry him home.

How we loved Heron's legends,
     the way she'd recite them,
          so truly,

With never a word out of order, nor concept unclear
To her listeners. Each of the stories had more than one meaning,
A lesson embedded, to dawn on the mind in repose.
For the children, a magical tale. For adults there was always
A hint there was more to be learned, to be taken to heart.
Hard-earned wisdom of ancients all neatly condensed, entertaining
And useful, and easily stored in the minds of the next
Generation, to guide them and shape them as we had been guided.
But during the legend of Flute Man, his music, and Bear
Woman, one summer evening, I sensed that my next child was ready.
So Kona and Lame Fawn and I took the path to the glade
Where I'd wanted Snow Owl to be born, was determined that this time
I'd reach it. A birthplace of fortunate omen, long life
And fine looks, many talents, and everything powerful Spotted
Whale's birth there had given her. Place where the wolf first appeared
To us. Sacred, secluded, and suited it was for a birthing.
Fat Moon, and the odors of balsam and pine on soft air
All combined to make welcome our second-born child on this hasty
Arrival. I'd barely stepped into the glade on the arm
Of strong Kona, when water broke free and hard thrusting took over.
I squatted. Lame Fawn quickly went to her knees in the leaves

            Right behind me and caught,
                  with sure hands and much practice,
                  our bundle.

"A boy. Very big," she announced as she placed him at once
In the arms of his father to show to me proudly. Still squatting,
My body completed its work in an instant. This birth,
Although wrenching, was rapid, the walk to the glade beneficial
For speeding the process. When Medicine Otter arrived,
After settling the children with Mother, he whooped in amazement,
"This man child is huge!" And the baby agreed with him, loudly.
Each wail he let loose with made cramps in my belly responsive
And hearty, no need to massage long the home he'd just quit.
The white moon overhead gave enough of her light so his washing
And wrapping was easily seen to. No need for a fire.
The night air was the warmest late summer had ever afforded.
"And what will you name him?" asked Lame Fawn when done with her
        chores.
"I don't know," I said, "Kona?" But he only gazed at his baby,
Transfixed by continuous howling. "He ought to be Wolf,"
He said finally, grinning, "He knows how to howl in the moonlight
Already." Remembering she-wolf, who stood at the edge
Of the glade on the day we collected dead Spotted Whale's scattered
White skeleton bones, I agreed. "Do not bury his caul.
Set it out on that rock at the edge of the woods for bold she-wolf,
In case she returns," I said. "Sit here a while and we'll see."

So we waited.
        But I never saw
            the caul suddenly vanish.

A rustle of leaves in the shadows, the snap of a twig,
And then She-wolf appeared on the rock, her notched ear slowly
     twitching,
And showing in moonlight the proof it was she who had come
As in dreams I had seen her so often approach and sit watching.
"Wake up, Ellacoya," said Lame Fawn. "It's time we returned."
"Was I sleeping?" I asked her. "Did she-wolf appear? For I saw her.
And where is the caul?" "You were dreaming. We've buried the caul
At exactly where Spotted Whale chose to lie back in her dying."
"I saw it on rock," I protested. "It lay there a while
As we dug in the soil. You had fallen asleep before Kona
Was finished with prayers of thanks and of praise to the wolf."
"I was tired," I admitted. We stood up to go. Proudly Kona
Presented our son to me, quiet at last and asleep.
What a chunk of a child he was, heavy and round-faced and solid.
No fears for him tainted my thoughts. He would make himself man
In our finest tradition and we would relax and enjoy him
The whole of our lives. Would rely on his care when old age
Would require. I was certain he'd outlive us both and would bury
His parents with love and with dignity many moons hence.
What a comfort it was to believe this, to trust in his future
So surely. I wondered what White Crow could see of his life.

        "He'll be first among equals,"
             Crow cried
                  as we entered the village.

There many still waited. When vision of baby's quick birth
Was revealed to her as it was happening, such was her magic,
She knew it was boy before Fawn did, delaying the news
Until we had returned. While the moon was still high, brightly lighting
The circle, our infant was handed around and admired.
Even Snow Owl awoke and came running to hold her new brother.
Song Maker and Little Fox crooned jolly lullaby airs
They'd been practicing. This was so different, so merry in summer
With everyone there to surround us and celebrate. Not
As it was, so alone on the ridge when our Snow Owl came early—
A worrisome birth. "He has eyes keen and bright as the wolf,"
Said my father, "wide set and strange colored." "Oh. Hush," cautioned
        Mother,
"The color will change in a matter of days." I then took
Him from Father and sat with him closer to flickering firelight
To see for myself. It was true. As he gazed open-eyed
And unblinking, my son had the eyes of the wolf in my dreaming.
He might have been her pup in spirit. Twice gifted, as stout
In his soul and devoted in heart as the wolf, but two-legged,
To walk on Earth upright. Accepting these truths, I then put
Him to breast with thanksgiving. And tiny Snow Owl settled cuddling
Against me, still sleepy, to stroke her new brother's black hair.

    Kona sat down beside us.
        The people filed past
            chanting blessings,

Then left for their separate shelters to sleep through the night.
We had little enough of that sleep, for our Wolf Pup was ravenous,
Feeding at intervals so close together I thought
It was constant, but Kona said, "No, you both slept at rare moments."
I knew by the sag of his lids and his slackness of jaw
He had not slept at all, was exhausted. Snow Owl was impatient
To start on her rounds, having slept through the night like the child
She still was, undisturbed, feeling safe and secure in our shelter
As usual. Happy, she kissed and admired the new being among
Us, then left him to us for pursuit of her own obligations
As she had determined her role in the village to be.
She was first very often, the one to discover an elder
Who'd suffered distress overnight, and went running for aid,
Or gave news a death vigil impended. No aspect of everyday
Living, or sickness, or sadness, or dying gave shock
To her. All was acceptable, proper, and richly rewarding.
No judgments beclouded awareness, for nothing repulsed
Her nor stunted responses.. Where laughter and happiness flourished,
She laughed and was happy. Where grief intervened, she would weep
With the mourners. Unguarded in feelings and fully expressive,
This sensitive Snow Owl, our daughter, embraced everyone,

> Found the treasure each heart,
> > whether shriveled or luscious,
> > > provided.

And so the days went at the end of that summer. Routine
And so peaceful we hardly believed the occasional traveler's
Stories of troubles to southward. For nothing touched us.
Crops abundant, mild weather persisting, good hunting and fishing
Made promise that winter supplies would be ample. Our Wolf
Pup was thriving and jolly. Lark, Hawk, and his sister and Dewdrop
Amused him by day. He soon slept through the nights without fuss.
Little Fox and Song Maker grew closer than ever. Their music
So fine, and so popular at the Fall Gatherings, word
Of them spread. And my dancing was noted, original, worthy
Of many requests for performance. We formed a good team.
Even Heron and Weasel combined to act out many legends.
The seasons passed quickly in sequence. White Crow, growing old,
Still insisted she could not divine Snow Owl's future, but Wolf Pup
She said would be chief in his time. No more babies were born
To Lame Fawn and her Medicine Otter, but Kona made children
With me. Two more sons. How I loved each arrival, Lame Fawn
As the midwife, and Mother and Father the grandparents sharing
Our joy. The whole village was flourishing, healthy, well fed.
And the weather seemed warmer each summer, felt milder each winter.
So much so that elders remarked it a worrisome change.

> Winter harshness
>   was our best protection
>   against pale invaders.

The stragglers from southward increased to a regular stream
Bearing tales of lost hunting grounds, summer encampments now
    occupied,
Forests cut down to make forts and stockades, meadows burnt
And the soil turned to dust in the wind. A wasteful and arrogant
Peoples these aliens were, so the wanderers said.
Some fell ill who came stumbling along the lake shore and collapsing
At last at our fire. They were treated by Lame Fawn with care
And the help of Snow Owl who was training with Fawn to be healer,
Her natural calling since childhood. Owl, old enough now,
Was preparing to go on taboo. Although proud, I was worried
Again. The old fears for her, felt since before she was born,
Were resurfacing. Nagging disquiet arose as she soberly
Dressed for departure. I wanted to stop her. Instead,
With wan smile wished her well, safe return, a swift journey, fine visions.
Her figure, so small as she walked away, purposeful, caught
The sun's rays, then the shadows, before disappearing completely.
Mere five days to wait and I'd see her once more by the fire.
Share the sweat lodge we women would make for her, combing and
    bathing
Her. Hear of her vision. Be told of her spirit name. Give
Her the medicine bag that Lame Fawn and White Crow were preparing
To honor her outstanding skill diagnosing the sick.

    Came the fifth day.
        Owl never appeared.
            And Black Hornet had vanished.

My heart was in tatters. Where was she? And Kona, who tried
To amuse me, "Our tender young daughter is probably mending
Some squirrel's hurt tail, or is setting the wing of a bee,"
Unconvinced of his own reassurances, fretted, as fathers
Will do about daughters. Our firstborn, so tiny at birth
That we marveled she lived, had a courage and will her small stature
Belied. "She is safe. She'll return," Lame Fawn urged us, "Believe."
On the sixth day I begged our tall Medicine Otter to shape change
And fetch her. "I cannot," he said. "To cut short her taboo
Would invalidate all she has worked for. Remember how Kona's
Brief meetings once threatened your own." But he worried. We all
Did. The village grew somber as day seven passed. The sun set.
In the morning, when no one had slept, our unrest was intense.
Every shelter soon emptied. The people all gathered at Council,
Insisting a search party form, set out quickly to find
Their beloved young butterfly visitor, Snow Owl, whose caring
Concern for them all fostered lightness and love in each heart
From the time she could walk. "I agree," said Lame Fawn. And she added,
"My own broken ankle and tedious crawling to home
From taboo did not take me eight days. She has met with some trouble."
The party was chosen—Loon Diver, Grey Hawk, and Red Elk—

    Snow Owl's uncles.
        They treasured their niece
                as their very own daughter.

My faith they would find her was strong, but the waiting was hard
To endure. Neither Kona nor I could give comfort the other
Accepted, each closed to the other, cocooned in numb fear.
I could understand now what my mother once felt at my going.
She held me all day in her arms, while grave Kona paced, wild
As an animal wounded, to walk off a pain unrelenting.
The villagers tried to get on with routine, but their hearts
Were not in it. Sun set again. Morning, the ninth day, came dawning,
A bright day of beauty with blessing of Springtime's warm air.
Around noon, a great keening arose at the edge of the village.
I ran to the sound. The three uncles surrounded Sweet Fern's
Son, Black Hornet, who carried the body of Snow Owl, not letting
Her go, or be touched. His face glistened with tears as he clutched
Her with fierceness I'd witnessed so often whenever he loitered
Around us. Full certain he'd harmed her, I leapt to attack
Him. But Loon Diver seized me and held me away from my daughter's
Limp body. Both Grey Hawk and Red Elk used all of their strength
To keep Kona from knifing him, not even knowing the story
Behind what had happened. But, seeing her fingertips blue,
Her mouth gaping, her moccasins missing, clothes tattered and bloody,
I knew that my daughter, my sweet one, my Snow Owl was dead.

All sat down at the circle
    and Black Hornet
        gave me her body.

"Belongs in your arms," he said gruffly, and stayed on his knees
In the dirt right in front of me, helpless to speak any further,
Arranging her feet and her hands and her braids.
His hands, shaking and caked with dried blood, were enormous yet gentle.
I watched them fuss over her, straighten her jacket, her belt.
My arms under her cradled her knees and her shoulders. Her body
Inert in my lap was familiar yet foreign and cold.
No responsiveness flowing between us. No sparkle. No serious
Frown of apology. Nothing. Then Kona was there, crouched beside
Me, supporting her head, his thumbs smoothing her brow. Disbelieving
The evidence stark there before us, we sat on the ground
While the fire was built up and the people stayed moaning and swaying
Around us. Our Spotted Wolf, too grown for Pup as a name
Any longer, led both younger brothers to see her and touch her,
Their sister, who loved them so much, who was there every day
Of their lives for them, gave them their infant names, Beetle,
Grasshopper, affectionate names they still answered to when
She would call them. Though Beetle sensed something was fearsomely
            empty
About her, Grasshopper, the youngest, pulled free of the hands
That reached out to restrain him and flung himself onto her body
Expecting her usual laughing embrace. "Ho! Wake up,"

    He implored,
        as he did every morning.
            But nothing could wake her.

Recoiling and baffled he groped for a reason she stayed
In my arms unresponsive and dirty. "You smell," he protested
And pushed at her shoulder, enraged that she paid him no heed.
He was building a fury his taut little frame, needing outlet,
Could barely contain. Snow Owl never had failed to embrace
Him, to laugh with him, help him to dress and to eat, and to tickle
Him jolly. Now here she was taking his place on my lap,
A big sister too old for such coddling he seemed to be thinking.
Her arm, because jostled, slid lifelessly onto the ground
At his feet, her hand open, revealing deep cuts and wrist bruising
Not noticed before. Huge Black Hornet, still kneeling in front
Of us, reached out and cupped it, like holding dead bird in a pitying
Palm. I had never suspected he loved her like this.
He was always so grim and so taciturn. Excellent stalker
Of game, a fine scout, but he kept to himself, gone for days
At a time. Outraged Grasshopper flailed with both fists at him, punching
And punching his back and his head and his shoulders. "Bad man!
Let her be," he was bellowing, childish voice rising in panic.
I saw all that happened around me with clarity. Sharp
And distinct every sight, every sound, but all distant and meaningless.
Mother took Grasshopper, gave him to Hawk. Hornet opened a pouch,

Laid before us a scalp
of red curls
and a man's severed member.

They lay in the dirt. Told the story. "I found her too late,"
Mourned Black Hornet. The horror of what had befallen her, obvious
Now, caused an outcry enough to split rocks, splinter trees.
In the tumult, the uncles raised Hornet and led him to Council,
While Lame Fawn and Mother bent tearfully down to kiss Owl,
And tall Medicine Otter coaxed Kona with whispers of courage
To leave us, the women, to tend to Owl's body while they
Chose the men who would tend to the grave. I saw White Crow
Explaining Owl's death to her brothers, who listened with awe,
Faces solemn, so open, so wounded, with no way to spare them
The grief that deranged us all equally, struck us all down.
They had no understanding of evil, knew nothing of cruelty.
Here lay long fears now fulfilled. Nothing more in my life
Could approach this affliction of fate. I was certain that whatever
Would happen already had. I went mindless and numb
At that instant. I watched myself give up Owl's body to Mother
As though again birthing her. Nothing was real any more.
Why would time not reverse itself? Give back sweet breath to my daughter?
Start over? I stared at that scalp. I remembered that hair.
"There's no kindness unpunished," I said to Lame Fawn as I thrust out
The scalp to her, parting those curls and exposing our seam.

    "I wish now we had killed them,"
        she said.
                "Our forbearance taught nothing."

Young Lark came to sit with me, silent, sweet smelling, bereft
At the loss of her very best friend and her lifelong companion.
Her warmth and her nearness, the sounds of her breath strangling sobs,
Were exactly the presence I welcomed the most. This connection
That lingered, when all else was broken, kept heart in my chest
Though it strove for escape with its pounding and flinching and flutter.
I wanted to run and to howl but my body refused.
There was nothing to say, so Lark wisely said nothing, remaining
Beside me as long as she felt she was wanted. Her gift,
Freely given, was comfort enough when no comfort could reach me.
My life must proceed. There were children to care for and teach.
Husband Kona, as stricken as I by this senseless destruction,
Might look for my strength when I had none. Each need seemed too
        much,
I had nothing inside me to draw on. A husk, dry and empty.
The blank of a smothering fog for a brain. Then a wave
Of enveloping calm overwhelmed me. Great pity for everything
Living suffused me. I felt a connection to all.
And with every least thing I sensed kinship. No boundaries, limits,
Or blindness remained to prevent full awareness of life
With its grandeur and glory, its haphazard pains and its agonies—
Final submission. This was the way of Our Earth.

    Snow Owl, traveling now
        with The Many,
            was safer than ever.

A part of me knew she'd accomplished her purpose on Earth.
I accepted that knowledge with gratitude, wanted to share it
With Kona. But no. I had faith he would plod his own path
Through this grief, realize revelations peculiar to his way
Of seeing this world. In the future, with senses less shocked,
If that ever could happen, perhaps we would talk and remember
Our daughter's unusual nature. Existence, though brief,
Leaving nothing undone. An Old Soul sent to visit a moment?
"I must be insane," I kept thinking. "I'm crazy. I'm stunned.
Such a horror as this hasn't happened. It cannot have happened.
No one is so evil. No man is so vile." But one was.
And Black Hornet, avenger, had brought us the scalp and ridiculous
Member as proof. Only Lame Fawn and Lark now remained
With me seated and silent, allowing my madness to eddy
And swirl as the flames of the fire sank to cinder and ash
And the offal that once wore a killer lay shriveled and filthy,
Commencing to rot in the dirt of our circle. How long
I sat senseless I cannot recall, but a restlessness seized me
At last and I stood. "I must tend to her body," I said,
And walked stiffly to fetch from our shelter fine clothing and treasured
Small items of hers Owl would want to keep near in her grave.

   Mother's shelter was where
         they had taken her.
               Women were washing her.

White Crow was crooning and smudging the air all around
Owl's scarred body as I brought her things. I could see dried blood
    staining
The flesh between thighs where the women had not quite yet reached
With their bathing. Sweet Fern saw my glance. Her jaw worked as,
    disgusted,
She answered my unspoken questions by nodding. "She fought
Like a fish on a line, with a vengeance," Fern told me. "She didn't
Submit. She was forced. She was no easy prey. See her wounds."
Fern would know all about being forced, being used, being prey,
The lone woman among us who did truly know. "See the cuts
On her hands and her arms from defending herself against slashing.
The soles of her feet have been shredded from running. Her wrists
And her ankles are bruised where she struggled to break loose the bindings.
The man had to kill her to get what he wanted. When Black
Hornet found him just lifting himself off her body, he bludgeoned
The brute with a blow to the neck with the man's rifle stock.
He determined that Snow Owl was already dead before scalping
Him living, then more, as he showed you. Then letting him bleed
To death slowly, my son cut Owl loose." Every woman was listening,
Motionless. Fern seemed transformed in the telling. Her rage
Was as clean as a blade in a flame. It was sharp. It was freeing.
No trace of distaste for son Hornet—just pride and relief.

    Crying Woman no longer.
        No longer defeated,
            She'd rallied.

This tragedy broke the last lacing of tyranny rape
Had once wrapped around her bound spirit. The proof of Owl's
        struggle
Made flesh there before her released her in some way profound.
And her anger lit mine. How I wished that the killer'd been captured
Alive. I would kill him twice over myself if I could.
My mind played rapid scenes of the painful revenge I'd administer
To him. A death in the end he would scream for, denied
To him over and over and over again. I would torture
Each finger, pry nails from each toe. Sear his tongue. Slice his nose
Up each nostril. I'd gut him and save his blue eyes for the watching
Of entrails erupting. Knock teeth one by one from his mouth
With my pestle. Smash bones and then twist every limb, every sinew.
No pity. No stopping me. Such were my fantasies wild.
I was angry with Snow Owl, as well, as I stared at her, lifeless,
And tiny, a victim. How could she have let herself be
Overpowered, be slain, be the cause of such grief, so much sorrow?
Brought home to us dead when her duty demanded she live
And return to us, woman of healing and caring and beauty
All lost now. A memory only. Too soon. Much too soon.
I collapsed, began wailing and howling. A gasping and retching
Convulsed my robbed belly. Full feeling at last had its sway.

    I kept kissing and stroking
            one hurt little hand,
                    a foiled mother.

The women allowed me my grief. No one offered to stop
Me by touch or by word. I was grateful. Tears flowing, they waited
In silence until my long seizure abated. My breath
Came again in deep hiccupping sighs, a sure signal exhaustion
Had conquered, that I was available, ready once more
For the bathing and dressing of Snow Owl so Kona and others
Might see her at rest before burial. Evening had come.
We would sit with her body all night. When the bathing and dressing
Were finished, I lay down beside her, imprinting her face
On my memory. Peaceful she seemed to me now, although energy
Quivered about her. The crooning, the murmurs, the love
That the women expressed to keep soothing us both formed an aura
Around us, a comfort of sorts, that, wherever Owl was,
I was hoping she felt it as I did, caressing her spirit
Though flesh had gone cold. I was grateful that Hornet had found
Her and carried her home. For she might have been out there forever,
A mystery where she had traveled. Still living? Or dead?
We might always have wondered. I could not imagine her vanishing,
Never returning, or having to live with that void,
Feel the anguish of no explanation, expectations of seeing
Her rife, hope persisting, yet wearing despair 'til I died.

    In the morning
            men carried her body
                    to lie in the circle.

I followed, tear stained and unkempt, with no care how I looked.
I saw Kona the same, wan and shaking, still sleepless and haggard.
His eyes in dark hollows found mine but they bore me no love,
The first time in our marriage I sensed such a distance of feeling.
Grief piled upon grief chilled my bones. This could split us apart
If we let it. Blame had to find outlet, strike somewhere. The culprit
Was dead, but that wouldn't ease anger, disperse blazing rage.
As the men were preparing to set Snow Owl down on a pallet
I told them to stop. "I have something to cushion her. Wait
While I get it." I grabbed Kona's hand, made him run to our shelter.
Inside, I embraced him and asked had he something to put
With her, something he'd carved, or an old treasured plaything
He'd made in her childhood perhaps. I was desperate to crack
His blank stupor. He'd hadn't the night with her body as I had.
Shut out of the care we had lavished upon her, his heart
Had no target. Our boys, who'd not seen us since yesterday, crowded
In with us, heartbroken and needy, yet wary, so strange
And so absent the jolly attentions they'd always been given.
I feared we were hopelessly shattered. But then Kona said
To them, "Gather the presents you made for your sister's homecoming.
We'll take them to her, but first tidy yourselves as she taught."

This was better.
        I rolled up scarred bearskin
                and took it to Snow Owl.

Black Hornet stood guard as they waited for me to return.
It was barely sunup as he helped me with spreading my bearskin,
The one with the scar that my mother had cured, my taboo gift,
From so long ago. What a happy day that had been for us,
So unlike today. The men lowered Owl onto the fur
Where her tunic and leggings, so white upon black, were a snowflake
Afloat in night sky, moonlit smoke, a white owl poised for flight.
How our beautiful girl glowed before us. The dew was still dripping,
Mist weaving its faint final wisps around shelters and trees,
As her brothers approached with the things they had made to present her
So proudly upon her return from taboo. Spotted Wolf
Laid a pair of low boots he had fashioned from moose hide with rabbit
Fur trim at her feet. We all sensed from his tension how much
He desired her to wear them, but Beetle pushed in with the lanyard
He'd braided of deerskin all threaded with feathers and shells.
Bold Grasshopper, who'd flung himself on her before, was reluctant
To go to her now, so he clung to his father's large hand
And hung back. Kona honored his fears, did not coax nor chastise him,
But stood by and waited until he was ready. At last
He stepped forward and held out his favorite stone of split agate,
Red stripes in the white of the broken rough edge he thought fine.

Understanding escaped him
when she didn't reach out
to take it...

Knew animals died, but he hadn't known people did too,
Until now. Would he even remember his sister, I wondered.
I knelt down beside him, one arm 'round his waist for support,
As I whispered that Snow Owl was dead, like a deer or a rabbit,
And no longer in her own body. She couldn't reach out
For his gift, so he must set it down for her. Carefully stooping
He set the small agate stone next to her elbow, said, "Here!"
Kona knelt at his other side, praised him, then tucked his own offering
Into her hands: a carved owl of white oak, taking flight.
A magnificent bird, every feather detailed on an object
So small as to fit in an amulet bag. He had meant
Her to carry it always. A fine piece. Artistic. Authentic
In form and so graceful it seemed a thing vibrant, alive.
I had watched him at work on it, saw it take shape in his fingers,
Well out of the sight of our daughter. He carved at low fire
Many nights to complete it, the flickering light lending semblance
Of motion, a trick to the eye, so mysterious. Weird
Intimation of vigor in sliver of wood wisely chosen
By Kona, the figure he'd seen within needing his skill
For release. I was sorry she never would see what her father
Had made for her, never would thank him, embrace him with joy.

> Little Fox and Song Maker
>> came forward to sing
>>> their goodbye song.

And Lark, her twin Hawk, also Dewdrop, presented their gifts,
Faces solemn and crumpled from efforts to muffle their weeping.
Then White Crow and Lame Fawn brought to her the medicine bag
They had made she so richly had merited, now had no use for.
I stood with my husband and children to watch the long line
Of shocked people file past, bend to gaze at her face. Our son Spotted
Wolf, restlessly scuffling in dirt with his toes, leaned against
Me and sighed. "Shall we put the new boots you have skillfully made
         for her
On her?" I asked him. A sob, quickly swallowed, convulsed
Him. He nodded. "But you'll have to do it. I can't." he protested.
"We'll do it together," I said as I led him to kneel
At her feet. "We must hurry," I said as I took off her moccasins,
Old ones, well worn. "Rising sun will soon shine through the trees,
Touch her body and she must be buried right after." Wolf conquered
Reluctance to touch his dead sister and fitted the boots
On her feet, one by one, as I lifted them. Great satisfaction
Relaxed his taut frame. This prized gift he had made was received.
Not the way he had hoped, but a way he accepted, could tolerate.
All of the village had now said goodbye. It was time
For her burial rites to begin. Fox and Song Maker, silently
Stood by while Lame Fawn and Mother and Sweet Fern and I

      Sewed my bearskin around
         Snow Owl's body
            and wrapped it with lashing.

"You'll like where we've chosen her grave," whispered Kona to me
As we finished our task and stood up. While I couldn't imagine
My liking her grave, I could see he had put careful thought
Into choosing a site, found some peace in preparing her placement.
The uncles and Hornet, the four who had carried her home,
Now stepped forward and lifted the pallet upon their broad shoulders,
And, following Spotted Wolf leading the way, we set out
For her gravesite. We passed through the glade of Old Spotted Whale's
          dying
And all my sons' birthings. We climbed past the ridge where we spent
Every winter to high on the mountain where trees were not growing.
Just lichen on boulders, low bushes between, on a slope
Facing westward. The Lake of the Smiling Great Spirit lay distantly
Shimmering, dotted with islands, including the one
Where we'd sheltered for days from the storm interrupting our wedding
Canoe trip, and where we believed our sweet girl got her start.
When the men set her down, there was no earth disturbance, no digging
Apparent. The mountainside rose high above us, rock face
Sheer and solid except for a cleft at the height of a perilous
Climb. Kona came to my side, pointed upward, "See, there?
Hornet knew of this recess, explored it on one of his forays
And stayed in it during a blizzard, kept dry many nights."

     "It is good she should be there,"
          I answered.
               "Her own secret aerie."

Song Maker and Little Fox sang their goodbye song again
And then led us through all of our usual chants as Black Hornet,
Amazingly quick, scaled the rock face, sat poised on the ledge
At the opening where she would lie and let down in a slithering
Coil a stout line he securely had tied 'round his waist.
At the base of the rock face we watched them as Kona and Medicine Otter
Lashed Snow Owl's wrapped corpse and the pallet with line he had
        dropped.
The two lifted her high as they could before Hornet took over
And, hand over hand, with enormous brute strength hauled her up.
Not a wonder some feared him, so big and so awesomely powerful,
Dark in his moods, ever sullen and watchful. He'd long
Ago ceased his old game of surprising unwary lone walkers
By jumping in front of them onto the path, but we sensed
He was sometimes nearby honing stealthy and shadowy talents.
The pallet, now empty, he lowered, then waited while rocks
In stout basket by basket were fastened one after another
For him to draw up. Thus he filled and then sealed the high grave,
Toes and fingers the only slight holds he relied on for purchase
While placing the last granite slab in the opening's gap.
I was startled when one clap of thunder boomed over the mountain
As Hornet descended. A storm had been brewing that none of us saw.

    Heavy rains hit,
        and I thought it fit
            the whole world should be grieving.

I walked toward home with my face to the rain, let it beat
On my forehead, accepting its sting, and its cold, and its purity.
Drenched and not caring, I sloshed through the puddles. Wet leaves
Drooping low slapped my head and my shoulders. I relished reminders
My body could feel though my mind was numb, swaddled and dumb.
No one spoke as we trailed one another downhill. Beetle followed
Big brother ahead but young Grasshopper stumbled. He fell
And lay trying his best not to whimper. This trek was a trial
He could not sustain. Had he fallen a few days before,
Sister Snow Owl would surely have gathered him close, brushed his
        clothing,
And checked him for scratches or cuts in that magical way
She possessed of adoring him out of each hurt or each misery,
Easily sending him back to his playmates all smiles.
Instead, I was the one who now hoisted him up, let him straddle
My hipbone and bury his face in my blouse, his frustration,
Fatigue and bewilderment too great to suffer unaided.
I carried him, lagging behind, being careful to shield
His small head from the rain pelting down on us, searching good footing.
He soon fell asleep, an exhausted warm bundle. My arms
Felt the press of his weight as I clutched him protectively. Precious
Small boy of my belly, alive, and so newly arrived.

    Merely three winters old,
        just beginning to talk,
            chase adventures.

I prayed I would not grow too fearful, would not squash his will
With anxiety, overprotect him at every least turning,
Or stifle his spirit with motherly fussing. A rage
To avert any further disasters swelled fierce for my children.
I came to a stump at the edge of the glade of his birth
Where I rested, allowing the others to go on without me.
I rocked him and sang to him fitfully sleeping. His breath
Came in snatches all ragged, his dreaming bedeviled by phantom
Pursuers that set his legs twitching, distorted his mouth.
"Spotted Whale," I breathed softly, "if you can now see us, please help me
With this little boy and the loss he has met. Benign wolf
Of the forest, watch over his grieving, and visit his dreaming
With gaze reassuring as you did for me long ago."
Rain had stopped sometime during my pleadings. The plops of the
        droplets
Still dripping from needles and branches made whispering taps,
Near and far, in the woods as they landed. Grasshopper ceased dreaming,
Fell into calm sleep at last, peaceful. Black Hornet appeared
In the glade, as he always did, silent, and sudden and frowning.
He paused at a distance to give me a chance to accept
His dark presence, reluctant to startle me, waken the youngster.
I nodded, then motioned him nearer. He came and sat down,

> Sighing, "She was the only child
>   who never feared me.
>   She trusted."

"You taught her that, early," he added. "The first time I jumped
At you, trying to scare you, you stood unafraid and spoke calmly.
You praised me, in fact. My first notice of worth and of skill."
"I remember," I murmured, unwilling to wake my Grasshopper
By speaking too loudly. We sat a long time in the glade
As he talked to me openly, pouring out words with an eloquence
So unexpected I listened and wanted to weep.
He recounted the tangled emotional shifts in his character
As he kept struggling to grow from a troubled young lad
Who, rejected, uncared for, and angry, saw love all around him
But none of it his, into manhood, earn honor, respect.
Most of all, earn the love of his mother, Sweet Fern, Crying Woman.
"I watched how you mothered young Owl," he said. "That was so new
To me." Late afternoon sent long shadows to cool the slight breezes
As Hornet talked on. So unusual for him. The men
Of our village were not in the habit of showing their feelings,
Or questioning personal history. This was a spate
That would not come again. Soon Grasshopper yawned, stretched, and
            grew restless.
He opened his eyes, looked at Hornet, who gestured and said,
"Here's another child having no fear of me, daring to pummel
Me. Hard little fists you have, boy. You're a brave one, you are."

    My son blinked and then grinned at him,
        went to him,
            climbed on his shoulders.

"Give ride," he demanded. "We've done this before, many times,"
Explained Hornet, who seemed to enjoy having Grasshopper grabbing
His ears while he stood up, and shrugged to position the weight.
We walked down to the village together, my son full of chatter
And happiness, no comprehension how permanent death
Was. Expecting to brag to his sister, expecting she'd be there.
We'd need a long time to undo expectations we'd see
Her as usual, going her rounds, being helpful and playful
And caring. A presence more real by her absence she'd be.
I had new understanding of Hornet as he swung Grasshopper
To ground from his shoulders and stalked away, wordless and stiff,
From the front of our shelter. Inside I found Kona and Otter
And both of the boys sitting listless, together but each
Isolated by pain. Somber Beetle showed keen disappointment
At our reappearance. His eyes glanced behind us as if,
Despite all that had happened his sister might follow, though knowing
She couldn't. His spirit was crushed once again by the fact
Of her death's confirmation. No matter how much we all wished it,
She'd never come back, never sleep in her bed, never eat
With us hurriedly, rush to her duties. Raw emptiness threatened
Cohesiveness. Froze precious family. I could not help.

> We crouched each one alone.
> Full of grief. Full of fears.
> Full of fury.

We might have remained there forever, immobile, adrift,
Each one staring at nothing. But Meadowlark's voice interrupted
Our mutual stupor. She called us to come to the fire,
Share some dinner with people who needed to do us the kindness
Of feeding us. Medicine Otter suggested the boys
Go with him to leave Kona and me by ourselves for a moment.
We welcomed his gesture and watched them depart. But alone
We were strangers, had nothing to say, were reluctant to reach out
Or touch one another. I studied his face with its lines
Of fatigue and distress newly drawn, to remain etched forever,
While he studied mine as though meeting me now the first time.
And it was like a first time, both altered and grim, unfamiliar.
Not seeing small changes with passage of time, we ignored
Them and saw only youth in each other. The figures we had been
Persisted in everyday dealings. Today we were old
In an instant. We'd buried our firstborn this morning. A future
Unpromising loomed, with no energy left to confront
What we must. The fine shape of our everyday lives had been stolen.
And more dire disruptions were coming. Invaders were close,
As the presence of Snow Owl's vile killer in woods we thought safest
For girls on taboo trek had proven. Soon Lark's turn would come.

    We would have to give up
        old traditions,
            curtail young girls' freedoms.

I hated the thought. And the boys. How would they deal with quests
For their visions in forests conscripted, and plundered and lethal?
The man that Black Hornet had killed would be missed, prompting search
By his kinfolk, I feared. I felt hunted already, incredibly
Closed in, and almost not caring. I sighed. Kona stirred
And said, "Come. You must eat." "I'm not hungry," I answered in protest.
"I know. But our people must feel they are helping," he said.
"We must let them." If anything should have been asked of me presently,
Being polite was not something I thought I could do.
But together we walked to where others were waiting to serve us.
Unable to give us the one thing we wanted, our child
Back, they gave what they had—food and presence and care. In their
      bustling
And scurrying, fussing with stirring and scooping hot stew,
Seating children with bowls full of everyday fare, feeding little
Ones, serving the elders, and adding more sticks to the fire
Gave a thin imitation of normalcy. Watching their busyness
Heartened me somewhat. A sense of belonging once more
To the living took hold. "This is good," I said softly to Kona.
"We'll make it," he promised, voice husky and crushed in his throat.
"Yes, we will," I agreed. We were welcomed, embraced, and surrounded
By generous people all mourning this shocking great loss.

    The aromas of cooking
        seduced me.
           I found I was hungry.

The simplest of life's plain necessities, food, human touch,
For example, took on a significance rarely considered
Of cosmic importance, and yet my detachment was pierced.
Like a puncture through shelter flap letting in light rays and visions
Of outside occurrences, simple attendant routines
Were restoring connection to people and places, familiar,
Reliable, constant, despite this upheaval of death.
I was slowly awakening out of confusion and numbness.
My grief became agony now. No protection, no shield
Against painfully sharp recollections. These last days were vivid,
Unbearable, cruel. I understood Meadowlark's lapse
Into madness before I set Dewdrop to suckle and rally
Her senses. The simplest of life's plain necessities—child
Needing nourishment, moss needing changing, demands of the body—
Conspiring and plotting, all pulled us relentlessly back.
We kept living and living and living. Enduring, resilient,
Magnificent, awestruck and questioning though we may be.
I felt better, without knowing how I could possibly feel so.
Then White Crow and Lame Fawn and Mother, conversing apart
From the group, signaled Kona and Hornet and Father to join them.
With serious faces and urgent low voices they talked a long while.

My three boys, Lark and Hawk,
        and grown Dewdrop, now Spider,
            surrounded me.

Grasshopper, sated and sleepy, contented himself with his head
In Lark's lap, let her comb back his hair in slow strokes with her fingers
As Snow Owl so often had done. The young people recalled
One by one, with shy smiles, their fond stories of Snow Owl in happier
Times. They were needing to keep her alive in their hearts.
And I, too, found great solace from hearing her name in their voices.
Her life had been real, not a dream after all. Spotted Wolf
Seemed most stricken, unable to say Snow Owl's name. His expression,
However, allowed a faint grin now and then as the stories came out
Of the things they had done for their youthful amusements and daring
Adventures. I heard a few things I had never been told
And had never suspected. Hawk's tree climbing feats and Owl's treatment
Of cuts and of bruises sustained when he fell, but concealed
From his mother for fear of a scolding. And contests of swimming
Too far, to a rock or an island offshore after dark.
And of snow fights, and races, and scaling of crumbling cliff faces,
And more. Each shared tale sparked another outrageous event
Recollected, until even Wolf burst out laughing, confessing
The one of his own with his sister when he hurt his arm.
She had bound it snug then did the bulk of his chores for him, hiding
His hurt so as not to explain how he'd courted a sprain.

> I had thought I knew everything
> mothers should know
> of their children.

Not so. But the best thing to know was how Owl as a child
Tamed Black Hornet's mean temper by showing no fear of him, coaxing
Her playmates to laugh with delight, make a game of surprise
When he sprang at them, ask him for help, and invite him to merriment.
Stiff as he was, he would sometimes unbend, become boy
Again briefly. Though older and stronger, well able to bully
Them all if he chose, he did not. As I listened I held
My breath, often uneasy, and wondered if they ever realized
How very dangerous he might have proven to be.
He had now become hero. Had found Owl. Had slaughtered her killer.
Had carried her home to us, buried her high in the cliff.
No one other than he had the strength to accomplish
That feat. I was worried Owl's death might undo the effect
She had had on his growth work, might tumble his still fragile outlook
To depths of dark rage he had barely forsaken. I spoke
Of my fears to them. Dewdrop, now Spider, acknowledged my worry
By saying, "He'll always be moody, be struggling to deal
With self-loathing that stung his young heart when a boy. But his spirit
Is rich with desire to live up to the trust she has taught
Us to place in him now we are grown. We have seen how his nature
Has opened to let him approach us assured we'll be pleased."

"He will always be tinder
     awaiting a spark though,"
          Hawk added.

The group of adults who were talking so long seemed agreed
Upon something at last, stepped apart and moved off to the others,
Conversing again with new urgency, shaping a plan.
Soon my father sat down with us, saying a party was forming
To go to the site of Owl's slaying and bury the man
Whom Black Hornet had left there, conceal the corpse scalped and
    dismembered.
A body would only prompt strangers' revengeful attack
If they found it, not knowing that justice itself had been rendered.
Tonight, in the dark, men would find it and carry it off
Then restore the disturbance of leaves and of ground where the episode
Happened, leave nothing to show he had been there at all.
A wise plan, but I thought of the son who'd be grown, who would miss him
And probably search for him soon. "Lame Fawn mentioned a son
Who was there by the ocean," said Father, "described your encounter.
We need to move quickly, so Hornet and I go alone."
"Take me with you," cried Spotted Wolf standing, intense and determined.
His grandfather almost denied him, but looked to me first.
"Find your father and Hornet," I said. "We'll decide on your going
Or not." To my father I added, "He needs to take part
In your mission, do something to discharge his smothered emotions."
When Hornet and Kona approached, they said sternly to Wolf,

    "Fetch your knife. Wear dark moose hide
        for cover. Keep up.
          And keep silent."

And so they departed. The moon not yet rising, the clouds
Scudding low, and the wind making promise of southern rains coming,
Provided incentives to keep searching strangers holed up
Until morning. Son Beetle sat curled close against me, not dozing
But quiet, not knowing just how to behave, where he fit
In a family broken, its balance upset. Seven winters had given
Him many good lessons but never prepared him for loss
Such as this. He sat studying Lark who caressed baby brother's
Small head in her lap the way Sister so often had done.
Then he glanced up at me, brown eyes wide, full of doubt and of questions.
"Will Lark be my sister now? Take Snow Owl's place?" he then asked.
"I imagine that Lark will stay Lark, same as always," I answered.
"That's good," he replied, which surprised me. "And why is that good?"
I was curious what he was thinking, this pensive young Beetle,
This deep child of mine. "Because no one can take Snow Owl's place,"
He announced in a passionate protest, tones startling Grasshopper.
Lark looked at him sadly. "You're right," she assented. "I love
You, however, as she did. You know that, my handsome brave young one."
"Oh, blgghh!" he went, shy and embarrassed and making us laugh.
Lame Fawn, smiling to see us content with each other and able
To laugh, came to join us, suggest it was time to bed down

> And in parting
> say prayers the men
> would be safe and successful.

We went to our separate shelters for sleep as the wind
Commenced driving hard rain from the south, bringing lightning and
    thunder
To flash and to shiver the ground with each rumble and roar.
Branches crashed in the forest. Small rivulets ran, sounding burbles
And tinkles, through ditches diverting the flow. We had dug
Them for runoff. I thought of my father and son and Black Hornet
At work in wild storm on a task necessarily grim.
Spotted Wolf, from this night, would not ever be boy again. Childhood
Had passed for him now, whether ready or not. He was man
In his bearing, and sober too soon for his age was my feeling.
When Kona came in, he was dripping. He stripped to the skin
And then crouched at a fire barely starting to glow, barely warming
The shelter. "The boy will need heat on return," he said, "good."
I was tempted to let myself feel quite insulted. Did Kona
Assume I'd forget to prepare to attend the boy's needs?
It seemed nothing we said to each other brought real understanding.
Some vital connection had ruptured between us. "Where were
You," I asked him, "so long in the storm?" "We hiked far off to bury
The scalp and the member that Hornet brought back," he explained.
"Should have thrown them for bait in the weir," I spat angrily, shoving
More sticks in the fire. "Would you want to eat fish that ate those?"

> Kona's question provoked
>   my hysterical laughter,
>   then sobbing.

He stared at me. Out of control and insane once again,
I gave vent to my heartbreak. The world had gone mad and I with it.
Outside, the storm worsened. The boys' sleep was restless and light.
They lay huddled together for warmth and a sense of security.
Kona, still naked, was shivering. Far from the heat of the fire
Now, appearing distracted, in shadow, abandoned and aching,
He was the same Kona I'd met on the mountain above
His old home in Long Bay half a lifetime ago. He'd been mourning
The death of his father, had asked to remain with me then,
But I'd sent him away on account of taboo. Was he thinking
I'd do the same now? Well aware wretched feelings will link
All together unbroken, bind earliest hurts to a new felt
Disaster, resurface old agonies once believed healed,
I said, "Come to the fire. Share my robe. Stay beside me forever."
He did. His cold skin was a shock when I touched him to wrap
My robe 'round his hunched shoulders. I built up the fire, began rubbing
His feet as I would for the children to counter a chill.
My hands worked every node in the soles of his feet, restored blood flow,
Sensation and color to heels and to ankles and toes.
How I loved this good man who was suffering so along with me.
"I wish I had killed him," he muttered. "I yearn for revenge."

> "It is not in your nature
>   to harm any person,"
>   I cautioned him.

"Killing would bring no relief, would provoke a great grief
In your heart worse than this one, I fear." Kona shook his head sadly,
"But what do I do with my anger?" he queried me, eyes
Full of fury, with tears of a frustrated helplessness glittering.
"Have it," I said, with a shrug of my shoulders. "What else
Can you do? For myself, in my mind I have already tortured
And killed him so many times over I'm tired of my thoughts."
"I can't tolerate being unable to make our lives whole again,
Being so helpless, defeated, and sad as before,
When my father was killed." There it was, the unbroken connection,
Hurt plaited to hurt for a lifetime, with nothing to say
That could close opened wounds. So we sat in the wavering firelight
Together and waited for Spotted Wolf, wordless and tense.
If taut muscles were proof against future disasters, our bodies
Right then might be holding off hurricane, earthquake and flood
For the whole of the land. If not breathing were cure against suffering,
We should be pain free at once. And if sleeplessness lent
Understanding, we'd know what to do for each other, and do it.
Instead, we just sat. The boys slept. The storm rumbled and flared.
Night seemed never to pass. Each suspended and sealed in a bubble
Of agony nothing could burst, we endured until dawn.

    The boys woke wanting food.
        Spotted Wolf soon returned
           with Owl's amulets…

Still in their bag, though the thong that had held it had snapped
In the struggle. Relieved for his safety, we rallied, attempting
To honor his deed with our thanks, not reveal our distress.
"Tell us what did you do with the body?" asked Kona with interest.
"Eat first and get dry," I encouraged him. "Then you can tell
Us what happened." Wolf laid Snow Owl's amulet bag on her bedding
And sat down to eat his food quickly, quite eager to talk.
"We did not have to hide the man's body," he said. "An enormous
Black bear was there tearing the stranger to pieces. A cub
With her, gnawing and pawing the parts, fairly well destroyed evidence
He had been killed by a man. So we left him there strewn
On the ground with his rifle a few feet away from his body.
I saw Snow Owl's amulet bag but we three had to wait
Half the night until bear ambled off and her cub scampered after.
And, Mother, I swear that bear laughed as she stood on hind legs
Before ordering cub to go with her." It was a good omen.
My totem was roaming the woods in my stead. "But what else
Did you find? Her small basket? Her moccasins? Traces of clothing?"
We wanted assurances nothing forgotten remained
To suggest that a woman of ours had been anywhere near him.
"Grandfather searched long, found her basket, and Hornet her shoes.

She had run very far
from the site of encounter
while fleeing."

We needed to hear every detail of what she had done
In her last freedom moments, for knowing was better than mystery,
Though it was hard. I could picture her confident stance
Upon meeting a stranger. No fear, only curious interest
And misguided trust. He could mean her no harm. No one had
In her lifetime been anything other than kind and accepting.
Her bafflement must have been total. It cost her her chance
To react fast enough for escape, I surmised. Then Wolf mentioned
A startling direction her flight took. "She didn't head home.
Flew the opposite way, as if trying to lead him as far from us
As she was able." "Protecting our village her aim,"
Kona sighed. In his voice was a mingling of pride and great sorrow.
"But might she have reached us?" he wondered aloud. "She could not,"
Answered Spotted Wolf. "Sister strode far, went to visit the ocean
We think. There's a shell from the shore in her amulet bag,
Which Grandfather confirmed." So our wandering girl reached the
       seashore.
A dream she had cherished since childhood, from stories of sea
And horizon and dawning, and whales with their breaching and spouting.
She'd seen for herself those extensive bright wonders at last.
What a daughter was this! Admiration and love filled my bosom.
Forever from this moment onward I'd picture her poised

     On a bluff
         overlooking the ocean,
            arms outstretched to sunrise.

"The man was much older," said Kona. "She should have outrun
Him." "He shot her," I said. "I have wanted to keep that fact hidden.
Too harsh for repeating. While washing we found a round hole
Through her thigh. It had hampered her running, though not stopped
    her fighting."
Her story was out now and all of it worthy of praise.
I could feel a great difference in telling of everything fully.
Acceptance, that Snow Owl had done all she could to resist,
Had completed taboo trek, was on her way happily homeward
Before the attack, lent a semblance of peace to our hearth.
I could see this in Kona, whose tension seemed eased as he listened.
For me, I felt better not harboring secrets from him.
A mistake to believe I could hold something back yet stay open
And honest, when all I could think of was how she'd been brought
Down in flight, made to flutter to ground and be captured, lie tethered
And kicking and terrified, dying her only escape.
Now we shared the same images, knew all there was to be knowing.
Together we bore the unbearable. Death was the worst
That could happen. No detail could make us feel worse that we already
Felt. "Go to sleep now, my son," Kona said. "You've done well."
I was thankful Black Hornet and Father had taken him with them.
A wise thing to do. It empowered his spirit once more.

    So we gathered his brothers
        and left him asleep
           on Owl's bedding.

Outside at the circle stood Mother and Sweet Fern apart,
Sharing details they'd learned from their own men returning exhausted.
They were motioning to us to join them. The boys, running off
To their friends, left us free to converse without softening gruesome
Descriptions the men had recounted in brief before sleep
Overcame them. Though when we heard one of the children exclaiming
"A bear?" we all knew it was futile to try to protect
Them. My young could accept all events except something kept from
     them.
For then their minds conjured up horrors and monsters and fears.
Nothing solid to face down and grapple spawned bad dreams and night
     screams.
A bear in the woods eating somebody dead was all right
Because real. And, besides, it was bad man, an enemy. Rough sorts
Of justice sat well with their view of the world. In their play
What was fair was forever an issue discussed and debated
Until resolution was reached and their game could proceed.
Kona went to find Medicine Otter. Then Lark and my sister
Emerged from their shelters and joined us suggesting we go
To White Crow with the news, though she probably already knew it.
Her visions were clearer then ever as age overtook
Her. I wanted to ask if she really had seen Snow Owl's killing
But would not reveal it for fear she'd misread awesome signs.

     But I never could ask her.
          She'd died in her sleep
               before morning.

Dear Lame Fawn was with her, had been there beside her all night.
"Her last words were 'Snow Owl,' just as though she were seeing Owl
          standing
Before her to welcome her," Lame Fawn said. "So like Snow Owl,"
Said Sister. "She's still taking care of us, keeping her vigils
For those whom she loves." This was too much to bear in my heart.
I went walking alone, leaving others to handle Crow's body,
Arrange for the burial, do all the things now required
To be done. I walked far by myself, soon was climbing the hillside
Above winter camp, to the base of the cliff where Owl lay.
There Black Hornet sat gazing across the big lake at twin mountains
Beyond it to westward. So peaceful it was there. The world
Was all washed, and the sky had no cloud. Air smelled fresh and Earth
          earthy.
So richly alive, yet resenting existence without my brave daughter,
I marveled at how strong the spell was of nature
Suffusing my senses, a pleasant serenity loss
Could not steal. There was no need for talking. We both treasured silence.
The wind was more comfort than words. This was such a fine place
Just to rest and breathe deeply, and try to stay sane inside sorrow's
Sharp talons, enduring and hoping someday to prevail.
I would never get over the death of my daughter.
I envied White Crow's having seen her. Was willing to die for that sight.

      It was strange that Black Hornet
            should be there.
                  I thought him home sleeping.

"I sleep very little," he said, though I'd not said a word,
Never asked him a question. "I guessed you might come here this morning
Once Spotted Wolf told you Owl's story," he added, his glance
Raised to indicate where we had chosen to place her forever.
"A fine place to think and remember," I said. "You chose well."
"She'll be safe there," he said. "Farther south they are plowing up
      graveyards
And burning our ancestors' bones for enriching the soil."
What a foul desecration, how sad, disrespectful and evil, I thought.
Nothing sacred was left to us where they were come.
"There'll be war very soon," Hornet warned, "and especially after
These killings. Our peace-loving leaders will have to resist."
He was ready to fight I could see. "They are mean to their children,"
He growled. "At least one I have watched get a beating, left out
In the rain a long time. A small yellow-haired girl, she stood ragged,
Defiant, not crying, not making a moan until told
To fetch water. I stayed in the woods. She walked by me and saw me
With never a quiver of fear. Her worst fears lay inside
That log shelter. I wanted to bring her to you and the village."
"Then do so," I said. "I have heard they don't value their girls
As they ought. What you've seen that you tell to me now only proves it."
His wish had been uttered aloud and agreed to. He slumped,

> Let the weight of an actual kidnap
>   oppress
>   his bold fantasy.

I never doubted he'd fetch her and carry her here.
"They have slaughtered the best of us. Now we shall take up their
    fairest one,"
Hornet resolved. This was roughly hewn justice, and rash,
But to know of a child being beaten, abused, and neglected
Offended us both. "Ah, but Hornet," I said, "it is she
Must be given the choice. And the village will need to agree to it,
Such a grave risk to our safety her seizure will court."
"We're already at risk," he said angrily. Traveling often
And deep into lands overtaken, he knew at first hand
What we merely had heard. Soon the village might split into factions,
Some choosing to stand and to fight, others choosing retreat.
There lay plenty of space between seashore and rivers, though
    mountainous,
Where we might live on in safety and peace our whole lives.
Our true skills in the forest would let us be everywhere, nowhere,
Unseen, unsuspected, yet watching and wary and strong.
This was Kona's way. I would go with him and live in the sunlight
And shadow of woodland's protection, concealed, like the elk
And the wolf and the deer in magnificent stealth and in glorious
Vigor, no matter how hard the conditions might grow.
These newcomers, invaders, would know we were there, feel our presence,
Would fear us perhaps, but could never detect nor subdue.

    We would vanish as mist
        or Spring snow
            yet be constant as seasons.

Departing the cliff side, we talked of abducting the girl.
How to do it, obtain the consent of the village, hide yellow
Hair while on return should she show herself willing to run
With Black Hornet. The scheme was a rich kind of madness I cherished.
In my mind no parent deserved any child she abused.
After White Crow lay buried beside our beloved Red Feather,
And Council, with little dissension, resolved it was right
To allow an attempt to persuade that one child of the strangers
To flee from her torment, we plotted a way to effect
Her escape without conflict. Our clever, lithe Spider was boldly
Prepared to accompany Hornet, to carry old clothes
As disguise for the girl. I gave blouse and some leggings of Snow Owl's,
Now useless, quite worn, that Black Hornet assured me would fit.
Beetle brought out a pair of his sturdiest, very best moccasins.
Lark added hooded hide cape that would cover bright hair.
The whole village approved, which astonished me. No one objected
Or fretted lest strangers come searching, or mount an attack.
It was reasoned that finding remains of Owl's killer, all scattered
By bear, would convince any searchers Girl met the same fate.
As they left on their mission, both Spider and Hornet gave warning
They'd wait many days, test the trust of the yellow-haired girl,

> Would not bring her unless,
>   understanding her choices,
>   she wished it.

I did not know how, in their languages different, he'd talk
With her, prove his intentions benign, lull anxiety, offer
Her rescue and safety, not kidnap, by signal and gesture convince
A mistreated young girl that these tall woodland creatures would treat her
More kindly than family had. I could find no small shred
Of compassion for people who cared not at all for her welfare,
Might not even question her unexplained absence. One less
Mouth to feed deemed a blessing, perhaps. For these were the people,
So Meadowlark said, who believed every child born in sin,
Doomed to suffer and die into punishments awful, eternal.
No joy, only sacrifice, judgment, great anguish and shame.
Not the kind of life she would discover with us should she join us.
I found myself loving this life, and its mystical cloak
Of enveloping energies keeping me company. More so
Than ever, I lived in two worlds now, one spirit, one flesh,
With no chasm between them. A seamless, expansive existence
Invested my days. Snow Owl's death punched a hole through the sky,
Let me see far beyond dirt and bones, harm and hatred and warfare
And fear. Ancient Woman I'd be, in these mountains and caves,
As was promised me once on taboo. Laughing Bear was my totem,
And she-wolf, with notch in her ear, was aprowl in my realm,

     And my people still lived
          all around me.
               Tribe no one could conquer...

Tribe no one could poison with sicknesses rampant, or theft,
Or subversion of spirit. Oppressive beliefs that sap energy,
Plunder the earth, and humiliate pride would not touch
Us. Apart, and above, and around them we'd live on in glorious
Freedom and wellness and purpose. Our women and men
And our children would cherish our heritage as we had taught them.
They'd carry pride down through the ages as always we'd done.
This strong shift in my thinking, I knew, came a gift from The Many.
As Medicine Otter had told me to do, I had learned
To invite and enjoy these far visitors. Trust. Not feel crazy.
Accept who I was. I was never alone, anymore.
And I never had been. Now I relished Their presence, accepted
Their guidance, no matter how subtly delivered. A whisper as good
As a loud revelation, for now I had met with validity.
Often imagining scenes of the future, I saw
My own children at home in two cultures, their own and the strangers',
With no one suspecting our origins. Here from the first
But so skillful at blending and working and flowing with harmony
Through the new culture, my children would come and would go
In blest safety. Like boulders on beaches, be rolled and be tumbled
By waves of wild hurricane yet maintain character true.

     Thus the life that The Many
         had shown me
            would manifest for them.

Convinced of survival, I disallowed fear, and resolved
We would prosper, all working together. It seemed I had taken
White Crow's role of seeing and forecasting future events.
Such a power felt natural now, and as welcome as dancing
Had been in my youth. With light step and with confident heart
I emerged from my reverie into my everyday duties,
Prepared, with the women, a feast for the evening meal.
The whole village would eat with Black Hornet and Spider and yellow-
Haired girl-child. I'd seen they were well on their way on the trail.
Soon the promised arrival occurred as predicted. My people
Accepted my sight without question. And Kona was pleased
When he sat with me, eating and smiling, and easy of manner.
"So now we see Spotted Whale's wisdom in choosing you. Young
As you were, she could recognize talent inherent your nature
Possessed. You were meant for this honor," he told me, amused
And yet proud. The estrangement between us, imposed by our grieving,
Had softened at last. We were once again tender and close.
Our attention went now to the yellow-haired girl-child before us.
She leaned against Spider and ate with a greediness born
Of denial and long-suffered hunger. We thought she might vomit
Up most of her meal when she finished. She didn't. She slept.

     This was one hardy child,
         very skinny yet trusting,
            who'd chosen us.

Blue-eyed and freckled and frail as she was, there was much
To admire in her spunk and her daring. To put herself into
Our alien circle, forsaking her own, took strong will.
In the days and the seasons that followed our Goldenrod's coming,
We saw, in her stubborn persistence at learning our ways,
And at teaching the children her language while she became fluent
In ours, she believed herself destined to travel two paths.
She grew tall, could outrun any boy in the races, was graceful
And happy and generous. Living by turns within each
Of our shelters, she stayed independent of any one family,
Spoke her mind clearly on matters of tribal concern,
And moved with us deep into the woodland, away from encroachments
Her people inflicted, not letting her figure be seen.
Fully half of our village resisted. Resolving on warfare,
They stayed on to fight for the sites we had camped in so long.
Her low words were a warning. "You cannot prevail. They're too many.
Too greedy. Too brutal. Believing that men can own land,
They will drive you away and will kill to possess your most sacred
Of spaces. I've seen this too often to doubt it, 'though young
When I first witnessed slaughter." Hawk's warrior body, when carried
Home riddled with shot, proved the cost she foretold we would pay.

> At the sight of him, Goldenrod
> tore from her neck
> her bright emblem...

An amulet worn since her childhood. "Dead mother's," she said.
Shiny metal, two pieces, one crossing the other. She treasured
The trinket and tried many times to explain what it meant
To a child's understanding. A symbol of torture and cruelty
Anciently used was the story she told of it when
Others asked. Now she placed it upon him and let it be buried
In dirt with whatever its magic. She no longer claimed
It but gave it to Hawk, with more weeping that ever she'd shown us,
Knelt broken in spirit. No pride in her birthright remained.
An old anger rose up in her, sparked her blue eyes, flushed her features
More red than had any bad burn from the bright summer sun.
Her sweet fury was high and her grief monumental. Then, striding
To Hornet, her savior, and speaking so all at the gravesite could hear,
She announced a bold plan. "I return, now I'm grown, to the people
I came from. I speak against fighting and killing and lands
Being taken." My heart swelled and pained as I heard her bold promise,
For nothing would stop this dire onslaught. As soon part a flood,
Sweep storm tide out to sea against hurricane, flick away blizzard.
Come sooner sunset in the East, or sunrise in the West,
Than a woman of theirs would be listened to, heeded, respected.
"You cannot go dressed as you are. I support brave intent,

    But your clothing will not
        be accepted," I said.
           "Then I'll steal some."

Her purpose unwavering, will strong and bold, stance erect
As a warrior headed for battle, our Goldenrod dared us
To stop her. "I've gone many times with Black Hornet to spy
Out my people. My father is dead, and my stepmother wanton.
My brother, mature now, a scholar and preacher, is steeped
In belief that all killing is contrary to their religion.
With him, once he sees me alive, I may have some success."
So she had been preparing for this, even living among us
And feeling our love, for a very long time. She would go.
In a deep meditation I asked that The Many assist her,
Achieve in the end for us all a benevolent blend
Of two peoples, an outcome that seemed an impossible fantasy,
One that I clung to as she did herself, despite strife.
Once she'd dressed in the billowing cloth, the high boots with bright
         buttons,
The mantle and bonnet she'd stolen, now no longer ours,
She departed transformed. Many prayers went with her, but wisely
We quickly moved camp. From now on she'd have need of a guide
If she wanted to find us. Black Hornet, or Beetle, or Spotted Wolf,
Running between, would keep watch, see her safe, intervene
If so needed. A modern taboo quest our Goldenrod crafted,
Inventive and perilous, fraught with uncertainty. Grand

     In its scope, and unique
          in its origins,
               Goldenrod's journey.

Black Hornet, or Beetle, or Spotted Wolf, from time to time
Down the seasons, reported the shape of her life with her people.
"They go in a white empty structure to sing and to kneel
And to listen to Goldenrod's people speak endlessly to them.
One scolds and cajoles, makes vague promises, threatens of fire
From a being most angry, describes to them walls that are falling
And gates made of gold in great cities where good ones will dwell
After death." I was saddened to hear that her people went inside
To shut themselves off from our glorious Earth's ample gifts,
From Her wonder, and beauty, and power, and odors, and comforting
Presence, to conjure up terrors, mold conduct with fears.
"They behave as though they are the only ones worthy of value,
That we are inferior beings. They see us beneath
Their contempt, like wild animals," Beetle now often complained.
"They have changed our brave Goldenrod's name back to Hannah,
     ignoring
Her voice. She's not happy, not willing to marry the man
Who has chosen her." "Ah, but Beetle," I said to him, "animals
Have equal value with everything earthly. There can
Be no insult. Great Spirit inhabits it all." He agreed,
But stayed sad. All my sons were grown men now. They had wives and
     small children.
While Kona and I, with tall Medicine Otter and Fawn,

    Were content to live hidden,
       the young ones soon lived
          among strangers.

Our language was dying. Our lands had been seized, and disease
Had reduced us in number. Our grandchildren, brought far to see us,
Could not understand us, wore garments impractical, cloth
That got wet and that tore at the rub of a rock or a sapling.
The wolf and the bear had retreated from sharing our cave
For the winters. Our hair had turned white, and our balance uncertain
Prevented swift travel. Stooped Medicine Otter died first.
And then Kona. We dragged them to rest very deep in the cavern,
Assembling a cairn of loose fallen coarse granite for each.
When Lame Fawn had lain down for the last time, I lived on in solitude,
Ancient and singing my death song, my Otter-swim song
From taboo. My people now blended and thrived with the strangers.
The woodlands, inhabited still by our ancestors' ghosts,
Kept me company, rustling and bustling and murmuring sweetly
As ever.
    "Walk softly.
        Be quiet and listen.
            We're here."

And so Herima ended the story of brave Ellacoya.
The children and grownups who'd gathered to hear the long tale
Sat enthralled, each unwilling to let it be finished, be over.
The rustle of leaves of the oak and the aspen, the hiss
Of small wavelets assaulting the shoreline, the splash of the heron
Afishing, the cry of the loon in the distance, gave song.

    The sun set. The moon slept.
        The wind died. The Earth rolled.
            And they heard it…

Ellacoya's Death Song:

THE OTTER SWIMS WITH ME

(REFRAIN)
Again the otter swims with me.
She circles, dives and rolls.
When I am drifting off in dream
She gently leads me home.

Herima sighed on her stump then. And everyone privileged
To be in the circle felt deep satisfaction.
There flickered above them bright fingers of light,
A green glow of green fire that soon spread a great blanket
Of red overhead, turning everything scarlet in hue
'Til the Lake surface burned like a meadow ignited
By lightning on summertime's driest of nights.
Then a yellow-haired woman, caressing dark heads of her children,

Begged, "Tell us the story
Of Goldenrod,
wild and courageous."

The End

CHARACTERS

Herima (HEH-ri-ma), outdoorswoman, present-day storyteller

RED HILL GROUP

Ahanton, Chief, **Grey Goose**, his wife
    Loon Diver, Ellacoya, Little Fox, their children
Lame Fawn, midwife, Ellacoya's best friend
Red Elk, Grey Hawk, Lame Fawn's older brothers
Yellow Snake, Lame Fawn's first husband
White Crow, seer
Red Feather, historian, storyteller, educator
Weasel, apprentice storyteller
Heron, storyteller

LONG BAY GROUP

Kona, son of slain chief
Medicine Otter, brother of slain chief
Spotted Whale, great, great grandmother of slain chief
Song Maker, young musician
Black Hornet, half-breed son of Sweet Fern
Meadowlark, widowed flood survivor
    Dewdrop (Spider) her daughter

MERGED GROUP AT RED HILL

Kona, Ellacoya, husband and wife
  Snow Owl, Spotted Wolf, Beetle, Grasshopper, their children
Medicine Otter, Lame Fawn, husband and wife
  Lark, Hawk, their twins

FOREIGNERS AND STRANGERS

Yellow Snake, unknown origin, married into Red Hill Group
Sweet Fern, runaway from the south, married into Long Bay group
Red-headed father and son, roving white hunters
Goldenrod, daughter of white settlers adopted into Merged Group

WHERE TO FIND IT

ABOUT THE AUTHOR

Jeanne Clark is a direct descendant of Thomas Clark, who arrived in the New World on the ship *Anne* at Plymouth, Cape Cod, in 1623. She has spent much of her life in New England, and now lives permanently in the Lakes Region of New Hampshire, absorbing stories from its woodlands, lakes, streams and mountains.

Photo by Mel George

After some undergraduate work at Tufts, she married, had three children, and graduated from the University of Miami at Coral Gables, Florida with a Bachelor of Education, *cum laude*, under the name Jeanne Clark Simon. She later earned a Juris Doctor from Temple University School of Law under the name Jeanne Clark Benjamin and practiced law in Bucks County, Pennsylvania. Now widowed from Mel George, who generously supported her desire to reclaim her birth name, she spends her days writing.

Jeanne's stories, essays, and poems, under the various surnames listed above, have appeared in *Yankee, Bucks County Panorama, Women Outdoors Magazine, The Frost Place 1986 Festival of Poetry Anthology, Contemporary New England Poetry: A Sampler, VOL II (The Texas Review), The Northern New England Review,* and have won honorable mentions in *The Writer* and The Poetry Society of New Hampshire.

Jeanne Clark is the recipient of the 2009 New Hampshire Senior Poets Laureate Award.